November 2013

To my dear Friend, Kate —
Am so looking forward to
seeing you soon —

Better To Have Loved

A TRUE STORY OF LOVE, LOSS, AND
RENEWAL

By

KATHRYN TAUBERT

You're in here — and you and
Charlie will always be in my
heart — Hugs,

Edited by Jay Schlichter

Kathryn

Printed in the United States of America.

Contact the author for information:
P.O. Box 2331
Dunnellon, Florida 34430
Email: kataubert@yahoo.com
www.kathryntaubert.com

ISBN: 9781619275805
LCCN: 2013918943

Kathryn Taubert's story offers hope and guidance for anyone starting over after the death of a spouse. From the depths of despair, this twice-widowed, retired 57-year-old widow with Tourette syndrome and a self-described "couch potato," built a new life as an athlete, jazz recording artist, international volunteer, and successful author.

Better To Have Loved is a love story, an illustration of what caregivers of the desperately ill endure, and a testimonial to the power of determination in surviving bereavement. For anyone who ever asked themselves *why* and *how* to go on, this book is for you.

Praise for Better To Have Loved

"Prepare for a journey like none other. Join Kathryn Taubert as she takes you on an intimate ride through a very personal, moving and heartbreaking tale. Strap yourself in as she chronicles the day-to-day details of watching her husband suffer from a debilitating disease.

Struggle to stay aboard as you hope this story will have a happy ending and beg for mercy that the ride will soon be over as Taubert makes you realize that some doctors were all any patient could want, while others were there for the paycheck. Come to the realization the author has been through this before.

Travel with her through depression, smile as newfound friends give her a reason to laugh again and be overjoyed as she finds an entirely new life in her 60's that she never thought possible. As you get ready to disembark, find yourself agreeing as you realize that it truly is better to have loved and lost than never to have loved at all."

Jay Schlichter, Naples Daily News, Naples, Florida

I hold it true, whate'er befall;

I feel it, when I sorrow most;

'Tis better to have loved and lost

Than never to have loved at all.

Alfred Lord Tennyson, In Memoriam

FOREWORD

This is a true story that took 12 years to complete. Part I is the hardest to read, especially for those who endured the pain of fighting to save a spouse's life and losing. For those who haven't, perhaps it will help you better understand what it's like. What you see or hear on the surface is merely the tip of the iceberg.

Much of Part I was taken directly from letters, emails and journal entries as things happened, the raw emotion evident. Emails or letters written to me are highlighted in ***bold, italicized*** print and ***indented*** on the page.

My replies and letters to others are *italicized* only.

Journal entries are noted as such until the year 2000, when email and letter exchanges no longer represent substantive portions of the text.

Part II gets easier to read as my grief waxed and waned. Surviving bereavement requires finding reasons to go on. Starting over, especially after multiple losses, seems almost impossible at times. Healing is a zigzag journey of unanticipated stops and starts. No one ever said it would be easy.

Part III is as much an adventure story as a diary of events that occurred during my search for a new life in a new place. I don't know how well I conveyed the fact that at times it seemed surreal. A writer can only do her best to convey feelings using words that are often inadequate to the task.

Some names have been changed to protect the privacy of specific individuals. Some individuals are introduced gradually as chapters unfold.

Since Part I was basically written in "real time," to thoroughly identify each person when first introduced would interrupt the flow of events as they occurred, I chose to let readers see and feel what was happening at that moment, without interruption. People merely referenced in Part I who played a more significant role in my life are fully identified later, as the "story" unfolds.

Accuracy sometimes suffers as a result of intense and vacillating emotions as are apparent, especially in Part I. Every line and event written about in this book is as accurate as I can recall. Some dates and times have been reconstructed to the best of my recollection since I didn't always record them.

It's important to note that some of the therapeutic strategies described in this book are controversial. We believed our use of them was beneficial, but it should not be construed as proof of value to everyone.

Any errors in this book are solely my responsibility.

Any resemblance to others living and dead is entirely intentional.

I owe a great deal of gratitude to everyone who supported me during the most difficult times of my life. There are too many to cite in this book, but you know who you are. Without your support, things might have turned out much differently.

I also owe a debt of gratitude to those who weren't always there when I might have benefitted from their presence. They helped me better understand my own strengths, and develop a greater capacity for forgiveness and compassion. People do the best they can with the tools they have.

Better To Have Loved was written to help others, as well as close the book, so to speak, on chapters of my life that at times still seem like a dream. But it wasn't a dream. It really happened.

To my editor, Jay Schlichter, I can't thank you enough for helping to make this book the best it could be. Your gentle insights, advice and counsel have made me a better writer. I'm still amazed at your "eagle-eye." You see something I can be *staring* at and totally miss!

To those who have or will be required to start over, there are checklists in the addendum that I hope will help. To those who have completed the journey of renewal, perhaps this book will give others insight into just how far you have come. God bless you all.

Kathryn Taubert, Florida, October 1, 2013

For Albert

Journal entry: December 26, 2001, 10:00 a.m.

I try hard to burn his image in my brain as he lay dying on the pillow beside me. I know the memory of his still-handsome face will fade in time when he is gone. I can't bear the thought of him no longer next to me, where he's been the last, best 12 years of my life.

I never tire of watching him. Although he can no longer move as much as a finger, I know him well enough to see the almost imperceptible changes in his fine, patrician features as I tell him I love him, how happy he's made me, and that I will be okay.

Some part of him will live in my heart forever.

Some part of me will die with him.

PART I

January 1999-December 2001

1.

Monday, January 18, 1999, 12:04 a.m.

To Denise:
From: Kathryn

Denise, don't look for me for a bit. Admitted Albert to Danbury Hospital tonight through emergency room with severe back pain. CT scan shows obstruction of right ureter.

Al on heavy pain meds and sleeping now. Doctor doesn't think this is kidney stone, but says not to speculate too much at this point. Possible surgery based on orders tonight.

Keep us in your prayers.

Kathryn

Tuesday, January 19, 1999, 8:59 p.m.

To: Kathryn

>I just read your email. How is Al? What is the latest? Do you need anything? Who is the MD on the case? We will call to check in. Our thoughts and prayers are with you both. Anything you need, you know we will be there to help.

>Denise

Journal: 10:00 p.m.

From the moment the doctor said "obstruction," I knew. Vague discomforts evolving into severe pain, vomiting. Sterile emergency room clerks, preternaturally calm clinicians, sick and injured lining the walls, curiosity overcoming discretion as they stare at the writhing man on the stretcher and his frantic wife.

Triage they call it - "to sort."

Sometimes I think the "sorting" comes at the expense of sensitivity. Condescending clerks shush my demands for help *now*!

Don't they know that he never complains about anything? Can't they see he is in *pain*?

Finally, a vacant cubicle, scant privacy for this agony. Probably a kidney stone, they say.

Averted eyes of attending clinicians rotate in sudden interest to the CT scan revealing the mass in his abdomen. This was more than they expected.

His pain was *not* exaggerated. Her frantic demands for help *were* justified. This was no mere kidney stone.

Wednesday, January 20, 1999, 9:00 p.m.

To: Denise
Denise, thanks for calling today. It was a bit difficult to talk. Al was on his way into surgery. It's probably cancer in the duct between kidney and bladder. Tumor doesn't seem to have spread. His attitude is very good. He's a serene man. He'll be home from the hospital within a few days.

He was already out of bed and walking after surgery. He's in excellent health otherwise. Tumor probably hasn't been there more than a few weeks, months at most. That worries me. If it's growing that fast...

Al will probably be a shining beacon of strength and resolve through all of this. It's one day at a time from now on. My volunteer stuff has taken a lower rung on my list of priorities.

If anyone asks, Al has an abdominal tumor, treatments are beginning next week, and the outlook is good. We're taking this a day at a time. We're still processing this, getting all the facts, ducks in a row.
K.

10:00 p.m.

> ***To Kathryn:***
> ***>I won't mention it to anyone else unless you want me to. Let us help you and Al in any way. You know the expression, "what goes around, comes around." Let it come your way! Denise***

I appreciate that, Denise. It's always been hard for me to ask for anything. Life keeps throwing opportunities at me to do it. This is going to be one of those times when I won't have any other choice.

> **>I guess God gets your attention one way or the other.**
> ***Denise***

Right now I can't let myself think too far ahead, Denise. My dear little mother has been a real trouper, answering the phone, keeping information flowing at a modest level, cooking. Jackie has been keeping my mother company and bringing her to the hospital to see Albert. I've been at the hospital all day and into the evenings.

Tuesday we'll begin the treatment consultations. Al's classmate is an oncologist. I'm also going to write Jim Leckman at Yale for a referral. He's always been so helpful to those of us who volunteered as study patients for the Yale Child Study center's research on Tourette syndrome.

We're being positive. The good news is that it is so new it hasn't spread beyond the immediate area. But it grew so fast, in a dangerous place.

If anyone can beat this, it's him. He's so calm from years of flying. I don't think Dory has processed the seriousness of her father's situation. She hasn't called since he's been in the hospital. I don't think she's able to handle it yet. I'm not sure she ever truly processed her mother's death.

And of course, we have no idea what to expect of Adam. His narcotic addiction is so profound. I've often wondered if he ever truly recovered from his mother's death from cancer. And now this.

Albert will want to protect everyone, including me. I am struggling from moment to moment. This is what I dreaded most. I've tried to live every day as though it could not *happen again.*

Al is the strong one. Somehow, I have to find the strength. He trusts me. He will need me more than ever. His intense look at me tonight spoke volumes: "Get on the Internet and see what you can find," he said.

I think we both know the initial treatment recommendations came too easily. They're offering only palliative care.

We're thinking ahead to clinical trials, if there is anything. In the last 24 hours, he's processed more. We haven't talked much about it yet. We'll deal with this at home. There is no privacy here. I am scrambling to get as much together off the Internet that I can find. He hasn't yet asked me to tell him what the doctors have said.

I tell him only what he asks, as his doctors seem to be doing. Perhaps he doesn't want to know. Or perhaps he already does? He asked me this afternoon if the final report was in yet.

All those years he suffered with his wife's cancer, he knows what comes next. My heart is breaking as I write this. Keep us in your prayers. And thanks for being there. I need that.
K.

Journal: 11:00 p.m.

Agonized waiting for results. Hope. Dread. Sleeplessness. I told the doctor not to sugar coat it. I need the truth.

Maybe if I impress this doctor with my strength and knowledge he will see that this patient is worth his best efforts, as though somehow that would make a difference.

They just opened his abdomen and closed him back up again.

A vicious, insidious spider crawling through his body, laying webs of destruction over vessels and nerves in agonizingly effective obliteration of everything in its path.

"Inoperable." Killing its host slowly, inexorably, and me with him. How could one word strike such terror into my heart?

I can't bear to lose him too. Not after losing Jim. Please God let me wake up and find this another bad dream. Al is my whole life. What would I do without him?

2.

<u>Journal: Friday, January 22, 1999, 12:00 a.m.</u>

The raw familiarity of it. The nightmares are back. I told everyone I've been sleeping okay. But how *can* I when he's lying alone in the hospital bed?

I couldn't sleep in that room with some stranger on the other side of the curtain, hearing every breath, move, tear-filled moment. I need to keep strong for Al.

How could this be happening *again*?

How can I think of myself when he's beginning the hardest fight of his life and needs me most? How can I handle all the details, calls, questions, visitors and still be strong enough for the fight ahead?

I must find the strength to do it.

Can I handle the truth for both of us? He hasn't asked for the prognosis yet. I marvel at his ability to live each moment as it comes. How I wish I could live life as he does, one day at a time.

I couldn't miss the doctor's almost imperceptible nod when I asked him if *this* was something that would go fast. I try so hard to pretend everything is going to be okay.

God, what a fraud I am.

12:00 p.m.

To: Denise
It's a high grade, aggressive and inoperable tumor. We're looking at alternative treatment options too. Throwing everything we have at this.

Al's attitude is wonderful. I'm keeping busy trying to organize the information for him to develop the "plan."

The doctors told me his prognosis is "guarded."

It could go very fast. The tumor is too close to major blood vessels and nerves. I'm afraid. I'm reliving memories of the horror of losing Jim. Somehow I have to find what I need to get through this.

Albert is my life, Denise. He's the best thing that ever happened to me.

For now, I can only think of one day at a time.

Al hasn't heard "guarded" yet. He knows it's a rare tumor that wasn't removed because it was too integrated in surrounding tissues.

His friends are coming by. Jackie is a big help. Dory is coming tomorrow. Adam doesn't answer his messages. Thanks for being there. I do need your counsel. I've discussed this with no one else. You are a blessing.
K.

Journal: Saturday, January 23, 1999

I spend hours searching the Internet for ordnance that will send this monster back to the Hell it came from, calling and writing friends who might have answers or know someone who does.

There are so many “cures” and attesting “survivors.” How do I interpret everything? I’m in so far over my head. The blizzard of information, options, and testimonials with no one to help sort them out.

Telephone numbers for “cancer hotlines” no longer in service.

Clinicians who say they’ll call back and don’t.

Doctors too busy to talk on the phone, making appointments to see you weeks hence.

Well-meaning friends who know somebody cured of cancer by this or that treatment, but don’t remember who, where, or when it was.

We don’t have *time* for this. We need answers *now.*

God, if only you could give the cancer to *me* instead! He’s so much better at living than I am.

He still has happy dreams. I never knew anybody like that before. He’s convinced he’ll beat this thing. He’s done things *right* all his life.

He should be the one to live….

He needs to be surrounded by friends and loved ones. I need to get the information for him to make the decisions that will save his life. Our lives.

This will be what keeps me going: finding the information from which he can choose his *cure*.

God, give me the strength and energy to do this.

3.

Tuesday, January 26, 1999

To: Denise
Pathology report confirms transitional cell carcinoma that responds to both chemo and radiation. That's the good news. Bad news is that it's a high-grade tumor, which means it's growing fast.

We have two appointments with oncologists. Al's friend Dr. Joe Bertino got him in on short notice with a surgeon specializing in this cancer. I'm continuing to collect data off the 'net and through a variety of other resources. It keeps me moving forward from moment to moment.

Al is his usual serene self, but with sobering moments of reflection. Both daughters here today, thankfully. He tires easily, the effects of two surgeries in two days, 20 staples across his abdomen, a stent inside the ureter.

He and girls are on their way out for a walk. I'm so glad Dory came to see him. Adam is spiraling downward again and trying to get into yet another methadone program.

Will keep you posted. Not much more to say till we see the specialists. Keep your prayers coming.
K.

Wednesday, January 27, 1999

To: James Leckman, M.D., Yale Child Study Center
From: Kathryn Taubert

Dear Jim,

We have appointments at Memorial Sloan Kettering Tuesday, and Columbia Presbyterian on Thursday. Please tell your friend that we've no doubt it was the use of his name that helped us get in so quickly.

We're seeing an oncologist in Danbury tomorrow afternoon and considering the concomitant use of alternative therapies that might help.

THANK YOU for your help. Whatever the outcome, the help, support, and prayers of our friends means the difference between being able to move forward and falling apart.
K.

9:43 a.m.

> ***To: Kathryn***
> ***>Please, for your own well-being and for Al's, let us help…you need to let someone help you take care of you as well.***
> ***Denise***

To: Denise
Mornings are always better for me, Denise. Each day seems like a new chance. I've collected volumes of information and options. The urologist, Ray Craven, removed stitches this morning. Ray's positive, conversational manner helped. Albert has always been a day-at-a-time kind of guy. He's so positive. I draw strength from him.

I've always managed to survive somehow. Your friendship helps so much, Denise.
K.

Journal: 1:00 p.m.

Is he really that serene? Or is he overwhelmed by the blizzard of information and what's happening to him? Pilots learn calm in the face of disaster. But I think this man was born that way. How I envy him.

Am I doing the right thing? He hasn't asked, sparing me the need to tell him that the tumor is in a dangerous location, growing fast and *inoperable*. That word again. Oh God how it scares me.

3:20 p.m.

To: Denise
Al holding his own although he has some discomfort from the stent holding the ureter open. He's limited to doing little exercise except walking.

Today, he's a bit low. I think too many people are asking too many questions: the hopeful, the curious, the well-intentioned. I'm encouraging him not to be so considerate of others at his own expense.

He told me I should practice what I preach.

He smiles from time to time. We have many poignant moments, recalling how we began. We've been practically inseparable these last years. I can't bear the thought it will end. I've lost too many people I love. All I can do is pray for the strength to get through this, for him. For us.

After Albert, there won't be much else for me. He's everything to me. He's given me strength and hope and love I never thought possible. All that happened before led me to him.

I'll keep fighting to keep him alive one more day, week, month. It's all I can do. He's all I have. He's all I want or need.
K.

Thursday, January 28, 1999, 5:22 p.m.

> ***What time is your appointment tomorrow? If you need to talk, get a hug, anything, I'm available...***
> ***Denise***

To: Denise
Our appointment is at 3:30 with oncologist Bob Cooper in Danbury. Dr. Joe has given us the name of a "heroic" surgeon at Columbia and another oncologist at Memorial Sloan-Kettering.

Albert told me again today he believes he'll beat this thing. If anyone can, he will.

Having a hard time. I've heard people say losing a child is the worst. I don't know, but I cannot imagine anything worse than losing someone with whom you literary share everything, day in and day out.

Al centers me, giving me strength, stability, love. I barely survived Jim's death. Years of grief therapy and antidepressants, struggling day by day for survival to get to a point where I wanted to live again.

Albert's love is the crowning jewel of my life.

Anger may be the only thing that gets me through this. I'll turn it on this monster inside of him and beat it to death.

I don't dare think of the alternative. Maybe I'm learning to do what I've so admired in Albert: live in the moment. I always wanted to be able to do that. God, you have to be careful what you wish for.
K.

Journal: 8:00 p.m.

How can they think of food? Al and my mother eating, laughing, and joking, as I sit there pretending. I envy them. *They* won't die alone. I know the devastation that will come as I bury them both one day.

9:54 p.m.

> ***>Kathryn, we love you. You and Al are in so many people's prayers…Good luck tomorrow. I'll be in touch tomorrow again.***
> ***>Denise***

To Denise:
I have to manage, somehow. It's surreal. I wasn't able to eat anything tonight. He and my mother are so close. They're cheerful, laughing at each other's jokes. How lucky they are! They know where they're going. Al says dying is merely getting "transferred."

He can't lose. If he lives he has his good life with those he loves. If he dies, he gets to go Home.

How can I be strong enough for this? If he doesn't make it, I can't imagine being in this place. Part of me has already gone. Thinking this way is the only way I can survive the devastation I know will come, yet again. Has it only been nine days since the diagnosis? It seems forever.

I have to stop thinking this way. Al is the one who keeps me going. He needs me strong. I've been working 15 hours a day looking for the magic bullet.

The raw pain of waking to the knowledge it's not just some awful dream. It's happening again.

The nightmares are back. I'm lost in an airport somewhere in Texas, desperate to get back to Connecticut, not knowing what time my flight leaves or even where it is, searching for it frantically and feeling as though I'll never find it in time.

I can't bury another one, Denise. I just can't. As God is my witness, I can't do this again.

Not yet. Not him.

Journal: 11:00 p.m.

How I love this man. How weak and powerless I feel in the face of my selfishness, crying over the fact that I know there isn't much hope. Do I tell him? How do I know what's best? How do I say the cancer will probably kill him in a few months?

"Don't bury him yet," they say. What do *they* know about what it's like to have the ones you love most dying in your arms? *Twice.*

5.

<u>Journal: Friday, January 29, 1999</u>

Today, we got hope. First we poison it. If that works, we cut out what's left and burn the rest away.

Chemotherapy for a few months and then rethink surgical options and possibly radiation.

It's no coincidence that "M-5" chemotherapy sounds like a weapon of war. Seventy percent of people treated get some reduction in the size and scope of the tumor.

Is "reduction" enough?

What about <u>cure?</u>

Saturday, January 30, 1999

Dear Dr. Bales:

We wanted to update you on Al's consultations. We were unable to reach Dr. P. for another opinion, so we secured an appointment with Dr. Derek Baines at Memorial Sloan Kettering for February 2.

We've arranged another surgical opinion as well with Dr. Carl Olsen, chief of renal surgery at Columbia Presbyterian for Thursday, February 4.

We've been asked to hand-carry copies of all reports to these physicians. We're also looking into complementary therapies. Al is feeling pretty good. He believes he can beat this. If anyone can, it's him.

Thank you for all your help.

Regards,

Kathryn Taubert

Journal: Sunday, January 31, 1999, 5:00 a.m.

It finally caught up with me. The horrible reality, sleepless nights and the terrible secret I keep.

People coming and going all day yesterday. I saw so little of him. This morning, the phone began again. I fell apart, wanting time with him this afternoon, just the two of us.

I was wrong to leave the house that way. I don't know how much more time with him I'll have. I was worried about him, the fatigue of all those calls, visitors. But even with cancer, he's got more energy than I do.

I ran out of the house and drove for hours. I ended up on the beach in Old Lyme, screaming at the top of my lungs in the car where no one could hear me.

I counted the pairs of ducks on the water. I *felt* the loss of the solitary one, whose life-mate was gone.

I found a beautiful stone in the sand amidst the broken shells. I imagined it a magic talisman and made a wish. I knew I'd recall that moment all my life. I don't know why.

How can I pretend things are like they used to be?

When I got home, I could see he was worried.

Mother was quiet. My guilt set in. How could I do this to them in the midst of their need for me to be strong? How could I fall apart so badly?

I needed time alone. I didn't want to come back to face losing him.

I'm being worn away like the sharp edges of that stone. If only I have the strength for it. I have to believe that there is a reason in my life for all this loss. It almost killed me when Jim died. I came out of that stronger, but how can I go through that again?

God give me strength. I am so tired.

11:00 p.m.

I wish we hadn't gone to the movie. He was uncomfortable because of the stent in his back. We went to eat afterward. I barely held myself together. Even Al was distracted. We tried to act normally.

How can others pretend nothing is different, and then when he's out of earshot, ask quietly, "How's he doing?"

They laugh, talk about the weather, Super Bowl, food. But they don't talk about the fact that my husband has inoperable cancer and nothing will *ever* be the same again.

How come I went straight from happiness to devastation and they got off at denial?

Journal: Monday, February 1, 1999

Stronger today. This roller coaster of hope and fear, hope and fear. How to explain the meltdown this weekend? I couldn't help it.

He understands my way of dealing with pain is different than his. He needs people around him. I need solitude.

He always forgives, forgets, and moves on. He hugs me and suddenly everything's okay. How I admire his compassion, his strength.

Maybe he gets to go Home now because his work here is finished. He's such a serene man.

We have such a wonderful life in lovely Newtown, CT. The life we've built together since meeting in 1988 seems like a dream sometimes. Both widowed, we knew the pain of losing a spouse. He lost his beloved Wilhemina after 29 years of marriage. I lost my husband Jim Holbrook after only three and a half years of marriage.

When Al and I married in 1991, I was 45 and Albert was 60. In spite of our age difference, I had to work hard to keep up with him! Now, at 68 years old, he looks a decade younger, still plays soccer with the "Over 40" team, and does everything "right." He's the most balanced person I've ever met.

Tomorrow we go to Memorial Sloan-Kettering in New York City. Will we find more hope there?

6.

Building a Team for Cancer Fight by Al Taubert

My diagnosis of January 24, 1999: tumor around the right ureter, about one inch above the bladder, which began probably within weeks or months at most.

Transitional cell carcinoma the size of a walnut, beginning in the wall ("lumen") of the ureter and growing outward.

Prior to this recent pain, I had other problems which were probably masking the pain in abdomen: Lumbar-4, L-5, S-1 disc herniations, found in a December 1999 MRI. I was under treatment with physical therapy.

Arthroscopic knee surgery in August '99. Physical therapy for that completed at the end of September. After rehab, the pain came on in lower abdomen. Routine colonoscopy in October showed diverticulosis. Gastroenterologist recommended high fiber and review in five years. Pain persisted, back to physical therapy for back, the pain now emanating to lower abdomen.

MRI in December revealed herniations. Physical therapy supposed to help.

January physical therapy for herniations and 6 days of antibiotics for possible diverticulitis didn't do much good. Had side effects after six days so stopped pills. Two days later, I went back to the doctor, who ordered another antibiotic, and recommended CT scan down the road if this didn't help. Vomited once in morning and at doctor's office. Later had an acute episode of pain in region of my right kidney (not previously noted).

Called doctor back and he ordered CT scan that night.

Vomiting began again. Kathryn took me to the emergency room where I had a CT scan which revealed a mass around the ureter.

On January 21, urologist Ray Craven inserted a stent into the right ureter and recommended surgery to biopsy the tumor that was constricting the ureter.

Tumor biopsy showed malignancy. Pathologist suspects high grade transitional cell carcinoma, confirmed by path report Tuesday, January 26. Tumor was not removed due to integration in surrounding tissue.

Had appointment for January 29 with oncologist for possible chemo/radiation to begin immediately on an out-patient basis.

Team members:

MDs for conventional therapy
MDs alternative medicine
Surgeons
Oncologists
Nutritionists

Health food store
Websites for clinical trials, alternative therapies in USA and other countries
Websites for support groups, alternative medicine strategies
Therapists for complementary medicine (acupuncture, hypnotherapy)
Pathology labs
Hospitals and doctors; medical records departments.
Insurance companies
Family, friends, spiritual support

Journal: February 1, 1999

I was both relieved and chastened. He took back control today.

He's so deferential with employees who see only blank spaces on calendars to fill in with faceless names. They don't realize that some of us don't *have* another week to wait.

There isn't *time* to be so nice. One of us has to *demand* action.

I edit his conversation while he's on the phone, tell him to *insist* on speaking with the doctor *now*."

"YES, IT IS AN EMERGENCY!"

He grows irritated with me.

My God, we are going to have to fight this disease with *poison!* Is there any choice?

What one can learn in so short a time? A few minutes of consultation with a doctor. Scrambling for information on your own with so little time to do it. Sorting through the blizzard of options for help. Something this important shouldn't have to be done that way without time to thoroughly consider all options. It's just *wrong*!

7.

Journal: Tuesday, February 2, 1999

It's the latest treatment, but with huge risks. The alternative is dying sooner rather than later.

The house usually wins in any gamble. This "house" is inhabited by a demon that strikes without mercy. I have more hope than I did last week. But I'm still afraid.

This town is no place for widows and orphans. Without him, I will be both.

Dr. Baines at Sloan-Kettering says the cancer is localized. Based on recent studies they no longer use M-5 for this.

What if we'd accepted the initial recommendations for the few months of palliative care they gave him at the beginning?

Albert is a possible candidate for a six-month, Phase I clinical trial of "sequenced drug therapy." Although his particular cancer is rare, as a study patient, he's in a category that had greater survival rates in early tests.

Those patients hadn't lost weight, had good "performance data," and no other disease.

Chemotherapy is to be administered every two weeks along with injections of a recombinant DNA biological "growth factor" to enhance immune function during days 3 through 11 of the first round of chemotherapy, and days 6 through 16 of the second round.

Al may not be eligible because of hearing loss from decades of flying. He has an audiology test Thursday. We need to collect urine for 12 hours for kidney function tests, as well as get blood and urine samples.

I have to call Danbury hospital pathology department for additional slides for the surgeon at Columbia-Presbyterian.

Journal: Wednesday, February 3, 1999

Yesterday we also saw the surgeon associated with the clinical trial. After chemotherapy, this doctor will remove almost the entire right side of Al's urinary tract: kidney, ureter, top of the bladder. He said this will help prevent recurrence.

Something doesn't feel right.

Take a perfectly good kidney too? I guess the desperate nature of our situation is still sinking in.

I called a psychiatrist today. I can't afford to be sick now. I have too much to do.

My Internet search revealed that taking a healthy kidney is no more effective than sparing it, as long as the chemotherapy shrinks it first.

MSK's surgeon admitted they are "very aggressive" in treating this cancer.

It seems so drastic to take a perfectly health kidney too!

Journal: February 4, 1999

Today we met for a second surgical opinion with Dr. Carl Olsson of Columbia Presbyterian Hospital in New York, armed with the new information about kidney-sparing surgery.

I entered the office towing a barge of grief as surely as my husband was buoyed by his ever-present optimism.

Without so much as a glance as we sat before his desk, Dr. Olsson's first words brought us up a bit short.

"And what is your problem?" he asked, emphasizing *"your."* We were just more in a long line of appellants.

Fountain pen poised over ruled pad, perfectly tailored suit, dark comb-over and smudge of a mustache, Dr. Carl Olsson was all business.

Warily glancing at each other, Albert began to talk as I took notes.

I liked the fact that Olsson took the medical history himself. Repeating details of one's illness to a succession of nurses and doctors is frustrating. I've often wondered how often many doctors refer to those notes, having had to remind them before of an important detail.

Albert spoke as I glanced around the office to the models of tall ships and various sailing paraphernalia adorning the walls. On one wall was a photo of the younger Olsson standing proudly at the wheel of an ocean-going sailing vessel.

Another wall contained a shelf with books about sailing and the sea. I searched for some means of penetrating this man's stern façade. I wanted to reach him on a level that would make him especially interested in saving the man sitting across from him.

The one at whom he hadn't even yet glanced!

"You're a sailor," I said during a lull, as Olsson pondered his notes.

Suddenly, *he was there.*

Lifting his head and laying down his pen, Dr. Olsson sat back in his chair and looked directly at *me.*

"Yes, I am," the barest hint of a smile beneath the dark smudge on his lip.

"We were told by another surgeon that he'd remove the kidney, ureter and top of the bladder after chemotherapy. Is that what you would do also?" I asked.

"Perhaps not. Removing a perfectly healthy kidney upstream of the tumor might not be necessary, since disease usually recurs downstream," he replied.

I was encouraged.

"We've also been told that you're the best. Is that true?" I dared.

Suddenly mortified at my temerity, I tried desperately to hide my intimidation from the man who just might literally hold my husband's life in his hands.

His mustache twitched ever-so-slightly as his dark eyes penetrated mine.

"Well, I wouldn't want to suggest that," he replied. *"But cancer is all I do."*

There it was. The *passion* we'd yet to find as we drowned in the medical sterility of the last two weeks.

My God. Had it only been two weeks?

I could practically feel the atmosphere lift around us. Olsson's passion was our hope.

Rising from his chair, Dr. Olsson walked around the desk to escort us to the door.

We *heard* the clunking of his *wooden peg leg* first, elevating this man to metaphorical heights befitting the *humanist* we'd only just perceived.

Al and I were speechless. Olsson's prosthesis wasn't apparent until that surreal departure from his office.

This Ahab's white whale was *cancer*.

We departed realizing just how far down we'd been until that moment.

"He's the first doctor I've seen that's made me really feel like he was going to save my life," Al said.

Suddenly, I had more hope than I had since this nightmare began.

"You can help us beat the demon, Dr. O.," I thought.

And we will. For us, *and* for you.

Olsson recommended another CT scan after about six weeks of chemotherapy in the clinical trial. If the tumor shrinks, we'll continue it for another four cycles (May or June), then operate.

If it doesn't decrease in size, we're to see Olsson for immediate surgery.

Optimistically we made a future appointment for surgery in August, well after the conclusion of the clinical trial.

We rode home to Newtown in relieved silence. For the first time I felt the initial prognosis could be wrong!

I was glad I hadn't told Albert what I knew about his condition.

He never asked.

I never said.

He's too smart *not* to have known it!

But in typical Albert fashion, he lives one optimistic day at a time.

8.

Journal: Friday, February 5, 1999

We're trying to get the results of his hearing test 10 days before our scheduled appointment. We can't waste another 10 days if Albert isn't eligible for the clinical trial!

I used to work in a hospital clinical lab. Test results that take minutes to complete often sit for days on someone's desk before the patient gets them.

Ten days for the results of an audiology test? Don't they know that with this tumor *we don't have time!*

I'll keep calling until I get an answer.

I also made an appointment for nutritional therapy with a naturopathic physician, Dr. Ron Schmid of Middlebury, CT. We're putting Al's team together person by person, piece by piece.

Saturday, February 6, 1999

Al just barely passed the hearing test for the clinical trial! We made appointments for the required pre-trial heart and bone tests. The large doses of chemo could damage his hearing as well as his heart function.

I'm struck by the irony of letting a man die of cancer because his hearing isn't good enough to participate in a trial that might save his life. To live, one has to be well enough to risk dying of the treatment.

9.

Sunday, February 7, 1999

Hi Everyone:

Thanks to everyone for your concern. It's three weeks after Al's diagnosis, and we're just now getting to a point where we have things to report.

Please forgive the delay, but it's been a whirlwind trying to find the necessary information to make a plan.

Al will be participating in a promising clinical trial at Memorial Sloan-Kettering Cancer Center, conducted by an authority on his kind of cancer. We've seen several specialists and after factoring everything into the equation, Al chose this route, with surgery to follow.

Preliminary results of the treatment have been exciting. The MSK group believes they are "onto something big." Al's overall health profile suggests the possibility of especially promising results, with a number of individuals remaining cancer-free after five years. The downside is that the chemo lasts for 24 weeks, compared to a standard regimen about half that. The upside is that toxicity levels for these meds seem lower.

It's called "sequenced drug therapy," which basically means that all the meds to be used have been tested previously, but not in this format.

There are potential side effects as there are to any of these medications, but Al is such a healthy guy, we're confident he'll fare very well.

Should he respond as hoped, surgery will occur after chemotherapy.

Processing everything in crash course fashion is more challenging than imagined. Were it not for our good friends, family, God, and the Internet, we'd have had much less success navigating this gauntlet.

What do people do who don't have the ability and resources we have? The key is finding information that's not always readily available. We wouldn't have known about these options had we not searched for it ourselves. Sorting through the blizzard of information and making difficult decisions is overwhelming. It points to the need for advocates to help people sort through the maze.

Clinicians need to link patients with advocates and support groups who understand treatment options, insurance issues, legal matters, and so on.

Al is a marvel. He's always been pretty much a day-at-a-time guy, optimistic and serene. There is something very special about him. He still has his happy dreams.

With both the conventional and alternative treatments we've already implemented, his wonderful attitude and spirit, the prayers and encouragement of friends and family, we're going to beat this thing. As Albert says, this is "merely another journey in life."

We're back and forth between Danbury and New York City with tests to finalize the treatment plan. We're required to go to Memorial Sloan-Kettering every couple of weeks, but most of the treatment will be administered locally thanks to Dr. Bob Cooper's willingness to work with the MSK doctors.

I have to give Albert periodic injections myself. He jokes that I'm looking forward to that.

Thanks to all of you for your prayers. I'm also sending this to you who haven't been aware of the drill we've been going through since January 18. It's hard to believe it's only been two weeks!

It's happened so fast we've not had time to keep in touch with everyone. We know you understand.

Al says he already feels the tumor shrinking.

If you don't hear from us, it's because we're busy setting up for treatments to begin about February 16. Email is much easier than the telephone, tied up with calls the last couple of weeks.

Your love, support, and prayers have meant so much, and will continue to do so. We are lucky to have so many friends who care. That's helped more than you know.

Love, Kathryn and Al

10.

Journal: Tuesday, February 9, 1999

It took two days to reach the doctor. Later he said his secretary didn't tell him it was a priority call.

He gave me his personal number, agreeing to administer Al's chemotherapy in Danbury, as part of the clinical trial.

I left the message with the doctor in charge of the program in New York. I hope he gets it soon. I take a page from Al's book, trying to be as polite as I am persistent.

Unless I keep calling, I have no idea if or when the messages get through.

Sometimes, I wish everyone who works in a doctor's office could be a desperately ill patient just once.

How *can* they know the desperation we feel without having been there and kept waiting when *there is so little time*?

I have become far pushier than I like, but there are too many delays in the system for desperately ill patients.

These last months have again proven to me that it's necessary to take charge of one's own medical care.

People must become educated consumers of treatments and services.

We need to speak up and make demands when necessary, find clinicians willing to have us as partners, not mere supplicants.

It's horrible waiting for phone calls never returned, test results completed in minutes but not reported for days, sitting for hours past appointment times waiting for doctors only to find out they never got our reports or, worse yet, *lost* them.

Albert has been stoic. In addition to bags of medical records, I've taken to carrying a bag of magazines as he does to pass the time. We've waited as much as three hours beyond our scheduled appointment to see a doctor.

Al's stent makes him uncomfortable, sitting so long. Walking helps, but the minute you leave the waiting room, they might call you and you lose your place in line.

Lost CT scans and medical reports have led me to carry duplicate copies of *everything* to appointments. I have a filing cabinet full of them now.

When calls don't come or reports don't show up after a day or two, I get on the phone or show up at the door. I'm pleasant, but persistent.

Don't these people know how difficult this is without having to fight the system that's supposed to help?

Well-meaning "patient representatives" don't seem to have any real authority to change things. We're not the first to endure this, I know.

The most efficient of all is Dr. Olsson's, run with military efficiency. His nurse returns calls promptly and is able to provide answers herself, inspiring further confidence.

Al is scheduled for surgery in six months on August 27, leaving sufficient time to recover from the clinical trial at Memorial Sloan-Kettering. Assuming it works. It has to work.

Dr. Olsson once returned our call at 9:00 p.m. I wondered how he managed to have a life, too.

I was felt grateful as well as sorry for him, more cognizant of the difficulty dedicated clinicians have managing their own lives while battling to save others.

Cancer takes a toll on more than just the patient.

11.

Journal: Wednesday, February 10, 1999

Life almost seems normal after a glass of wine. I wish I could find something else that would help without giving me such a headache.

We've got the plan pretty much in place, but it shouldn't be this way. The mad scramble against time, looking for the magic bullet with whatever resources one can assemble on one's own.

How do people manage this alone? As capable as Albert is, he's still desperately ill.

I watched him process it slowly at first. Initially he treated it as though nothing was different, while I was frantic, desperate. He was so calm, matter-of-fact. Each of us deals with things in our own way.

Each day the clock ticks off another 24 hours of a life already threatened by inoperable cancer. Without an advocate, the patient is at a terrible disadvantage. If the caregiver can't maintain her own strength, they're both doomed to the mercy of others who may have good intentions, but not the requisite *passion* required to save one more life among many.

It's understandable why cancer clinicians distance themselves. They see so many patients die. But emotional detachment has a cost. The patient often becomes just one more in the long line of desperately ill.

It really *is* about what and whom you know. We have options: good insurance, medical contacts, and many friends.

Will it save his life? At least we have more hope now. At this point, I *need to believe*. I don't dare let myself think otherwise.

People mean well, but questions about our choices erode my confidence. I wish I didn't know what I know. I hope the prognosis was wrong. God, please let it be wrong.

I've learned more about cancer than I ever wanted to know. I've crammed for the hardest exam I'll ever have to take to become a suitable partner in Al's war against it. I gather the information for him to do the most important job he's ever had: make the decisions, endure the treatment, and *heal.*

He's taking dozens of supplements daily, following nutritional guidelines recommended by our Dr. Schmid. I'm following a similar program to make it easier on him. It certainly won't hurt to get myself back on a healthy food and supplement routine as well.

Every week I fill three small paper cups of supplements for each of us per day. That corner of the kitchen looks like a pharmacy. Nutritional interventions and supplements cured me of advanced endometriosis 30 years ago. Can they help him now too?

Friends say *"You're in our thoughts."* Then they launch into details of their own lives.

I can't focus on their kids' slumber parties, school plays, or family vacations. I try to be polite, but find myself tuning out.

Those who've been there *know*. It's in their eyes.

"*We love you. We're here.*" That's all they need to say. Anything more is too much.

At times I want to disappear to a place where the sun never sets and the water is blue and soothing. I want to forget this pain, this fear.

I feel so selfish thinking of myself when Albert's facing the hardest fight of his life. I think the caregiver suffers as much sometimes as the patient.

I don't want to be out of Al's sight for a moment. I need to build as many memories with him as I can.

Maybe, just maybe, he'll be the textbook case that beats this monster. If anyone can, it's him.

How ironic it would be if he survives it and I don't?

I know I'm not supposed to bargain with You, God, but give me just five more years with him. Please. Don't take him from me now.

12.

Journal: Thursday, February 11, 1999

I was able to get copies of Al's pre-clinical trial tests without going through the usual hurry up and wait, thanks to a friend of Al's at the hospital.

What do people without such resources do, waiting for days for an appointment just to get the paperwork necessary for the next crucial steps?

It's not fair. Yet I'm thankful we're blessed with such friends.

Clinicians for the clinical trial told us what to expect and what they hope to achieve. They weren't happy with Al's list of supplements. I went prepared with clinical studies showing that these things do help reduce inflammation, scarring and toxicity.

"Absolutely not," Dr. Baines said.

I understand the need for consistency among study patients. But isn't there a way to balance the needs of the individual with the needs of the protocol?

I took an article from the ***British Medical Journal*** from the hospital's own website, reporting a recent study of patients with tumors similar to Al's and treated with high doses of vitamins A, C, E, and B6. It reduced the rate of recurrence.

Why does it take so much to convince clinicians that alternative therapies might help? Why does it take so long for demonstrable successes to become mainstream?

Is it because there's too much money in the status quo?

Cancer is an *industry*.

Al decided to pursue the "integrative medicine" approach, combining conventional and alternative treatments.

I feel guilty because I know I influence him, even though I try not to. Am I doing the right thing?

He's always been his own man. But he trusts me. I'll keep researching the information and encouraging him to make the decisions. It's his life and the choices should be his.

But when he asks, I give him my opinion.

We trust each other.

13.

Saturday, February 13, 1999, 2:24 p.m.

To: Kathryn
>You certainly do sound better, Kathryn. Taking charge and action helps. Beginning the plan/treatment puts things into another perspective. Until you had a plan, everything was unknown. Trying something gives hope. It sounds like the doctor at MSK is trying to be realistic.

No promises but there is hope. It always looked obvious that you and Al loved each other. It even comes through in your emails. As much as it is Al's ultimate decision, you play a key role here and it will always guide him.

It doesn't matter who else thinks you're bitchy. It only matters what Al thinks! It's so unfortunate that people have to be so frustrated by trying to get good medical care. There is something very wrong with our system and who has access to what care and all the red tape involved.

Your advocating for Al gives him the space to be in his own skin and stay centered enough to make choices and centered enough to stay focused and

strong. Fear can be disabling. He needs to keep his wits about him. You have an incredible way about you and I'm sure in this situation you haven't lost it. You will only help him feel the peace he needs to deal with what he needs to deal with.

But what about you? Although you sound more hopeful, are you really OK? Are you and Al able to have any fun time? Have you laughed together? Please, please remember to take care of yourself as well. You are no good to him if you aren't in good shape. Need anything?????
>Denise

<u>Journal: 10:00 p.m.</u>

Has it only been *four weeks* since this nightmare began? It feels like a year. I still can't believe how quickly life can change. One minute, you are happy, serene.

The next, you're devastated, facing the horror of losing someone you love more than anything else in the world and having him die in your arms, just like Jim did in mine.

Gone in five minutes and *your* whole life with him. I have everything I need with Albert. It's all I could ever want. Please, God. Not again. Don't take him from me too.

14.

Journal: Sunday, February 14, 1999, Valentine's Day

They're going to give him a drug that will help with some of the side effects. We'll have to get it directly from the hospital in New York City each time Al has a chemo treatment in Danbury.

As long as I've lived near the City, I said I'd *never* drive in it. Jim used to say, "Never ever say 'Never ever.'"

Al continued driving till now. But it was going to be up to me to get the medication for his shots. It couldn't be delivered and had to be picked up in New York City at the time of each chemotherapy treatment in Danbury, an hour and a half away.

Al said the best way to drive in New York is "don't look left or right so you won't know what's coming at you!"

I *think* he was kidding. He's so calm, and funny. How I wish I could be more like him.

That's when Charlie DeSantis stepped in. *"I'll be there to drive you,"* he said. He didn't just ask, he identified our need and met it. At times like these, you don't always know what you need. Charlie saved me that day, maybe literally.

Somehow, I'll find a way to drive there myself in the future. I've got two weeks to figure it out. I've gotten through a lot worse than New York City traffic.

How do people endure this emotional roller coaster?

15.

I came home from the grocery store to find two small, white wildflowers in a jelly-glass of water on the kitchen counter.

Al had been walking in the woods again.

I've never had a more beautiful Valentine's Day bouquet.

Journal: February 15, 1999

I haven't spent any time on the Tourette syndrome support group since this began. My friends Sheryl Keith and Joanne Cohen are taking up the slack. It never ceases to amaze me how one's life and priorities can change in a moment. I was never more aware of that than the night Jim died as I tried saving his life.

They didn't tell you in 1983 that CPR only worked in about six percent of the cases. My husband of only three and a half years, Jim Holbrook, wasn't to be among them.

God please don't let me fail *this* time.

16.

<u>Tuesday, February 16, 1999, 4:25 a.m.</u>

To: Dr. Derek Baines
Memorial Sloan-Kettering Cancer Center

Al and I worked out the attached schedule for the clinical trial directly from the statement of informed consent. It helped us with a visual representation of what the trial was about while making the final decision. We thought someone else might find it useful. Al and I both believe he is in the best hands possible with you and your staff at MSK, working with Dr. Bob Cooper in Danbury.

Thanks again for your time, effort and dedication to finding the treatment and cure for cancer. We're looking forward to Al's being in the group that represents your successful efforts on behalf of us all.

Regards,

Al and Kathryn Taubert

<u>Journal: 10:00 p.m.</u>

I'm doing everything I can so they remember who Al is as a person, not merely a research patient. I put together a chart based on the treatment plan. It's daunting. Perhaps someone else can benefit from it too?

Tuesday, February 16, 1999

To: Denise, Joanne, Sheryl.

Al had his first five-hour chemotherapy session today in Danbury. He basically sat in a lounge chair with all the other chemo patients, reading and swapping stories. We worked it out with MSK that he will have virtually all of his treatments in Danbury, through oncologist Bob Cooper's office. It'll save us many trips to New York City.

Side effects thus far are relatively minor and mostly the result of the medication to prevent them.

We're watching him pretty closely today. He's up and around, eating, doing chores. He went for a walk tonight. He doesn't feel 100 percent, but better than expected. I'm not too surprised. With the nutritional regimen he's been on the last month, he should be levitating his way through this whole thing.

We anticipate his white blood count will be its lowest within the next week or 10 days. Depending upon how well the growth hormone works, he may or may not experience the typical fever, chills, etc. Expecting some hair loss.

He's not at all worried about that. "I've got lots of hats if my head gets cold." The man has no vanity. He really is what I want to be when I grow up.

This wonder drug growth hormone (GCSF) is a genetically engineered, recombinant DNA product.

I'll be giving him a total of about 100 shots over six months, for a total cost of about $35,000 for that medication alone!

MSK developed the drug to help chemotherapy patients avoid some of the destruction of immune fighting cells during treatment.

It's still somewhat experimental. MSK is eager to see it absorbed into mainstream cancer therapy. It is prohibitively expensive at this time. We get it at no charge as part of the clinical trial as long as we pick it up in New York ourselves.

If we weren't part of this clinical trial, we'd never have heard of it, or fighting with our insurer to cover it.

The two chemo drugs he's receiving during this first 12 weeks are Adriamycin and Gemcitibine, both of which have been tested individually. The first round of patients received these to test for toxicity. Eventually he'll get Isofosfamide, Paclitaxel, and Cisplatin as well.

Al is part of the third group receiving the doses that worked best. He gets the first two plus the GCSF for 12 weeks. Then he'll get the other three and GCSF for the last 12 weeks. He's getting almost four times the "normal" dosage of one of the five chemotherapy drugs alone. I'm afraid.
Kathryn

Wednesday, February 17, 1999

To: Alt.Support.Tourette Friends and Colleagues,
From: Kathryn
Re: Hi Everyone!

We had some laughs yesterday. I took Al for his round of chemotherapy in Danbury. My mother and I then drove to New York City to pick up the first round of GCSF.

It was my first solo trip driving there, as well as my mother's. She went along for the ride, brave little soul that she is.

Every time mother is in the car with me, we find a parking space, no matter where we are. She's convinced Daddy is always riding with us. But finding a parking space in New York City?

Half a block from the hospital, a spot opened up in front of a fire hydrant. I figured if the guy vacating it got away with it, so could I since I wasn't going to be there long.

Mother agreed to keep an eye out for cops and tow trucks. This sweet little 85-year-old Texas lady remained in the car. I sprinted into the hospital to get the drugs, dashing back to beat the traffic going back to Danbury in time to pick up Albert after his treatment.

Returning to the car, I found mother next to the open window, hand on her open wallet!

"Mother, what are you doing with your wallet in full view of the open car window?" I asked worriedly.

"I was waiting for a policeman to tell me to move. I was going to give him a $10 tip to let us stay here a while."

Visions of her arrest leapt before my eyes: "Texas octogenarian arrested for attempted bribery of New York City police officer."

"Mother, were you REALLY going to bribe a cop?"

"I was just going to tip him to let us stay till you got back with the drugs," she replied innocently.

She really is that innocent, even at 85. She was surprised when I suggested that her "tip" might be thought a bribe. We both had a good laugh at what her friends in Galveston would say!

Albert later joked that the cop probably would have arrested her for not offering more!

Laughs these days are few and far between. I'm just glad I didn't have to bail mother out of jail while explaining the $5,000 worth of drugs in my possession as I sprinted out of the hospital.

She really got into the experience; "scolding" cabbies who wouldn't let us change lanes, threatening to "bribe" cops, guzzling water out of a bottle "like all the Yuppies do."

"It was fun, Kathryn. I never thought I'd be driving in New York City."

Neither did I, Mother Dear. Neither did I.

Albert looks, sounds, and feels pretty good under the circumstances. We feel the tumor shrinking. I'm doing better, stronger, more determined. He inspires me. We're taking life one day at a time. We believe we'll beat this thing. He already has, in his mind. He is serene.

I'm flying mother home to Texas Saturday and returning Sunday. Keep those positive energies and prayers coming. Albert looks at me with glistening eyes and says, "I just can't believe how much love I feel around me in all of this."

It means the world to us both. Thank you all for covering for me in so many ways. I may venture back to the Tourette's support group soon. It's been virtually non-stop and a drill I wouldn't wish on my worst enemy. I can't believe it's only been a month.

I've started to find the necessary rhythm to see this through. How can I not be strong, when Albert is the one with cancer and doing so well? He's always a tower of strength and inspiration for me. Now, more than ever.

I'm trying to take care of myself too, recognizing my vulnerability to depression. I'm back on antidepressants, dammit. It took me years to get off them after Jim died. But I can't take the chance of getting sick now.

You wouldn't believe how many supplements Al takes daily. I'm also taking 65, about half what he does. He drinks the equivalent of 12 pounds of organic vegetables a day in fresh juice and eats all the right stuff. His cravings for coffee, cookies have all but disappeared. He was bothered by a whiff of baking cookies yesterday. "My system is so purified that I can't even stand the smell of that stuff."

I'm consuming the same foods he does. At least Dr. Baines agreed to let him stay on the supplements, drawing the line at herbs, however. Since I'm not up on them enough to disagree with him, we relented. Albert called it "a draw."

Al feels good about the route he's chosen. His attitude and general health other than the cancer are very good. Like another New Yorker said yesterday while getting his own chemotherapy: "Sheesh. Cancer, schmancer. As long as you're healthy, what does it mattah?!"

That was laugh number two.

The days are filled with phone calls. Email is best. I can get to it as time and energy permit. I asked Albert what he wanted me to say about it to our Tourette syndrome support group colleagues.

"I have cancer. Maybe if they see that it has a face, they won't be quite so afraid of it. This is just one more

journey for me. Maybe there's a reason for this. It's part of God's plan."

Is it any wonder why this man is the center of my world?

Lv, Kathryn

17.

Journal: Monday, March 1, 1999

Al stepped out of the shower with a wad of hair in his hand. "I guess I won't get a haircut this week."

God how I love this man.

Journal: Tuesday, March 2, 1999

Terry visited Albert today. Al joked about it "getting chillier," as he swiped away yet another handful of hair.

The look on Terry's face reminded me that most aren't prepared for this, especially when it happens to someone who's always been the picture of health and vigor.

Maybe that's why some of his friends have yet to come to see him.

Sunday, March 7, 1999

Dear Dr. Eason
Re: peripheral neuropathy

My husband is on high dose Adriamycin and Gemcitabine as part of a clinical trial. After his first treatment, he had a few hours of discomfort in his hands. After his second treatment, his hands swelled a bit, became red and hurt so that he couldn't open a jar.

Soaking them in warm water and Epsom salts helped, but the pain lasted for more than 24 hours before the swelling went down and the pain went away. He also felt sensitive to touch all over. Is this a symptom of peripheral neuropathy? Many thanks for your help.

Kathryn Taubert

Monday, March 8, 1999

***>We're hoping no news is good news but just wanted to touch base. We hope you're both doing well.
Tim and Barbara O'Connor***

To Tim and Barbara:

Hi, Al is still snoozing, but will be online later. He's going to be glad to hear from you, I know. He's five days into his second chemo treatment. He had two miserable days afterwards, but he bounces back pretty well and fast.

It's a hard dose of chemo he's getting, but we both feel it working. The side effects are uncomfortable for a couple of days, but we're managing them.

The worst one so far has been his hands swelling and hurting for a day or two. He's lost most of his hair, but the only thing that worries him is that his head gets cold more easily. It would kill me, but the man has no vanity. As much as I love his thick, wavy hair, I think I love his flawless bald head even better.

The hardest part for him of this whole thing is that he's not able to be as physically active as he was. He goes for walks, but doesn't have quite the strength. No surprise with all that rocket fuel in him. He hasn't lost too much weight. Except for the relative inactivity, he still does pretty much whatever he wants to except for a few days after his treatments.

He has four more of these particular treatments before the "mid-term" check-up. He's handling this chemo much better than most. No surprise here.

But then, we're throwing everything at it: megavitamin and mineral therapy, hypnosis, acupuncture, modified macrobiotic diet. You name it, we're doing it.

The best medicine is as much normality as possible. His friends mean so much to him. Call, come over, send up a flare. The hardest medicine to locate now is the easiest to take: liberal daily doses of laughter. I can see the difference in the way he feels after that.

He's restricted only by how he feels, which is pretty good except for the few days after chemotherapy. He has to be cautious in crowded places. We can go to movies, but not when they're crowded. The week after chemo he's more susceptible to infection. We're telling people to come over any time, except if they are sick or have been recently exposed to colds or anything else.

Kathryn

18.

Journal: Tuesday, March 9, 1999

Dory came to visit today, coughing as she walked through the door. Alarmed, I asked her what was wrong. "The doctor says I may have walking pneumonia," she said.

I probably overacted when I almost shouted at her not to take one step nearer her father. "Don't you know how sick you could make him?" She just stood and looked at me. How did this happen? Didn't she know? She hasn't seen him much or even spoken with him. I don't know why.

He's always been such a good father. Denial about his condition? How did I fail to make it clear how vulnerable he is to infection right now?

Albert has so many good friends. I'm a little overwhelmed at trying to "manage the case" as well as visitors and everything else. But he inspires me with his patience, determination, good humor. I know he doesn't feel well, but I've yet to hear him really complain. His friends and family mean so much. I see the difference in him when they joke, or talk about merely routine things.

I am so tired at the end of each day. At least I don't have as much trouble sleeping now. The antidepressant helps. Dory left shortly after that exchange. I felt bad about the way I reacted toward her. I hope she understood.

Journal: Thursday, March 11, 1999

It took him more than an hour to eat dinner tonight. He has swollen hands and mouth sores after this latest chemo. I pureed some of his dinner so it would go down more easily.

He doesn't complain, forever stoic in the effort to do what he needs to do to keep his strength. He's losing weight from lack of appetite and inability to eat.

Mouth pain due to chemotherapy or radiation:
In a study conducted at the Yale Pain Management Center, capsaicin was shown to reduce dramatically the pain of mouth sores resulting from chemotherapy or radiation treatment. All 11 patients in the Yale study said their pain decreased--in two cases stopping entirely--after eating the capsaicin-laced candy.[1]

Today I made a recipe for Hot Pepper Candy for mouth pain. I hope it helps him. He just takes it one day at a time. Sometimes I wonder if he needs to let it all out. But he's always been so calm in the face of adversity.

---

[1] ***Nelson, C: Heal the burn: Pepper and lasers in cancer pain therapy. Journal of National Cancer Institute, 86, 1381, 1995, as reported in The Healing Power of Herbs, Second Edition, Michael Murray, N.D.,1995, Prima Publishing, Rocklin, CA, page 73.***

Thursday, April 1, 1999

>I take it as very positive that you are planning on going to the wedding. Have a great time and if you do need anything or Al needs something, we really aren't far.
>Denise

To Denise:
Haven't packed yet, but I'm not taking much. The really good news is that Al is doing better after this last treatment. We tried something new and iced his hands during administration of this time. During his last treatment, his hands were red, hot, and swelling. This time, however, they are a little red and swollen in places, but cool to the touch. He has very little discomfort at all!

He managed to swallow lots of ice during chemo. Tonight his throat is a bit sensitive, but not swollen. He was able to eat without discomfort! After the last treatment, he was getting nauseated. This time, he's been taking ginger capsules, and darned if his nausea is insignificant now. He's taken only one Lorazepam today so far as opposed to the three previously.

Previously in the process, he would be very tired and getting ready for bed. But this afternoon we went to a movie, came home and took a walk. He "danced" down the road and did a few push-ups! Then he ate a good dinner and is watching TV now!

Friday after treatment day is typically the worst day. All signs are very good for it being easier on him this time. Keep your fingers crossed.

He had a Pavlov moment Wednesday, getting nauseous before the nurse even inserted the IV. It made him realize just how much the mind can influence the body. He really dreaded going in there.

He's started doing more of the mental imaging he learned.

I asked the nurse if the doctor recommended giving him the shots this time for his lowered red blood count. She said she didn't know. When I got back from New York City, she still didn't know.

At the conclusion of his treatment, I asked again. She looked at his blood count and said things were just above the limit and the doctor hadn't said anything.

I asked her to please check. We know his blood count will take a dive after this treatment, and there are no side effects to the shots. Seems like it might be a good idea to give it to him before his blood count bottoms out?

The lowered blood count makes him short of breath when he walks. His blood pressure is low (96/64). Normally on the high side of normal, his vitals are way below normal after chemotherapy now.

After another hour, the nurse came back in and said "Doctor has approved your shot." Biting my tongue, I thanked her profusely. She apologized for taking so long. How many people would have just left without knowing they should insist on an answer? The office was very busy. The cancer business, it seems, is thriving. Meanwhile, as we were telling another patient with swollen hands about icing, the doctor entered the room and noticed the gloves/ice packs on Al's hands, and asked what he was doing.

"Icing my hands to help with the swelling."

"That makes sense," the doctor said. "Restricts access to the capillaries. Where'd you learn about that?"

"My wife figured it out," Al said proudly.

The nurse silently busied herself with his I.V. and looked away.
The doctor didn't say anything else before leaving the room.

I teared up at Albert's touching faith in me, simmering in silence.

Why isn't this kind of information available when patients start chemotherapy? No one has mentioned ways to help stave off side-effects. I wouldn't have known about these things had I not researched them myself.

I guess after what they see, swollen hands, mouth sores, upset stomachs, and fatigue are minor. But the quality of life for a patient in treatment shouldn't be overlooked either.

I'll be leaving for Texas Saturday for Amy's wedding and returning Sunday. Both of Al's daughters will be here this weekend. If he suddenly takes a turn for the worse, I won't go. But it looks as though he's going to do well.
K.

Journal: Monday, April 5, 1999

The bride was beautiful, the groom handsome, the wedding lovely. My dear little "Spook" is now a grown woman married to a fine young man. Amy and her father are also reconnecting. I'm so glad.

I've relocated so much in my life. It's hard to maintain long-distance relationships, especially when you're solitary by nature. But I keep connected in my own way. People don't realize I'm really kind of shy and need solitude to recover from the fatigue of each day's 30,000 tics.

Most people have no idea I have Tourette syndrome unless I tell them. I probably have more energy than most people, but use up a lot of it managing the tics so that most people don't notice them. Crowds, loud music, too much "sensory input" exhausts me.

But I wouldn't have missed Amy's wedding for the world. I was tired, and missed Albert. How he loves a party. It brings tears to my eyes recalling how he once said he loved going to weddings because it was like getting married to *me* all over again.

Of everything I've done in my life, to be loved by someone that way is the most important one of all.

I still wonder that Albert could have had any woman in the world, and he chose *me*.

Journal: Wednesday, April 7, 1999

There was an iconic moment during this last chemo. Albert was drinking a large glass of his daily dose of the freshly made green vegetable juice we call "swamp water," for its appearance.

Other patients were eating meatball sandwiches, sodas, ice cream. The doctor walked in, looked at Al's glass of juice, shook his head and walked out the door without saying a word. He didn't even ask what it was.

I suppose there isn't much on the doctor's desk to suggest Albert's diet might be one of the reasons he's doing relatively well. He's not the typical patient there.

The super-high doses of poison pouring into his veins scares me. Other patients are receiving traditional therapy in far smaller doses.

But Al's doing okay, relatively speaking. Could it be some of the things we're doing in addition to conventional treatments? Isn't anyone outside the alternative care community interested in *why he's doing as well as he is*?

19.

Journal: Thursday, April 8, 1999

After four chemo treatments, we saw another doctor and nutritionist in New York City. They told us the nutritional plan we're using is "very professional," making few suggestions. They agreed with our Dr. Schmid's recommendations for diet and supplements.

I don't understand why allopathic and alternative medicine clinicians don't talk to each other. Alternative care clinicians don't get the respect they deserve.

I know there's a lot of "snake oil" out there. But I know from my own research that there *is* hard data to support some alternative treatments. *Why* aren't more people on both sides of the issue working *together*?

Right now it only makes me angry to speculate and I don't have time for it. I pity those who don't have our resources for fighting their way through this maze. It would be so easy to give up. Patients need advocates for help and information. How many aren't getting it? The more I read, the scarier it gets. Cancer is an industry. People are dying in record numbers of it in spite of the propaganda. The "cure" rates don't cover patients who relapse after five years. In 1950, one in 30 of us got cancer. Now it's one in three!

Who stands to lose most if something as simple and relatively inexpensive as diet and supplements could reduce the incidence of cancer?

20.

<u>Friday, May 7, 1999, 12:47 p.m.</u>

Dear Friends,

It's three months after Albert's diagnosis. His mid-term CT scan shows the tumor has shrunk by 75 percent, reducing it to well under a centimeter in size!

What's left may be nothing more than scar tissue! No sign of metastasis or lymph node infiltration!

He's not only beaten the odds thus far, he's exceeded expectations and we're not even halfway through the treatment. We're convinced a contributing factor is the combination of alternative therapies and conventional treatment.

One hundred and 20 supplements daily plus a modified macrobiotic diet, hypnotherapy, mental imagery, prayers, support and love from our friends, relatives, and acquaintances, have contributed.

This has been one of the longest days of my life. I knew Dr. Cooper would walk into the room and I'd see the answer in his eyes before he even spoke.

He walked in with both thumbs up!

Nurses and receptionists were jumping up and down right along with me. Were Al not so anemic, he'd have been doing the same thing. He sat there grinning from ear to ear.

"I knew it was beaten. Judging by what the chemo did to the rest of me, my wife did five times a day with her vitamins, teas and soy beans, and with all the love and support around us, cancer doesn't have a chance!"

We see the doctor at MSK next week and Dr. Schmid the following day to determine next steps.

We're elated, exhausted, and even more hopeful than before. He's not only won this very major battle, he's winning the war!

Tonight we both ignored the soy beans and ate steak.

Love,
Kathryn and "Dr. Soccer"

Journal: 11:00 p.m.

Three months ago I thought he'd be dead by now. His faith was stronger than mine. He took it one moment at a time. I struggled every minute not to think too far ahead. The patient was the role model for his caregiver.

I'd already left our beautiful life behind in my mind, unable to imagine a future without him. Every day was a struggle for hope, vacillating between guilt for worrying about myself and admiration for his ability to deal with his illness without complaint. As sick as he was, he never lost faith. How I love and admire this man. How I strive to be more like him.

He's my coach too.

Monday, May 31, 1999

To: Joe Bertino, MD
From: Al Taubert

Dear Joe,

Update: I completed the MSK clinical trial round one: Adriamycin/Gemcitabine, on April 28. CT scan showed major shrink of original tumor, by 75 percent or more. Impressive!

Had a lot of annoyances, mouth, throat, nausea, hemoglobin 7.2, hand-foot syndrome, etc. A while later, got fever, no viral infection, but hypersensitivity pneumonitis to Gemzar. Lasted a week, small relapse, but now am through it.

For the last week, I've been feeling better every day, and I really enjoy that!

So I blessed you and cussed you out in the same breath for the last half year. Really, much gratitude from me, Kathryn, and family. So far, so good.

So now what? I've got more choices and opinions which I'm weighing. Probably decide next week, June 7 or 8, which road to take.

Please say hello to Pat and know that we appreciate what you've done by referring me to Dr. Olsson.

Your old friend, Al Taubert

Tuesday, June 1, 1999

To: Larry Larson
From: Kathryn Taubert

May I call you Larry? Jim gave me your email address and said you were interested in what we were doing. He was so helpful to us during the early days of Al's diagnosis. I hope this will help you and your wife in her treatment.

I also will send you a list of resources with whom you might speak about this sort of thing, including a urologist who has colon cancer and is using alternatives to survive his own "previously terminal" cancer. ("I may still die with cancer in my body but not because of it," he said.)

We don't know precisely what to attribute to Al's progress. And frankly, don't really care what did it. Something is working.

The clinical trial is certainly at least partly responsible. They said Al was in a patient category who had a better chance of doing well. However, according to NCI data, the odds for this kind of tumor were against him.

I am not a clinician. I have my own health story from 30 years ago. I was diagnosed with advanced endometriosis. I went into total remission after a complete overhaul of my diet. I had confirmation by five doctors, was taking twice monthly injections of then-experimental Depo-Provera to retard progress of the disease. I was scheduled for surgery within months. I'd reached the upper limit of the drug that I could take.

Many years ago I was a cardiopulmonary research assistant and a clinical chemistry technician. My formal education was biology. I've tried to stay current, especially with medical information.

If a little knowledge is dangerous, then I suppose I'm more than a little dangerous. I don't have credentials in medicine or nutrition, and neither does Al. He's a retired Pan American airline pilot.

We do know how to find people who know things we don't, however. I'll give you a list of resources to pursue.

Al and I wish you the best. Your brother is a very good friend, and has done many wonderful things for those of us with Tourette syndrome. It was one of the references he gave us that sent us in the right direction.

Best regards,

Kathryn Taubert

21.

Journal: Friday, June 4, 1999

I've tried so hard not to influence him. I search for information, sort the data, manage appointments, arrange schedules, prepare meals, supplements, and manage the rest of our lives. My job is "managing the case."

His job is getting well.

Familiar with my interest in science and medicine, my high school guidance counselor, Arthur Graham, encouraged me to join the "Industrial Cooperative Training Program" at Ball High School in my hometown of Galveston, Texas.

I was 17 when I started going to school half a day to complete my high school education while learning to be a laboratory technician in the Cardiopulmonary Laboratory of the University of Texas Medical Branch, John Sealy Hospital. ("UTMB")

The training was excellent, both in lab skills and life outside of high school. My boss, cardiology professor Dr. John Wallace, opened doors to me I might never have had were it not for his enthusiasm for teaching eager young students. Under his tutelage, I went from a shy high school student to a bona fide "cardiopulmonary research assistant." I also made enough money during high school and between college semesters to pay for college and buy a car.

Those experiences eventually landed me a job in a clinical chemistry laboratory of a general hospital where I honed further skills in performing various blood "chemistries" for hospital patients. I became familiar with medical terminology and procedures. I also learned to become a decent medical "advocate" for myself as well as loved ones. I had no idea just how important those experiences would later become.

People are asking Albert and me what we've been doing to fight this cancer. It makes me angry sometimes to think of how defenseless most are against this terrible disease and the too-complex system to address it. Without an advocate, what do they do?

Doctors have started administering the three new drugs for the last half of the clinical trial. These drugs are bringing Al way down. He's lost a lot of weight. He's so weak.

Now he's got this terrible skin rash circumnavigating his body. A skin biopsy says it's a chemo side effect. Doctors can't say which drug is causing it.

He's been hospitalized again because his blood count is so low. We're little more than halfway through the clinical trial.

He's already had four times the "normal" dose of chemotherapy.

Dr. Baines offered to remove the suspected drug from the next round, but couldn't assure us it wouldn't kill him anyway!

One of the nurses told me she was impressed how well he was doing considering the quantities of chemotherapy he's been on these last months.

I told her we believe the alternative therapies helped. She whispered her agreement conspiratorially, as though she felt she were committing heresy by saying it.

I was going to tell him today I think he should consider stopping the trial. I was agonizing over whether it would be the right thing.

I walked into the hospital room, roiling with doubt.

"I've decided to stop the trial, Kathryn. The CT scan was good. I believe the cancer is gone. I want to recover from this and have Dr. Olsson take out what's left and take it from there."

I hadn't said a word. He saved me, yet again.

The high doses of chemotherapy helped shrink the tumor. It was in such a dangerous place and growing so fast, only that drastic action could save him.

But now it was killing him.

It was time to stop.

Journal: Thursday, June 10, 1999

Al needs time to recover from the chemotherapy before August surgery with Dr. Olsson.

We'll spend the next few months rebuilding his strength. He's so positive and so relieved to have stopped the chemotherapy.

MSK researchers tried to talk him out of quitting. I know they don't want to lose a study patient who has shown such good results in spite of recent setbacks. But I can't help but wonder if sometimes the protocol is more important than the patient.

Their mission is to find a cure. But people die in the process. As strong as Albert is, he's almost 69 years old. Such high doses of chemotherapy kill cancer. But it kills patients, too! That's why they call it a "trial!" You sign your life away, literally, before being accepted into such trials. You agree to take the risk of dying.

We won't know if any cancer remains until his surgery. The CT scan still shows a small mass that could be nothing more than scar tissue. It could also be cancer.

Dr. Schmid told us about the *"Anti-Malignin Antibody in Serum" (*AMAS) blood test[2] that supposedly detects

---

[2] http://www.oncolabinc.com/AMASbrochure.pdf. Note: this test is controversial.

the presence of cancer anywhere in the body. Why doesn't anybody know about this?

What harm can it do? We decided to try it. The next few months will be an anxious waiting game.

Is the cancer really gone, or is it lying in wait to strike again?

It didn't register right away that the AMAS report I was reading said *no sign of cancer.*

I'd just opened the envelope in the car as we prepared to go into the restaurant. I reread it twice.

"Albert, the AMAS says there's no sign of cancer."

It still hadn't sunk in.

"I know. I feel it," he said matter-of-factly.

He's recovering well from the chemotherapy. CT scans show no cancer anywhere else in his body. This curiously unknown blood test says he's cancer-free!

We ate lunch in companionable silence. He still melts my heart with that spontaneous caress on my cheek as he turns to smile at me. I sit there almost numb, daring to believe this latest news. We'd just survived a horrible journey through the gates of Hell and back. I can now truly believe we'll beat this thing.

I'm still amazed he never asked me about the original prognosis. He's too smart not to have known. He read the initial pathology reports, but never said a word. He stayed focused upon the present, doing what he needed for survival. I learn from him every day of my life.

Wednesday, June 30, 1999

To: Dr. Richard Evans, M.D.

*Dr. Evans, my husband and I read your book, "**Making the Right Choice**," which is precisely what we are attempting to do.*

Albert had seven rounds of high-dose chemotherapy for transitional cell carcinoma of the ureter. The tumor has shrunk more than 75 percent in size to under 1 cm. Doctors cannot say for certain that's what's left is cancer or merely scar tissue. Al has decided against further chemo and is scheduled for surgery. The tumor was previously inoperable before chemotherapy.

Your insightful book about the "cancer industry" and the downside of chemotherapy reinforced my husband's decision to forego further chemotherapy treatment. Thank you for telling the "other side" of this story.

Best regards,

Kathryn and Al Taubert

22.

Journal: Thursday, July 1, 1999

Albert is driving again now. He continues to improve, and gain weight and strength. The painful skin rash is almost gone. He's walking for exercise and spending time on the soccer field, although still sidelined from playing. His beautiful bare head is fuzzy with new growth.

We spend our days decompressing from the intensity of these last six months. We're so grateful now for the mundane activities that seem so much more precious than before.

Every day is one day closer to Dr. Olsson hopefully telling us that Al truly is cancer-free. I didn't realize how emotionally exhausted I was until now.

Fear still simmers within me, but I can't believe how just a few months ago I thought Albert would be gone by now. It might have been had we not looked beyond initial recommendations. It makes me angry to think of it. But I don't dwell on it. I'm just grateful to be grateful.

23.

Friday, July 2, 1999

To: Friends and Family

Hi Everybody,

Al is doing very well, although faced with new choices. We hope our experiences will help some of you should you have to traverse this gauntlet someday. Statistically, one out of three of us will.

The "industry" behind cancer is daunting. The patient has too much to do in too little time. This makes truly informed choices difficult. The more resources everyone has, the better.

In our last update we told you the terrific news: Al's tumor had shrunk more than 75 percent, putting him in a whole new ballgame. His chances improved dramatically with this information. Our lives went from breath-holding to re-grouping.

For the first few weeks, we got used to the idea that whatever we'd been doing was working. In fact, working so well that conventional medicine can't tell us whether or not Al even has cancer anymore!

That brings us to the AMAS test. "Anti-Malignin Antibody in Serum" has been something of a medical enigma for about 25 years, according to one source. This antibody is present, according to studies, in the bodies of people with cancer regardless of location.

Unlike the few other cancer markers available, (PSA for example), that identify substances produced by the malignancy itself, AMAS identifies the body's response to all cancers (antibodies).

Claims are made that the AMAS test has been clinically proven in more than 3,300 cases, and identifies cancer with an accuracy of 99 percent!

Why don't you know about this? That's the question we asked our naturopathic physician, Dr. Schmid. He's been using it more than 5 years with his patients, and recommended it for Al to determine if the spot left on the CT scan is merely scar tissue or cancer.

We sent a half dozen copies of the abstract mentioned below to doctor friends of ours. None criticizes the science or the concept. In fact, several have called this test "promising." What they did say is that this test needs to be used more in order to replicate the startling results already achieved. Since few know about it, few use it.

Albert's AMAS results show he is completely cancer-free at this time. No sign of cancer anywhere. Nada.

We decided to use this test as merely one more tool in the medical arsenal. It's not as the sole arbiter of decisions relative to subsequent treatment.

He had seven cycles of high-dose chemotherapy in the clinical trial. We believe the combination of chemo and various alternatives were responsible for his outcome.

More than 120 capsules of supplements daily, fresh juices, a modified macrobiotic/vegetarian diet, guided imagery, chiropractic, moderate exercise (when possible), as much laughter as we could muster, lots of love and prayers from friends and family, have accomplished his remarkable result.

His cancer was aggressive, highly invasive, stage III, inoperable, and very fast growing. But somebody has to be part of the lucky group. Why not him? It's a whole new ballgame now.

The side effects to chemo were increasingly worrisome. Ironically, he spent four months fighting off side effects of chemo! He was hospitalized twice for allergic reactions. One has put him in the medical journal, "Chest," for his status as one of a mere handful of cases reported with "Gemcitabine Hypersensitivity Pneumonitis." He made the record books.

He therefore decided to suspend further chemotherapy in favor of other options. Since he's already had about 25 percent more chemo than patients not in clinical trials, he figured he'd had enough.

Although I've tried very hard not to influence him too much, I was shamelessly overjoyed at this decision. No one could assure us that his next allergic reaction wouldn't be far worse, even fatal. The signs were ominous.

So what's next? The surgeon at MSK wants to remove the entire kidney, ureter, and a piece of the bladder. This will remove any possibility of recurrence along that side of the urinary tract, and allow them to completely biopsy the entire area to determine the extent to which the treatment worked.

Although the odds of recurrence in that area are less than 50 percent, the MSK surgeon thinks them great enough to warrant the drastic surgery. People can survive quite nicely with only one kidney. But, as Al says, "if you're young and the kidney hasn't been chemo'd."

The Columbia-Presbyterian surgeon wants to remove only part of the ureter, a piece of bladder, sparing the kidney, and reattaching the remaining ureter to the top of the bladder.

They say the odds of recurrence don't warrant losing what may be a perfectly healthy kidney. Removing the entire kidney would compromise any future chemotherapy. Also, as we age, kidneys can lose some function.

Although both kidneys appear to be healthy now, one doesn't know exactly if the single remaining kidney would remain healthy or the extent to which it has already been compromised.

Still another clinician says no surgery at this time,

except removing the stent, since the AMAS test says he's cancer-free. This is the most conservative approach, saving all options for later. We're to keep doing what we've been doing with the alternative therapies. The risk with this approach is that malignant cells may remain. The AMAS has about a one percent rate of error.

Al still has a few residual after-affects from the chemotherapy, but seems to have escaped any permanent damage, which was a strong possibility. This is where we believe certain supplements were especially helpful. He still has a stent (tube) in the ureter (tube between kidney and bladder) which causes just enough irritation to keep him from his usual vigorous daily exercises.

His overall fitness is returning, but not enough for "even a substitute in a soccer match," as he says. (He's gaining on it.) His hair is growing back, although he says he might leave it off. He enjoys not having to comb that, and other advantages, like "faster showers, no haircuts, or time wasted parting it."

The next few weeks we'll get the information we need to determine which approach to take, continue recuperating, and enjoy feeling good again. He's getting a few pre-op tests, and needs to make the decision soon. Surgery is tentatively scheduled for August. Keep those positive thoughts and prayers coming.

They work. Kathryn and Al

Journal: July 2, 1999

Who would stand to lose most if, for less than $300, you could take a blood test to discover the presence of cancer anywhere in your body without further examination?

What if this test could also be used to measure your treatment progress without more costly tests?

What if cancer were manageable with nutritional therapies instead of chemotherapy, surgery and radiation?

Who would stand to lose the most?

24.

Journal: Thursday, August 26, 1999

Columbia-Presbyterian hospital's hotel-like accommodations for the surgical patient's family are beautiful. I can stay near Albert without having to drive back and forth to Connecticut. I am so relieved. The seven months since Al's diagnosis seem like *years*.

The last two months were a bittersweet compote of hope and anxiety. Diagnosis of cancer, once present, is always a threat to peace of mind. At first, you can't even say the word. It's a "mass, growth, or malignancy."

The first time you use the word "cancer" seems so final, yet it's the first step from denial to acceptance, and *action*.

Al has gotten stronger, gained weight. His color is better, he's exercising and maintaining his nutritional regimen. Dr.'s Schmid and Steinberg from New York City made a few adjustments, but he still consumes more than 120 supplements a day.

My little kitchen pharmacy is now just another daily routine. His chemo side-effects have virtually disappeared, with no sign of permanent damage. Though it all, he has remained positive.

"I know the cancer is gone," he says. "Even without the AMAS or surgery, I can tell."

Chemotherapy leaves scar tissue. The location of Al's tumor was such that this new surgery carries great risk. Olsson has elected to spare the kidney and remove only the diseased portion of the ureter, a small portion of the bladder, and reattach the remaining ureter to the remaining bladder.

Al could bleed to death, or lose the use of his right leg because of the location of the "tumor bed" and difficulty removing chemotherapy-induced scar tissue. That's why two additional surgeons will be on standby.

I'm grateful watching him regain strength. Each day is a blessing. We've been given more time. I now believe he truly can make it. This man should live to be a hundred. How this rare cancer could have happened to him, I can't imagine. It typically afflicts those who work around toxic substances.

Could it have been the two years he lived in post-World War II Japan, eating local foods perhaps contaminated by radiation? One of the medical tests indicated his extraordinarily high levels of "heavy metals."

Was it 40 years of flying and the ionizing radiation at altitude? Maybe it was years as a small boy going to work with his father at the Greenwich power plant.

I don't even know if these things cause cancer or not. His father died of liver cancer at 65. Is there a genetic susceptibility there? He was negative for one kind of genetic defect that causes cancer. There is so much science doesn't yet know. But he got cancer and now we are going to find out if he's beaten it. He is so *certain.*

We spent tonight together in his hospital room before tomorrow's surgery. We read together, sharing interesting passages with each other. He's never impatient when I interrupt him to do so.
Sometimes during breakfast at home, we end up talking an hour or more. Then the phone rings, he's off with one of his buddies on some soccer matter, and we're back in the world.

His friends have been so good to us. Chris and Ron and Joe and Charlie have been a constant presence. At times like these, friends are especially important.

Were it not for my own friends, I'd have been so much more alone. Al's rallied around the "Coach" in ways that lifted his spirits. Whether it's telling stories about soccer with his soccer buddies, or flying with his fellow Pan Am retirees, it's gotten his mind off cancer.

But the undercurrent of worry over Adam's drug addiction still simmers. Al's concern for the life of his only son is ever-present.

At times in the night, I hear the rhythm of his breathing change. I ask if he's okay. "I'm just wondering where Adam is," he says. It breaks my heart for both of them.

He rarely worries about the cancer, it seems. He truly believes it's gone. He's always worried more for the lives of those he loves.

Journal: Friday, August 27, 11:00 a.m.

I'm a wreck. I've wandered around the hospital, tried to read, bought a pink bromeliad at the gift shop to lift his spirits when he's back in his room.

If he gets back.

I'm going crazy. He's been in surgery for hours. I can only assume no news is good news. I can no longer leave the waiting room for fear they'll be looking for me.

My heart stops every time someone walks through the door. I'm in agony, praying as hard as I can that Al's is all right and the cancer is *gone*.

I trust Dr. Olsson and his chief resident. Dr. Saed's gentle manner is the antithesis of Olsson's abruptness. But Olsson's reputation, organization, open-mindedness, and willingness to include the patient as part of the team inspires confidence.

Dr. Saed told me that Olsson chose the kidney-sparing surgery in part because his medical team encouraged it. I don't know why it takes so long for so many clinicians to catch up with the latest research. There are no "sacred cows" in Olsson's medical service.

"Residents fight to get on his service," Dr. Saed said.

I can see why.

1:30 p.m.

Saed smiled as he approached me in the waiting room.

"We got it all. Didn't even have to call in the other surgeons. Dr. Olsson popped out the remaining tumor bed with the end of the scalpel with no problem. There was very little scar tissue."

I could barely see for the tears as he led the way to see Dr. Olsson.

"It had to be those anti-inflammatory supplements Dr. Schmid recommended. He told us they might help reduce chemotherapy-induced inflammation and scarring! Why don't regular doctors recommend it?"

"Mrs. Taubert, we're learning more all the time about these things. Medical schools are more open-minded as more studies are showing positive results. In time, we'll know even more, I'm sure."

Saed's calm, thoughtful reply was comforting and frustrating at the same time. How much more time would be required for medicine to "catch up?" How many patients would die in the process?

Barely keeping it together, I waited anxiously for Olsson.

Still in his scrubs, he stepped through the door of the small anteroom where Dr. Saed left me. I took Dr.

Olsson's hand in both of mine, barely able to speak. I thanked him as tears streamed down my face.

I didn't expect the emotion I saw in his eyes as the curtain opened on his normally reserved demeanor.

It must be awful to be a sensitive person in the midst of such pain, suffering, and failure as doctors often see. I'm sure it's why they appear to be so dispassionate. It's their own way of surviving the horror.

But for those with the strength, windmills can be tilted without losing one's humanity. There must be enough moments like this to keep them going.

"I didn't see any sign of cancer," he said. "We've sent the specimen to pathology to confirm, but I believe there is no cancer at this time."

The words for we'd prayed.

Albert is cancer-free.

3:00 p.m.

"May I see him?" I asked the nurse guarding the recovery room entrance.

"We just brought him down. It'll be a while before you can," she said officiously.

"I'm his wife. I won't disturb him. He needs to know he's okay and I'm here with him. Please let me see him. I promise not to stay more than a minute or two."

Looking thoughtfully at me for a moment, she picked up the phone and called for someone to take me to him.

"You can't stay long," the attending nurse said, checking his blood pressure.

"Albert, it's Kathryn. I'm here. You came through with flying colors. There was no sign of cancer. No need for the other surgeons. You were right. You're going to be just fine!"

"Mrs. Taubert," said the nurse quietly monitoring his vitals, "You can stay."

Tears streamed down my face as the hint of a smile appeared upon his handsome face. He wouldn't recall that moment. But I'll remember it the rest of my life.

25.

Wednesday, September 15, 1999

Dr. Derek Baines, MD
Memorial Sloan-Kettering Cancer Center
From: Al Taubert, medical authorization

Dear Dr. Baines:

Attached is a copy of my pathology report, performed after surgery at Columbia-Presbyterian Medical Center on August 27, 1999.

Consider this my authorization for you to consult with physicians there and/or obtain any portion of my medical record which you require for purposes of the MSKCC, sequenced drug therapy clinical trial in which I participated.

Please let me know if you require additional follow-up visits, and/or other information to complete your study. Also, when the study is complete, forward a copy of the published paper to me, if at all possible.

Sincerely,

Al Taubert

We never heard a word from them again.

Dr. Andrew Kalem, MD
The Center for Holistic Urology
Columbia-Presbyterian Medical Center
New York, NY 10022

Dear Dr. Kalem:

My husband and I read with interest about the opening of your holistic urology center. Al is a surgical patient of Dr. Carl Olsson's, having just had surgery for transitional cell carcinoma of the ureter. (Biopsies show him to be cancer-free.)

Diagnosed this past January with a T-3, NO, MO, Al participated in a Memorial Sloan Kettering clinical trial of sequenced drug therapy.[3]

We also used substantial alternative medicine under the care of Harold Steinberg, MD, formerly of the Schachter Center in Suffern, N.Y., now practicing in NYC. Also Ron Schmid, M.D., of Middlebury, CT. We believe that Al's remarkable progress in treating the difficult malignancy is due to the combination of alternative and allopathic treatments. We also used services of Columbia's own Complementary Care Center, before, during, and after surgery.

We want to let you know that we support what you and Columbia are doing, and wish you great success in

---

[3] Protocol called for 10 cycles of chemotherapy over a six-month period. Al completed seven: six of Adriamycin and Gemcitabine, and one of Ifosfamide, Paclitaxel, and Cisplatin. He discontinued treatment after 7 cycles due to side effects. He suffered no permanent damage.

bringing together alternative-allopathic medicine for the benefit of your patients.

In the event you are not already aware of the Anti-Malignin Antibody in Serum test (AMAS), you might want to examine it for potential use in your practice. Al tested cancer-free on this test some three months before surgery confirmed it.

Please don't hesitate to contact us if there is anything that we can do to help in your efforts, sharing our own experiences.

We hope to help others learn there is hope after a diagnosis of cancer. We believe the holistic approach worked for us.

Best regards, Al and Kathryn Taubert

Journal: September 15, 1999

We try to help spread the word. We hear back from almost no one outside the alternative medicine communities.

Columbia-Presbyterian's neurology department under the auspices of Dr. Carl Olsson clearly gets it.

26.

Journal: Thursday, September 30, 1999

These last few weeks have been a soft blur of peaceful renewal for us both. Al is healing well, but oh, what they did to him!

The long red scar bisects him from the middle of his chest all the way around his right side to the middle of his back. It's a testament to what the human body can endure.

Visualizing him spread open on that operating table brings tears to my eyes. His poor body so terribly ravaged by seven rounds of high-dose chemotherapy and then to endure this bi-section.

The final pathology report concluded there was no cancer. CT scans confirmed that there is *no sign of cancer anywhere in his body.*

He'll have regular CT scans at three-month intervals for a couple of years. We'll continue AMAS for verification.

He has no restrictions on activities. We'll continue alternative protocols developed by the naturopathic members of "The Team," as Albert calls them.

But he's so upbeat, positive, and happy.

We sent authorizations for release of all surgical records to the MSK Clinical Trials team. Even though

Al discontinued the clinical trial before completing it, and chose Dr. Olsson for the surgery over the one at MSK, we hope his results will be useful in their work. I know I was hard on them at times. I also know their research is vital. Al's participation in this clinical trial was his only hope. His aggressive cancer was in such a dangerous place he didn't have time for anything else.

We celebrated a wonderful evening with friends at Chuck's Steakhouse for Albert's 69th birthday. Still a bit lean and pale, he's coming back strong. It's barely been a month since that heroic surgery.

I lay beside him in the early dawn, watching him sleeping, breathing evenly. It seems like decades ago when I thought he might not be there anymore. *But he is cancer-free. It's just over a year since that horrible night I took him to the emergency room.*

He's talking about going to Montana this January. Knowing him, he'll recover well enough to be skiing by then. He'll be back on the soccer field by spring.

"I'm a soccer coach who flew," he used to say. Retiring a year before his beloved Pan Am went under, he just switched his captain's hat for a soccer cap. He slipped so easily into retirement. It was more time to indulge his love of the game.

"The Clipper Pioneers" are planning a transatlantic cruise next spring. The gathering of his fellow Pan Am retirees will be an opportunity for us to go on our first cruise together.

I'm back to working in the yard, taking care of the animals, reading, and thinking about resuming some kind of volunteer work. I like the Danbury Animal Welfare Society ("DAWS") no-kill shelter. I adopted my old cat Dinah there. I'm less involved in the Tourette syndrome Internet support group now. Others have filled whatever vacuum I might have left.

For the moment, I seem to be in a state of unnatural calm. So drenched in emotion this past year, it's as though I've been wrung out and hung up to dry.

I'm off anti-depressants again, thankfully. I hate taking pills in spite of the 65 supplements a day I still take while feeding my husband 120!

Friday, October 01, 1999

To: Jerry Weston
Hi, Jerry. Al here. This is a follow up on our conversation a few days after your surgery, during which I realized you were still getting banged by painkillers and other things. I realize you're not out of the woods yet. Hopefully, your recovery will be more dramatic and you will feel like your old self.

My own adventure with cancer involved a lot of searches of what's out there and available for possible treatment. This means everything from a "shaman" to the most conservative and conventional medicine available.

Having looked at all this, and having had some experience in the past, combined with what my wife,

Kathryn, has been studying for years, we came up with a program for me, which I will briefly outline here. After looking over this, if you have any questions, I'd be more than happy to talk with you about them.
Good luck. Keep us posted!
Al

<u>Journal: 3:00 p.m.</u>

Al is getting calls from people who want to know what he did. He gives so freely of his time. He's always been a role model and now he's got yet another example for others to follow.

He dictates, I type.

He likes that.

I love it.

Some part of me will live from CT scan to CT scan.

The first will be the worst. If the cancer is going to return, it will be with a vengeance say those who believe that to be a downside of chemotherapy. Only the most aggressive cancer cells survive.

It would most likely come back downstream of the original site, in the region of the bladder.

At times I railed against some of the doctors. But all of them contributed to Al's spectacular outcome. I am grateful to them all.

We have our lives back. Together, we are stronger now than ever.

27.

May 2000

It's been almost a year and a half since his original diagnosis. We had a real scare. Al's CT scan and AMAS tests suggested a recurrence.

Follow-ups suggested either the test interpretations were wrong, or whatever was there "disappeared."

I'd like to believe the alternatives we're still employing are working, banishing any remaining cancer before it takes hold.

Albert is fit as a fiddle.

We had a wonderful year. He's back on the soccer field, managing teams and playing with the "Over 40's."

He's volunteering with an agency that gives rides to the sick and elderly for doctors' appointments. He goes an extra mile so one elderly shut-in can buy groceries at the same time.

Albert is the kind of man who stops on the side of the highway to help a total stranger change a tire. He's got such a good heart.

We went to Montana in February. I love sitting in the lodge between the roaring fireplace and floor-to-ceiling windows. I waited for him to conclude his days of skiing.

The Grouse Mountain Lodge has the best coffee, breakfast, and view of Big Mountain in Whitefish.

He spent his days on the mountain. I spent mine playing with my computer, reading, walking to town, or volunteering at the county animal shelter. I found homes for 14 stray cats this year.

I'm most gratified about "Angel." She didn't live up to her name at the shelter, but was adopted from my home by a woman from a photo of this beautiful Siamese. It was prophetic that Angel, after having terrorized everyone else, quietly allowed herself to be carried away by the woman who took her home. We promised to keep in touch.

Al and I spent evenings alone or with friends.

We spent nights in each other's arms.

I realized during that awful year what "in sickness and in health" really means. As he lay near death next to me in what now seems a lifetime ago, the last thing on either of our minds was sex.

It's as though a toggle switch went off in our heads.

I knew at that time I could spend the rest of my life without it just as long as he was near me. I just wanted to hold him.

When he got well again, that switch flipped back on.

For both of us.

The "Clipper Pioneers" reunion cruise to Portugal was wonderful. We danced across the Atlantic to the Azores, exploring those beautiful islands off the coast of Portugal.

We spent three festive days in Lisbon with a side trip to Sintra, then east through the wonderful estancias to the walled city of Evora. We took an overnight train to Madrid before flying back to the USA.

Although other people rarely notice, my constant ticcing makes sitting in close quarters uncomfortable for me.

The long flight to New York would have been exhausting were it not for Al's status as a former Pan Am pilot. He would readily have sat in coach without complaint, but he asked for an upgrade for my comfort.

The flight crew offered us vacant business class seats free of charge. I was grateful for their gracious treatment of former Pan Am flight-deck crew. Al was treated almost like royalty by airline personnel who appreciated what Pan Am had done for commercial aviation.

My life is filled with so many blessings. Most of all, my Albert.

I've never been happier.

28.

February 2001

Although Al remains in good health two years after his diagnosis, he is worried about his children. So much has happened. After coming to the conclusion that letting Adam go was the only way to save him, Al now struggles with how much to intervene in his daughters' lives.

Adam is a handsome young man in his mid-30's who could have accomplished anything he wished. Once telling me he felt immediately compelled to use more after his first "hit" on marijuana, he soon progressed to harder drugs. Dropping out of college and losing his soccer scholarship, he moved from job to job, finding and losing one opportunity after the next.

I truly believed he meant it every time he said he was going to "get clean." But countless drug rehabs failed and he was soon back on the streets. So many times I worried for him and his father. Albert tried everything in his power to help his only son, to no avail.

One day Al said to me, "I've done everything for my son except let him go. I guess that's all I can do now, that and pray."

It was the hardest decision he'd ever made in his son's life. The risk of losing him was as great, if not greater, than not.

But letting go doesn't mean giving up. It means taking a chance that somehow your loved one has enough strength and will to eventually get clean and sober, staying that way and building a new and healthy life. I can't imagine what it took for Al to do what he did one night when Adam called. We'd already gone to bed when the phone rang. It was Adam saying he was halfway back to CT from his most recent state of residence. "Dad, I need a place to stay for a while," he told Albert.

After a moment of silence, Albert replied, "Adam, I love you. You're my son and always will be. I'll buy you lunch or dinner when you arrive. But you'll have to keep on going and find another place to live."

We still don't know the ultimate outcome of that decision. I do know, however, that it's always in the back of Albert's mind somewhere. He loves all his children very much. Adam's drug addiction has taken its toll on everyone. His daughters have suffered as well. No one can say, however, the degree to which it has influenced their lives too. Families often revolve around the sickest member, with collateral damage showing up in ways not always recognized.

Al's daughters have their own set of problems with which to deal. But Albert has great faith in and love for all of them. Although I've never had children of my own, having two sets of step-children taught me how difficult it is for parents to merely stand by and watch as their children are required to stand alone.

But in usual Al fashion, he takes it one day at a time. I know he's worried about his children when he's so quiet.

I tried to be their friend. Somehow, I'm cast in the role of "evil stepmother," no matter what I do. What could I have done differently?

They seemed happy that their father and I found each other at first. But things seem to change after we built our home in Greenleaf Farms.

It was our dream home, built with proceeds from the sale of his home and mine. When we met, I lived in the lovely town of Harwinton, in Connecticut's Litchfield Hills. Albert lived in Sandy Hook, CT. For a while we divided our time between them until we built our home on the border between Newtown and Redding Ridge, CT.

I know I'm sometimes hard to get to know. I think it goes back to the days when so many didn't want to know the "twitchy" child I was. I couldn't hide my undiagnosed Tourette syndrome in those days. My animal companions were my best friends.

By the age of seven, I developed head-shaking and vocal tics (throat-clearing, sniffling, whimpering sounds). After realizing I couldn't stop, my parents took me to the best doctors available. After batteries of inconclusive tests and several years of medications with no success, my folks let me decide whether to continue with the constant side effects and seemingly endless hours in doctors' offices.

I chose to stop, and we just went on with life.

Unknown to me, doctors had rendered the opinion that I had probably suffered a "shock to the nervous system" before or around birth. It would be 30 years before I got the formal diagnosis of Tourette syndrome (TS) that dismissed that hypothesis.

After reading a 1984 article in "***Science***" magazine listing the symptoms of a "bizarre condition" called Tourette syndrome, I found the answer I'd been seeking all my life. I was incredibly relieved to learn my condition had a name. I'd always known nothing was "wrong with my mind," as had been suggested on more than one occasion by mystified clinicians.

I would also learn that my parents had spent those same years wondering what "shock" they might have caused to precipitate my condition! I never knew how much they had suffered all that time thinking how they had caused it. They never told me until my diagnosis at 38 years old. They were vindicated as well.

I would later become active in the local, state, and the national Tourette Syndrome Associations (TSA). I founded a summer camp and educators' conferences for children with TS, Obsessive Compulsive Disorder (OCD) and Attention Deficit Hyperactivity Disorder (ADHD).

I participated as a study patient for the Yale Child Study Center in New Haven, CT, in a number of neuro-imaging and cognitive-behavioral research studies.

Two drug studies resulting in miserable side effects to me reminded me of those childhood years of untold rounds of experimental medications. I'd learned to "accommodate" my tics without resorting to medications. I would never take medications for TS again, nor would I participate in more drug trials.

Most adults with TS do not take medications solely for tics, unless they are among the most severe cases or are required to remain completely immobile for some reason (surgical procedure, for example). Most medications used to treat TS are "off-label," designed for another purpose entirely. They can result in sedating the patient to the point of interfering with the ability to think and act clearly. I can tell you from personal experience what the anti-psychotic drug "Thorazine" does to the mind and body of a nine-year-old child. It's not pretty.

I volunteered in the 1990's for programs with Yale because their first line of treatment does not include drugs until they have exhausted all other cognitive-behavioral and environmental options. Most children do not require drugs for TS alone. There is also enough concern about what drugs can to do a child's developing brain to warrant caution when using them for OCD and ADHD as well.

I was asked to write a chapter for the seminal medical text on the subject at the time.

Tourette's Syndrome: Tics, Obsessions, Compulsions: Developmental Psychopathology and Clinical Care, edited by Dr.'s James F. Leckman and the late Donald J. Cohen of the Yale Child Study Center, was published in 2001 by John Wiley & Sons, Inc.

My chapter, ***"The Role of Voluntary Organizations in Clinical Care, Research, and Public Policy,"*** was singled out for special mention by William M. McMahon, M.D., in the ***American Journal of Psychiatry***, Volume 158, No. 3.[4]

While I have "uncomplicated Tourette syndrome," OCD and ADHD are frequently found in those with this tic disorder. As I became a teenager, the "forcefulness" of my tics diminished, although the frequency and number increased. My vocal tics didn't include the most difficult ones such as "coprolalia," the uttering or shouting of socially unacceptable words. But friends I met through TSA have that and more. I've never ceased being amazed at the grace and dignity with which these people endure Tourette syndrome's most difficult symptoms. All too often they suffer public vilification and misunderstanding far beyond what I endured.

Although my life as a child was sometimes difficult with my symptoms being far more obvious than now, I've dealt pretty well with my "old ghosts." It always helped me to reach out to others who needed help even more than I.

---

[4] http://ajp.psychiatryonline.org/article.aspx?articleID=174690

But some part of me is still "hiding," I suppose. Sometimes it no doubt keeps me apart from those who don't understand.

I can be very sociable and often enjoy it. But I'm always relieved when I can finally disengage. I'm really a rather solitary person and not entirely comfortable in groups. I learned how to play that game in business, but it's not my natural state like it is Albert's.

I admire him for his ability to be anywhere, anytime, and with anyone, without anxiety.

Feeling as though I'm not welcome somewhere reminds me too much of those times as a child when I wasn't. When I sense it happening, I withdraw. I don't have the energy to keep trying.

I guess I've given up with Albert's children. But it makes me sad. I think they tolerate me because I'm married to their father.

At least Al can spend time with his grandsons. They love their "Opa." He took Jack to the World Trade Center, and is taking Josh soon too. One-on-one time is special for them. But he has to go to see them now. Dory rarely brings them to our house anymore.
I love those two little boys. They're the only grandchildren I will ever have. But their mother doesn't seem to like me very much.

I was a little hurt when I realized that the only photo of a grandmother they had in their rooms was not of me, but of Albert's first wife they never even knew. I know how much Dory loved her mother. I tried to be a good "step-grandmother" to the boys. We get along really well. But how does a child choose between a mother and a step-grandmother? The outcome is a foregone conclusion. I don't have a chance.

But I do still have Albert. To be so loved by someone you love so much is more than many ever have.

May 1, 2001

Today I asked him if they ever did a CT scan of his head.

"They didn't today. I don't recall if they have before. Why?"

"Just wondering," I said.

And I let it go at that.

June 4, 2001

We went to Newport for our 10th anniversary and stayed at the historic bed and breakfast called "The Jail."

We walked along America's Cup Avenue, toured the harbor from the sunny deck of a catamaran.

We sat and watched people at Christie's, read together before falling asleep in our "cell" at night. We shared early-morning pastries and strong, hot coffee at The Porch on Bannister's Wharf, watching sailboats gently rocking in the harbor.

Celebrating our anniversary at Castle Hill Inn, I snapped a photo of him as he turned his head to gaze into the setting sun.

The flash didn't work.

Something cold slithered around my heart. Al's serene gaze into the setting sun seemed agonizingly prophetic.

I said nothing, turning my head to hide my quivering tears.

July 2001

"Ocular migraine," the doctor called Al's intermittent visual disturbances. He told us not to worry about them. It wasn't serious.

August 2001

Our driving trip around the quaint Canadian province of Nova Scotia was a meandering 10-day time-warp into a kinder, gentler past. It was like stepping back 50 years.

Driving up the Atlantic coast above the thriving city of Halifax, we stopped for lunch in peaceful roadside parks.

A favorite dish of Al's is scallops marinated in fresh lime juice, cilantro, garlic, and scallions. I purchased the ingredients from small shops along the way and prepared them for our roadside repasts.

Lodging in out-of-the-way bed and breakfasts on the coast, we meandered through neat little villages and fell in love all over in quaint Lunenberg.

We met my "distant relatives" at a Highland music festival in Antigonish. It seems like every other person there was a McDonald, including me!

For my mother, we purchased in New Glasgow, a lovely pewter nightlight in the shape of an old Victorian home.

We pored over old ship's manifests in Pictou, searching for names of my Scottish antecedents.

Why this simmering anxiety? I can't shake the feeling something isn't right.

Am I slipping into depression again in spite of everything? I sleep well, my appetite's good. I've never been physically very strong, but I feel fine.

The "heaviness" that accompanies the depression isn't there. The dreams no longer haunt me.

We have our concerns about family, but we're managing.

Maybe it's the old ghosts again.

How can something this good last?

29.

Tuesday, September 11, 2001, 9:10 a.m.

I sat down next to the hospital bed, waiting for them to bring Al up from the emergency room. It's been two years and nine months since the diagnosis of cancer.

I barely noticed the T.V. suspended in the corner of the room. I was vaguely aware of a plane crashing into a building over and over again. I thought it was a movie.

Then I saw the CNN banner across the bottom of the screen.

This was no movie. It was really happening.

Planes had just crashed into the World Trade Center in New York City.

It was a surreal nightmare. My husband, who for years had flown those same kinds of planes, had just been told he had a tumor burning in his brain on the very day two planes were taking down the World Trade Center.

Once more, a frantic rush to the emergency room in the early morning hours after a sudden attack of terrible vomiting.

"There's a large mass in the cerebellum," the doctor had said. "It's probably a metastasis, but we won't know until a biopsy."

They brought Al into the room, lifting him onto the bed, heavily medicated and barely conscious.

“You’re aware what’s happening in New York City,” Dr. Markind said. “Since we’re part of the regional emergency system, we’re going to send you home for a few days to make room for casualties from these events.”

“These events” were the end of the world as we knew it, and the end of the life for which Albert and I fought so hard.

It’s in a “good place” for a brain tumor, Dr. Markind said. “We can remove a lot of it without permanent damage. But there are two little spots in the front of his head that may be in brain or bone.”

They sent us home with steroids to reduce the swelling in Al’s brain.

There were no casualties, of course, from the World Trade Center. They called us back in a couple of days for surgery.

The neurosurgeon said the tumor had to come out. Al apparently already has “gait” problems upon examination. How could we have missed this?

Why didn’t I ask them last spring about a CT scan of his head?

Thursday, September 13, 2001, 1:36 a.m.

Surgery is scheduled for Wednesday, Sept. 19. The doctor says the two spots in the front are inoperable.

2:18 a.m.

Make list of questions to ask.

Dr. Bass will order blood work for Tuesday, the day before surgery.

Arrange for hospital room.

Does Olsson recommend this strategy? Options?

Get information prior to surgery regarding Rational Therapeutics assay for possible chemo down the line.

Help expedite paperwork, get copies of reports to pathologist prior to surgery.

They say this neurosurgeon is the best in the area.

They say we need to take this one day at a time.

Again.

Albert is calm, resolved. His warm hand around mine in the night comforts me.

Thursday, Sept. 20, 2001

They got all the tumor in the back of his brain.

Al may be a good candidate for a non-invasive procedure called stereotactic radiosurgery (SR) that kills remaining cancer cells. It's highly focused radiation causing much less damage than so-called "whole-brain" radiation. It's as much as 80 percent effective on metastatic brain tumors, including inoperable ones.

We see radiation oncologists in New York next week.

Could SR have been used instead of conventional surgery if we'd caught the tumor earlier?

The thought of it almost paralyzes me with grief and guilt. If only I'd asked why they didn't do CT scans of his head.

I push the thought aside.

Monday, Sept. 24, 2001

We spent a quiet evening on Albert's 71st birthday.

Just two years ago we were celebrating his recovery birthday party at Chuck's. What a difference between now and then.

He's recovering well from brain surgery. He continues to take steroids for inflammation, which make him a little hyper, but he doesn't complain. Sometimes I wonder if he should.

Thursday, October 4, 2001

The two of them clearly disagreed with each other. The neurosurgeon believed Albert was an ideal candidate for SR. The oncologist clearly favored traditional whole-brain radiation.

"We'll do what you wish, since we offer both," said the oncologist, "but I urge you to consider the traditional procedure."

He seemed a little defensive when I cited statistics on the benefits of SR with which his neurologist colleague had confirmed.

Who was I to question the head of a major medical center radiation oncology department? I don't even have an undergraduate degree. But my husband's life was in his hands.

"Let's do SR," Al said. He read the same stuff I did and made his own decision.

Every time I falter, he is *there*. His gentle-handedness belies what others sometimes think. Al is *always* in control. He *is* the "wind beneath my wings."

30.

<u>Monday, October 8, 2001</u>

It was a real-life horror movie.

His head bolted into a metal “halo” that rose above the back of his wheelchair, Albert and two other similarly trussed patients were rolled down the hallway to the MRI lab.

I followed them as if moving through a dungeon in which the victims were being led to the rack.

When his turn at stereotactic radiosurgery came, the neurosurgeon immobilized his head and neck in the frame bolted to his skull. He then placed a “hat” with radiation projectors on the frame. Al lay on his back on the table.

With 200 bolts of highly-focused radiation burning into his brain, any movement whatsoever could kill him.

The neurologist’s part of the procedure completed, he left the hospital, apparently for a family vacation. It was just the radiation oncologist, his assistant, and us.

“May I come in the room?” I asked.

“No one is allowed in during the procedure,” the oncologist abruptly replied.

I remained in the door, however, never taking my eyes off Albert. No one said anything as they made necessary adjustments.
"We cannot do the procedure on this man," the doctor abruptly announced as he turned and walked toward the door.

"There is no alternative but conventional radiation," he said.

Back in the examining room, he told us the small tumors in the front of Al's brain were blocked by the head frame.

The doctor seemed somewhat perplexed as earlier, before that pronouncement, he had examined its placement, moving it ever so slightly this way and that.

"Doctor, isn't there any alternative at all?" I asked.

"Mr. Taubert is going to have to have conventional radiation. There is no choice in this matter. I will arrange for you to set up a series of treatments near where you live."

Was it my imagination that he seemed almost smug about this outcome? Was he feeling vindicated that his wish for Albert to have whole-brain radiation was the only option?

Removing the bolts from Al's head and bandaging the wounds, the doctor dismissed us with telephone numbers for the radiation facility near our home.

We were both depressed and deflated on the drive back to Connecticut. Even my normally upbeat husband barely said a word. I had no reserves left to try to lighten the mood.

Stereotactic radiosurgery had been our last hope. If Albert has whole-brain radiation, he might eventually lose some cognitive functions. I don't suppose most doctors think these patients will live long enough to worry about it.

Monday, October 22, 2001

"Do you want to give this one more try?" I asked as we drove away from New Milford hospital, having just arranged his series of radiation treatments.

"What do you have in mind?"

"I don't know. But I watched the oncologist in New York as he examined the position of the frame on your head. He seemed to be trying to reposition it somehow."

"Let's get on the Internet when we get home and see what we can find," Albert said.

3:30 p.m.

"Dr. De Lotbiniere's office," she answered.

"Good afternoon. My name is Kathryn Taubert. I'm calling for your help on behalf of my husband with metastatic brain tumors. He's just been turned down for stereotactic radiation in New York because they said the tumors were blocked by the head frame. I'm hoping Dr. De Lotbiniere can help. Is there any way I can talk to him if he's there? I'd be grateful for your help."

God was with us that afternoon. The receptionist was away from her desk and Dr. D.'s nurse had answered the phone. She seemed interested.

Alain De Lotbiniere's credentials were impeccable. He virtually built the SR department at Yale Medical School, not 40 minutes from our house.

His nurse asked me to fax a brief overview immediately.

Dr. D. was in the office that day. She would see that he got the information right away.

4:45 p.m.

"*Mrs. Taubert? This is Alain De Lotbiniere at Yale. I just read your fax. I have a few questions.*"

Shattered dreams coalesced into hope like leaping horses. I thanked him for calling, not believing the luck.

> *"Do you happen to know if your husband was placed on his stomach during the procedure?"*

"No, sir, he was not. I was standing in the door watching. He was on his back the entire time."

"*I think we may be able to help,*" he replied. "*I've learned a few tricks over the years. Can you bring your husband here for an MRI this Thursday?*"

Of course we could.

31.

Monday, October 29, 1:00 p.m.

Drifting in a simmering river of hope, tears streaming down my face, I listened from across the hall as Dr. De Lotbiniere's team prepared Al for the procedure.

De Lotbiniere believed they could simultaneously irradiate both the original tumor bed and the small tumors in front, killing the remaining cancer cells in his brain.

I could see Albert on his *stomach* on the table, head once again bolted to a metal halo and fixed to a crown of 200 radioactive thorns.

Dr. De Lotbiniere seemed so confident.

"*They said they couldn't do this in New York*," I overheard him tell his colleague.

"*What happened*?" replied the neurologist.

"*His wife didn't believe it*."

4:00 p.m.

"*Mrs. Taubert, we've finished the procedure. We'll be sending your husband to a room shortly in the event he has swelling, in which case we may keep him a day or two. You are welcome to stay with him*."

Barely able to speak, I asked if he would write the New York oncologist and tell him what they'd done. By simply repositioning Al on the table, they were able to successfully complete the procedure.

I wanted the doctors in New York to know. I was livid over what we'd almost allowed to happen.

"*The letter's already started,*" Dr. De Lotbiniere said gently as he turned to leave the room.

There is no measure of gratitude for these knights in white lab coats. I couldn't believe that only one week prior we'd been told that what they had just accomplished was impossible. I was angry that another "sacred cow" had cost us time and hope, and maybe Al's life.

I also learned that in Connecticut, the law requires both the presence of a neurologist and radiation oncologist throughout the entire SR procedure, unlike New York.

After positioning the frame on Albert's head, the New York neurologist left for vacation, leaving the radiation oncologist to complete the procedure alone!

I wondered if the outcome in New York would have been different had the neurologist remained.

If only we'd caught the tumor before it had to be surgically removed. Dr. De Lotbiniere didn't know if it could have been treated with SR. There was no way to determine now if it would have been possible.

If only they had performed routine CT scans of his head as well as his body! Cutting into a cancer releases cells to do more damage. But maybe we had another chance after all.

32.

Saturday, November 10, 2001

"*I do my coaching between games*," Albert once told me. I had commented upon how calm he seemed compared to the other coaches running red-faced and shouting along the sidelines.

"*All I usually do during games is make substitutions. The boys couldn't hear me anyway with all the racket,*" he said, chuckling.

However, today he broke his own rule about not shouting at a referee for a bad call.

"*Way to go, Coach*," said one of the boys after his display. He also got a hand and standing ovation from the team for it as well.

It's the steroids.

Tuesday, November 13, 2001

Dr. Nicholas Gonzalez told us we'd been doing most of the right things, but that Al's system was still "too acid." Cancer needs an "acid environment" to live, recommending changes in diet and supplementation to counteract it.

We found Gonzalez after an Internet search that revealed his unusually successful track-record with some cancers.

Practicing both conventional and alternative cancer treatments, he was well known in the New York medical community.

After an exhaustive interview process, Al had been admitted as a patient. Dr. Gonzalez said that specific changes in Al's regimen would correct the acidity, "if we caught it in time."

He seemed to hesitate as he said it. He'd seen Al's medical records.

Friday, November 16, 2001

I surprised Al with a weekend getaway to Newport, Rhode Island.

The problems with the lawsuit over a building lot Albert initiated a few years ago were escalating. I had to call police to stop people from harassing our driveway contractor. I had a previous legal issue over my driveway after Jim's death. I must have bad driveway karma.

We couldn't believe what was happening, this travesty of greed and town politics. Litigants were trying to force us to meet their demands, figuring Albert too sick to continue fighting. I told him I would handle it from now on.

It began a few years ago when Al got approval from the town to subdivide a property and sell a building lot. From there it escalated into a political football with us caught between the town and an unscrupulous politician with a personal agenda.

Using political influence, she got the town zoning board of appeals to reverse the decision. The zoning official, incensed over the reversal, resigned his job.

Little did we know this would escalate into a hugely expensive challenge to "city hall."
Albert isn't well enough for this. He was unusually quiet and seemed relieved when I said I'd take over.

I hoped the weekend away to one of our favorite destinations would cheer him a bit.

A seagull outside our harbor side motel room pecked at the glass so often that finally Al tossed a few crackers out the slider and sat back to watch.

Everything seemed in slow motion. Lying next to me, he later admitted his neck was bothering him.

Maybe he'd been sleeping wrong, he thought.

33.

Friday, November 23, 2001

He tires easily, moves more slowly than usual. I'm trying hard to be positive and keep things as normal as I can. He doesn't feel like playing soccer now. He's still trying to coach, but doesn't have his normal energy.

I make myself go to the DAWS shelter to volunteer. I can't focus on anything else when working with a formerly abused dog.

There's one in particular with whom I've developed a special attachment. Six years in a kennel, he's finally overcome his mistrust of people. He's among the most affectionate dogs I've ever seen. I cannot abandon Tony now. Our walks together are as good for me as him.

Albert and I had Thanksgiving dinner out with Adam and Jackie. Dory, her husband, and the boys didn't come. Al didn't feel up to traveling to see them. I didn't have the energy to cook.

Jackie is leaving for Eastern Europe to join her new husband. I hope her new life in Romania works out for her.

It'll be hard driving past her condo now, knowing she's no longer there. She and her Dad are so close. We'll miss her.

I wished I'd cooked. This holiday dinner out was too impersonal. At least Adam seems to be holding his own, staying clean and sober. Do we dare hope he's going to make it this time?

Monday, November 26, 2001

I could hear the neurosurgeon shouting at his receptionist through the phone. She had just told him I was in his waiting room, refusing to leave until he talked to me. I'd been trying to reach him for days.

Earlier he insisted there was no reason for the discomfort in Al's neck. The brain surgery was successful. The CT scans of his head showed no problem.

I knew something was wrong. Albert never complains. This was different. The Danbury neurosurgeon who had performed Al's brain surgery was about to go into surgery. He couldn't see me, and clearly didn't want to.

"Dr. Cooper, you have to help us," I said, crashing his office at the hospital shortly thereafter. Seeing my distress, his receptionist admitted us without an appointment to his office.

"Did they do an MRI of his neck and back?" Cooper asked.

"Not to my knowledge," I replied.

Picking up the phone, he called for an immediate MRI, ushering us to the upstairs lab himself. I'll be forever grateful for that small kindness. He was clearly distressed with the eventual result. Leptomeningeal carcinoma. Deadly, inoperable nodules of cancer creeping down Al's spinal column from the operated tumor-bed. It was beyond help.

Oh God, why hadn't I asked them last spring about a CT scan of his head?

34.

Wednesday, November 28, 2001

I wanted to run away with Albert as fast as we could.

The profound feeling of dread washed over me as we sat before this new radiation oncologist.

Was it his officiousness or what he was recommending?

The only option was irradiating Al's *entire* spine.

He admitted they didn't do much of it at that hospital.

I'm terrified.

Saturday, December 8, 2001

The angry red marks on Al's back frightened me as I took him for his next radiation treatment. He couldn't walk very well after starting them. He awoke this morning, after the last one, in a delirium.

The EMT's carried him down the stairs to the waiting emergency vehicle. I followed in my car, recounting the number of times I'd followed such a vehicle before. I always think of it whenever I see them.

They save lives. They also take them away.

Is it the cancer or the whole spine radiation that's killing him? Or both?

Monday, December 10, 2001

I was bringing him home from the hospital that morning. His weary eyes told me he was glad to be going.

"I'm still so attracted to you," he said quietly, holding my hand. "I can't wait to get you home."

He tries so hard to keep going. Giving up was never part of this man's game.

"Press on," he'd always say. No matter what.

Press on.

35.

Friday, December 14, 2001

The last radiation treatment was too much. I couldn't endure watching him suffer anymore. He said "No" when I asked him if he wanted to continue the treatments.

I'm relieved he won't have another of those Draconian irradiations.

Albert is dying.

His friends helped me rearrange the downstairs bedroom with two rented hospital beds. I wouldn't sleep upstairs knowing he'd be downstairs alone.

I arranged for hospice care. I'm exhausted from lack of sleep. His friends are calling so often I had to make a schedule to insure there's enough time for them to visit while attending to Al's needs.

I told his closest friends to come whenever they chose, however. Even though Albert speaks rarely now, he visibly brightens when they gather around his bed and talk about soccer. It's as though everything is normal.

Sunday, December 16, 2001

Jackie's back from Romania to live here with us for a while. Adam is here too.

Albert cannot get out of bed without help. With Adam's support on his left and Jackie's on his right, Al struggled to get up to go to the bathroom.

"I'm just like a baby," he sighed apologetically.

"That's okay, Dad. I'm here," Adam said as he held his father firmly. "You've done this for me my whole life. Now I'm here for you."

I quietly backed out of the room, silently sobbing. Albert finally had his son back.

Thursday, December 20, 2001

He's shutting down one inch at a time.

I know he hears me. At times, he still opens his eyes.

I taped a poster of Big Mountain in Montana on the ceiling over his bed for when he does.

The guys have been wonderful, visiting and talking to him, joking and reminiscing. He can't respond, but I see the slight changes on his face.

Jackie and Adam are taking such good care of him. I can sleep a little as we take round-the-clock shifts.

He can't get out of bed at all now. Hospice provided sheaths containing urinary catheters that don't require insertion, reducing the pain a bit.

I see the slight grimace on his face when I remove them, however. I tell him I'm sorry. I'll do better next time. At least there is no pain associated with this cancer.

We turn him periodically to prevent bed sores. I've learned how to change sheets with the patient still in the bed. I try getting him to eat, with little result.

Yesterday I left the room momentarily to visit a friend who'd stopped by. When I returned, the visiting nurse was trying to find a vein in his arm with the needle. I could see it was hurting him, but he couldn't speak.

I demanded she stop immediately. Backing away sheepishly from the bed, she had only been doing as ordered, but there is no further point to this.

I felt badly after admonishing her. But I felt worse that I'd left Al unable to defend himself.

Dr. George Anderheggen comes to pray quietly with Albert almost every night in the dimly lit room. George once told me if he'd had a brother, he'd have wanted him to be like Al. Earlier in our marriage, George, a psychotherapist, had counseled us when we were struggling over what to do about Adam's drug addiction. George, also an ordained minister, had also counseled addicts at one point in his career. He gave us insights which helped us better understand the depth of the issues with which we were struggling.

Karen Klein spent an hour or so sitting next to Al's bed, reminiscing about the soccer team she managed and he coached. Karen handled the important details of scheduling and team administration, freeing Albert to coach the kids, including one of Karen's sons. They made a good team.

Albert didn't reply the day the hospice nurse asked what he saw when staring at the wall at the foot of his bed. In her 20 years of hospice work, she'd seen many dying patients claim to see deceased loved ones gathering around them. I hoped she was right.

Sunday, December 23, 2001

It was dark. Jackie and Adam were at a movie. I was alone with Al, sitting on his bed. Suddenly he opened his eyes directly into mine, alert as he held my gaze. He couldn't say anything and didn't have to. I *knew* what he was asking.

"Sweetheart, if this gets too hard, it's okay to go Home. It'll be hard, but I'll be okay. Albert, do you know what I'm saying to you?"

A tear appeared in his eye. I held his hand, stroked his cheek. He closed his eyes. *He knew*.

36.

Monday, December 24, 2001, Christmas Eve

The kids and grandkids were in the family room. I was alone with Albert, watching him sleep. If it *was* sleep.

I don't know what to call this in-between place he is in now. But something I did told me he still heard me.

The barest hint of movement around his mouth told me he was still there. He had *smiled.*

Tuesday, December 25, 2001, Christmas Day

How he loved Christmas. A deeply spiritual man, he always knew where he was going.

"It should be celebrated for what it is," he'd say, lamenting the commercialism.

The kids and grandkids were opening gifts around the tree in the other room. I asked them to bring the gifts into our room, but they wanted to "keep things as normal as possible for the boys," remaining in the family room.

The little artificial firs with tiny white lights sitting in the corner of the family room served as decoration. I didn't have the energy this year to festoon the house with the usual ones. There didn't seem to be much point to it this year.

I couldn't get into the spirit. I put a small, ceramic tree in the corner of his room, however, because I knew he would appreciate it. If only he could.

Maybe they're right to want to keep things "normal" for the boys. But I couldn't bear leaving him alone on Christmas Day.

I lay next to him, listening to their voices as they opened gifts. I had placed envelopes on the little trees containing checks for each. I didn't have the energy this year to shop for gifts.

Albert surprised me a month ago with a collection of cassette tapes with some of my favorite old standards. I know it was because he knew he wouldn't be able to give them to me later.

He's never heard me sing those old tunes I used to perform so long ago. But he knew the music was always in my heart. He would of course know that, because he's in there too.

37.

Wednesday, December 26, 2001, 10:00 a.m.

He tried to take the small bit of food I placed between his lips. He'd eaten virtually nothing these last days. I knew from hospice to expect it. Still, he tried.

He began coughing, trying to clear the congestion. Jackie was rushing in and out of the room crying, *"Just go, Dad. Just go!"*

Adam left the house shortly before. I know what Jackie was enduring. Watching someone you love die is unspeakable. They call the last gasps of life "death rattle." He parted his lips to take the pill I offered to quiet him. He seemed to breathe easier when I told him to relax and not try so hard anymore.

I lay next to him as he gazed out the triple windows on the clear, cold Connecticut winter's day. Not a breath of air as the world seemed to hold its breath…waiting in the bright sunlit woods where we had lived and loved so well.

Suddenly he opened his tired eyes to gaze upon the beautiful world outside our windows, as I burned the image of his handsome face into my mind.

With a slight twitch of a lip, he closed his eyes for the last time as I held him. It was three years since his diagnosis of cancer.

He was gone.

PART II

JANUARY 2002-APRIL 2004

38.

Sleep, when it came, was indeed a *welcome little death.* Waking to empty dawns was unspeakable in a house suddenly too big, too quiet, too empty.

I lived in the bedroom where Albert spent his last days. The guys put the furniture back as it was before it became Al's hospital room, *but he was still there.*

Friends invited me to spend New Year's Eve with them, but I couldn't leave that room. I needed to be with *Albert.*

Family and friends resume their lives as you realize yours will never be the same.

It hits you like an anvil those first few weeks after the calls and sympathy cards trickle away, a call here and there, a card now and then before they stop.

Life gets back to normal for everyone but you. He's not there and never will be again.

I stumbled through days and nights in a numb blur, making arrangements for Al's memorial service, greeting those who called or came by, taking care of the animals. The dogs Maggie and Kip were strangely quiet. The cats padded softly about me, seeking more attention than usual it seemed.

Just as Maggie and Kip had stood quietly by with drooping heads the day Al, Chris, and Ron took their brother Jack away for the last time, they *knew.*

The church overflowed with mourners lined up out the door into the parking lot. I stopped in the narthex to look at the photo collage that Jackie had assembled of her father's life.

In the center was the photo of Albert I'd taken in Newport on our 10th anniversary, when the flash failed and that slithering premonition chilled my heart.

I don't recall how I got to the church or with whom.

I only remember seeing Al's children and grandsons filling the front row on the left. For me, there was only the empty pew on the right.

I was grateful as Denise and Tom Foster sat quietly beside me. Chris French rolled Annie's wheelchair to the end of the pew. My dear friend Harold had been more like a father than older brother to Annie. Annie loved Albert too. I met Chris volunteering with the Tourette Syndrome Association. Annie was almost like a little sister to me as well. Born with spina bifida, hydrocephalus, and a host of other serious birth defects, Anne Marie Knox was among the strongest people I ever met.

Not expected at birth to live more than a few weeks, if that, Annie not only survived, she became a guiding light and beacon of strength to all who knew her. For all the pain and suffering she endured throughout her life, I never heard her complain. She was always the first to offer a kind word or sympathetic ear. Her compassion and empathy for others never failed to inspire, no matter how pale in comparison their own troubles were to hers.

A couple of years after I introduced Chris and Annie, they married in a lovely ceremony in our home.

My mother asked if she should come from Texas to the service. Losing Daddy, then Albert would have been too much for her. No was else was available to bring her. At 88, the flight alone would have been too much. I couldn't have attended to both her and my own unspeakable grief.

I don't know how long the service lasted. I lost count of the shared vignettes through tears and laughter, remembering the man who meant so much to so many.

I recalled how Albert's eulogy in 1996 for my father had comforted my family. He described Daddy as only another man can. Al's comments were warm, funny, enlightening. I was determined to make my eulogy to Albert do him justice as only a wife's can.

I struggled for composure as George Anderheggen called me to the lectern. Robert Fulton focused his video camera as a hush filled the sanctuary. I began to speak.

I tried hard not to let the hordes of tics overwhelm me. I saw later I wasn't very successful.

I was a numb observer in the replay of our life together. I felt oddly detached, even remote. I told the story of how we really met, as Annie giggled from the pew. She was among the few who knew that Albert didn't merely *"pick me up in a dentist's office,"* as he used to say.

He had replied to a personal ad I placed in "*Connecticut Magazine*," as I hoped to demonstrate to a girlfriend a new way of meeting people. The outdated issue with my ad in it, was what Albert "picked up" as he waited for his dental appointment. I'd never done that before, nor had he. In the ad I'd requested a "short note" and photo. When his letter arrived, a three-line handwritten note and drawing of a *musical* note fell out of the envelope. It made me laugh. I'd also written that laughter was what I had been missing.

He couldn't have known the significance of music in my life and how once it had been a budding career that I left behind for love.

"Meet me for lunch or dinner," his note said. "If you don't laugh, *I'll* buy. If you do, *you* buy."

I'll always remember the first time I saw him walking through the door of the place we agreed to meet. Arms opened wide beneath a dazzling smile, "I'm here, and I'm even on time!"

I'd realize later that he wasn't as compulsive about time as I am. It never mattered. I adjusted our schedules accordingly.

I found Albert's grandsons among the blur of faces in the congregation as I spoke of their "Opa" and how much he loved them. I saw nothing for me in the eyes of his three adult children.

I didn't know it then, but after those few days, I would never see anyone but Jackie again.

After the service, the house filled with people. They found me by the dining room table that was laden with the food our housekeeper, Maryuza Prado, had prepared. She had tears in her eyes too.

Backed into a corner as the line grew, I felt simultaneously trapped and overwhelmed with gratitude.

"I should move this receiving line to another room and get out of this corner," I thought before wondering why. Some part of me was still detached. I don't remember what I did after that. The next days are a blur.

Most of the people at the service would go on with their lives without Albert or me. There wasn't much for a 56-year-old childless widow in what was tantamount to a bedroom community for Stamford and New York City.

Past experience taught me there would be no real life for me here without Albert. At least I wouldn't feel quite so abandoned this time. I'd grown stronger and wiser since Jim's death.

39.

January 15, 2002

It was just after dark when the doorbell rang. “I just came to see how you were doing,” she said in her Aussie accent. “Mind if I come in a while?”

I never even thought Cheri liked me. Her husband, Chris Armentano, is one of Albert’s oldest friends. There always seemed to be plenty of reasons for her to be elsewhere when we got together. Finding her at the door that cold winter night was a surprise.

But at times like those, you find out who your real friends are. Well-meaning people say they’ll invite you to dinner or come over, then never do.

“I’ll call you soon,” others say, but other priorities get in the way.

My inherent shyness kept me from calling them. I determined to do something about that as soon as I could get my feet back under me, if I ever could.

I’ll be ever grateful to those who included me in their lives even after Al was gone. Were it not for them, I’d have been even more alone than I was.

Frequently over the next few months, Cheri Hicks Armentano would come to my door in the evening with, *“I just came to see how you were doing.”*

Even those who think we know people miss a call now and then. She and I discovered we had more in common than either of us imagined.

She'll always have a special place in my heart for those cold nights when, were it not for her kindness, I'd have grieved alone.

I got a letter from my sister Mary, the first one ever. It's hard when you have a sibling with whom you've been estranged almost your whole life. It's never been easy between us, nor will it ever be.

Some part of her is as better off without me as I am without her. I bear her no ill will. I know she's doing the best she can as are we all. But sometimes one has to just let go and move on.

I could tell her letter had been written in an alcohol-fueled haze. Her normally precise hand wavered unevenly across the page as she wrote how sorry she was, hoping I would find "solace in Christ."

It was her way of trying to help and I was grateful. For that brief moment, she was the older sister for whom I'd always hoped. But I knew it wouldn't last.

My other sister Dorothy called about once a week for a while.

My mother called almost daily.

I told them I was managing, although at times I could barely speak for the fulminating pain.

What good would it do to tell them how awful it was to see that empty pew? I sensed their guilt at not having been there. There had been mostly good reasons, of course, and mother had offered.

But couldn't *someone* in my family have been there? Memorials are for the *survivors*.

It's my own fault. I never asked for them anything, leading them to believe I never *needed* anything. I was the independent, self-sufficient one. They needed to believe it. So did I.

On some level, I don't think my family could deal with the fact that I wasn't always as strong as they thought. Sometimes independence is wrongly perceived as arrogance. Most of the time it's just self-preservation.

It's too late to tell them now. It would only hurt us all more. I can't handle any more pain.

At least they have the videotape of Al's service. It was one of the last projects completed by Emmy-award winning cinematographer Bob Fulton, shortly before he was killed in a plane crash. Bob videotaped Al's memorial service as a favor to me at the request of our good friend, Joe Kugielski.

Robert E. "Bob" Fulton III won the Emmy in 1997 for *"Denali: Alaska's Great Wilderness,"* which he shot from his single-engine plane while operating a wing-mounted camera. Bob died 4 months after Albert's memorial service, when his Cessna A-185-F crashed in Pennsylvania, the result of a freak combination of thermal forces that caused his plane to break up in the sky.

Later, along with his family and friends, I would help search the field where the crash occurred, in hopes of finding the ring his daughter wanted so desperately to locate. We all thought it a wonderful "sign" that she was the one who found it. I thought it sadly ironic that Bob and Albert, who'd met not long before Albert's illness, would die so close together in time.

Robert Fulton was a good man. His offer to videotape Albert's service meant a great deal to me.

Pilots often stick together, it seems, offering to help when one of their own is in need, or makes his "last flight." Walking the field where he died in search of his ring for his daughter was the least I could do for his family, after what he'd done for me.

Joe and Anne Kugielski were among those who stood by me after Al was gone. Maybe in some way I was their last link with Albert, too. Joe was a professional photographer who had done work for National Geographic, Martha Stewart publications, among others. Albert had met Joe, Anne, and their children through their mutual love of soccer.

40.

Memories flooded my mind. Albert's absence and the long battle to keep him alive had left a huge void. I had flashbacks to a past I didn't want to leave. I thought about the day I told him I'd quit my job to join him in Montana.

It was January 1991. I'd been looking out the window of my Hartford office on a cold, dark winter evening, staring at the city lights.

Albert had retired from Pan Am the previous July. He had just left for Whitefish for a couple of months of skiing. Life without him was sad and I was very lonely.

That night I went to see the movie "Awakenings," loosely based on the experiences of neurologist Dr. Oliver Sacks, starring Robin Williams, Robert DeNiro, and Julie Kavner. Kavner's character had long been smitten with Williams', but had resigned herself to the fact his interests only seemed to be in his work.

At the end of the movie, "Eleanor" tells "Dr. Sayer" goodnight and leaves the building. Recalling that DeNiro's poignant character "Leonard" had once admonished the Dr. Sayer character to not let life pass him by, Sayer threw open the window to ask Eleanor if the offer for coffee was still open.

That movie changed my life. Monday morning, I submitted my resignation to The Travelers. The company had been good to me. I had a wonderful career.

But it wasn't what I really wanted *in my life.* Albert was.

He was a basically happy guy. Smart, well-read, funny, kind, generous and compassionate, he opened my eyes to the rest of the world. Having flown to almost every country on the planet except China and Australia ("takes too much time"), Albert routinely perused periodicals and T.V. programs with an international focus. Soon I was doing the same.

Born to German-immigrant parents, Al spoke German almost exclusively until he was five years old. His first day of kindergarten in Port Chester, N.Y., where his parents and uncle had settled, little Albert walked home after a couple of hours and told his mother he didn't want to stay in class because "Those kids talk funny."

Saying it was the only way he was going to learn proper English, she marched him right back across the street to school.

Al's father was an avid soccer player, as was his uncle, a former professional soccer player in Germany. Both men instilled a deep love of the sport in Albert.

Al went to college on an all-sports scholarship. Ice hockey was his favorite, but it was too expensive when he was growing up. Soccer became the sport for which he'd later become well-known throughout Connecticut and elsewhere.

As a youth, Albert played semi-professional baseball for the Philadelphia Phillies farm team and a Canadian franchise before enlisting in the U.S. Air Force to become a pilot.

Lt. Albert R. Taubert Jr. graduated with his wings in the class of 1953-A, subsequently serving on active duty for six years.

Captain Taubert left the military for a career in commercial aviation, flying briefly for Northeast Airlines and literally writing the FAA manual on calibrating flight navigation aids. Living several years each in Japan and Germany and flying 28 years for Pan Am gave him a worldly perspective not many acquire.

Albert was an urbane man with the warm and common touch of a man born the American son of grateful, hard-working immigrant parents. He once told me how glad he was that his parents had emigrated from Germany in the late 1920's. Albert was born in 1930, an American citizen by birth.

Another uncle had been a German U-Boat commander in World War I. Al imagined how differently his life might have been had he been a boy growing up Germany in the 1930's, as that country spiraled toward yet another world war and the horrors of Hitler's "Third Reich."

Al loved the USA for the opportunities it had given him and his family.

Even as he flew for Pan Am, he continued serving in the Air National Guard until the 1960's when about to be deployed to Vietnam as a "forward observer." Before deployment, however, the type of aircraft he would fly was grounded due to mechanical problems. Not long thereafter, the Vietnam conflict ended.

Al believed in "giving back." Among the first members of the Board of Directors of the Connecticut Junior Soccer Association, Albert also founded the highly successful Newtown Soccer Club in 1972.

As the first United States Soccer Federation "A" licensed coach in Connecticut, he was involved in every aspect of soccer. He not only continued playing until he was 70, he coached, administered team programs, and developed soccer training programs for coaches.

Still flying with Pan Am, he also worked as head soccer coach for Western Connecticut State University, and assisted his coaching colleagues at both Newtown High School and Fairfield University.

Referring to himself as "a soccer coach who flew," he made friends all over the world. While many flight crews on layovers were resting up or going to the pool, Albert sought out casual soccer games from Brazil's Ipanema Beach to Istanbul, Turkey.

He also captained the Pan Am soccer team, and served as Pan Am's aeromedical chairman and member of the Safety Committee during the 1970's initial hijackings. His devotion to volunteering and trying to make things better for those around him more than rivaled my own "chronic volunteerism."

I thought soccer was merely "kick-ball" until I met Al and saw a real game in action. I couldn't help but marvel at a well-played game. It's like a fast-moving ballet of skill and quick-thinking with agile athletes who never stop running!

Albert's friends called him "Dr. Soccer." It didn't take long for me to understand why.

By the winter of 1991, about a year and a half after we'd met, we hadn't spoken of marriage. We just knew we were a couple. I didn't want him to feel pressured because I'd just quit my job with The Travelers!

I called him in Montana that night and told him that what I had just done was something I did for *me,* which was true.

No matter what his response was, I knew I'd be okay. I'd already survived the worst thing I ever would with the struggle to rebuild my life after Jim's death. I was no stranger to risking everything for love.

I recalled the overwhelming relief when, after a heart stopping silence, Al said: "You don't know how honored I am. I know how you loved that job. I would never have asked you to leave it. You did it for *us*. Get yourself out here as soon as you can."

Three weeks later, I was on Big Mountain with him.

Waking softly together in the cold Montana dawn of that Valentine's Day, he turned sleepily to me and said, "So, you wanna' get married?"

"Sure," I said, waking to a dream. It was as though we already *were*. On June 1, 1991, we just made it official at a "surprise wedding."

I had left my position in 1980 as director of training with the March of Dimes Birth Defects Foundation to marry Jim Holbrook.

I was now leaving my dream job as management education executive with The Travelers Insurance companies to be with Albert.

Both the March of Dimes and The Travelers were outstanding companies for which to work. I learned much, met many fine people, and accomplished things I'd never have thought possible as that shy little girl of so long ago. Ascending corporate ladders was a sometimes daunting, but heady experience.

In 1990, as an internal management consultant for The Travelers Insurance Companies, my boss reported directly to the CEO and chairman of the Travelers Board of Directors. That was a long leap for a Southeast Texas country girl who didn't even have her undergraduate degree! But I'd never needed it. I'd always gotten in on the ground floor of disciplines for which degree plans either didn't yet exist or weren't required.

My employers sent me to one educational seminar and training program after another to gain the skills I needed to perform my jobs. I had hit my stride by the time I went to work for The Travelers. I was grateful for my employers' faith in me.

Over the years, I'd taken jobs which I enjoyed, and worked hard to succeed. I was free to go wherever they needed me, relocating frequently as the opportunities arose.

But those jobs, as great as they were, weren't what I really wanted out of life.

I left both the March of Dimes and The Travelers for love.

And I never looked back.

41.

Painful reminders merged with the devastation of losing Albert. I struggled hard to keep from drowning in grief.

There was no Harold this time around to pull me kicking and screaming back to life as he had during those grim days after my husband Jim's death.

No one told us in those days that CPR only worked on about 6 percent of heart attack victims.

My husband of three-and-a-half years, James Edward Holbrook, wasn't to be among them.

I could feel myself dying after Jim's sudden, tragic death. I saw through the veil of tears to the welcome relief beyond, but it was Harold who saved me during those years when grief pursued me like a hungry hound. I had prayed for death then too.

Jim Holbrook was the funniest man I ever met. I never laughed or cried as hard as I did with him. His sense of humor was legendary. His mantra, "Never ever say 'Never ever,'" always made me smile.

He scooped me away from a thriving career with the March of Dimes. A marketing executive with Eastman Kodak, he was the consummate salesman. He sold me for sure!

On December 2, 1979, I was attending a Manhattan conference at which Jim was presenting a program on the return on investment (ROI) of audiovisual training programs. Since I was developing an audiovisual training program for March of Dimes field staff, his presentation was exactly what I needed.

Taking a seat near the back of the room, I watched as this handsome gray-haired man in a sharp three-piece suit entertained as well as educated the room full of participants. He was an excellent speaker with the superb presentation he'd developed as a representative of Kodak's Motion Picture and Audiovisual Division. Training wasn't his profession, but a master's degree in economics more than qualified him to develop this program for those of us for whom training and development were.

As I was having dinner with a colleague later in the hotel restaurant, Jim entered the room, greeting us as he passed our table. A few moments later, he walked *back*, introduced himself and asked to join us. After chatting an hour or so, I excused myself and went to my room.

Not long after, the phone rang. It was Jim inviting me to lunch after his presentation the following day.

Lunch turned into an invitation to attend a Kodak reception. The reception turned into dinner with Jim and some of his associates that night and the next.

When "one gets caught between the moon and New York City," as the song[5] says, especially during the

---

[5] **"Arthur's Theme," 1981 Academy Award winning song by Christopher Cross, Burt Bacharach, Carole Bayer Sager, and Peter Allen.**

Christmas season, just about anything can happen. There is nothing quite like the *Big Apple* all shiny and glittering with holiday lights and cheer.

Jim and I barely left each other's side for the duration of the three-day conference.

Three months later, I left my career with the March of Dimes, and moved from Connecticut to Rochester in upstate New York.

On March 8, 1980, we married in a quiet ceremony at his home with a few family and friends in attendance. I was 34, he was 44. We might have married in haste after a whirlwind romance, but we fell in love at leisure.

He called me "Sunshine." When he died so suddenly three-and-a-half years after we married, my world was shattered.

On a night not long before he died, I was waiting at Chuck's Restaurant bar in Danbury, CT, in anticipation of our having dinner when he returned from his Manhattan office. It was the first week of October 1983, three-and-a-half months after we'd moved back to CT from Rochester, N.Y.

A soft voice behind me asked if the adjacent seat was available.

Turning to look directly into smiling hazel eyes, I fought an impulse to ask this man where we'd met. But I knew it wasn't possible. Jim and I had only been in town a few months and I hadn't met many people yet.

"You're married," he said after a few pleasantries, noting my wedding ring.

"Very," I smiled back. "My husband is on his way back from the City. And you?"

"Not anymore," the humor in his eyes clouding over. We chatted pleasantly until Jim arrived. I left Harold "Buddy" Knox feeling as though I left a friend. In another life, he and I might have been more than cordial strangers.

Two weeks later, Jim died of a massive heart attack at 48 years old. He'd just returned from a business trip. After dinner together in our new home in New Fairfield, CT, he stood up from the table, gathering me in his arms.

"I love my life. I love my wife. I love my job."

An hour later he was dead.

In 1983, at 37, I was widowed for the first time, having tried to save my husband's life with CPR, and failing.

Ten days later I went straight to our lawyer's office, after getting off the plane from burying Jim in Tampa, Florida, where his parents and brother were living.

"Don't sugar coat it," I told the lawyer. We hadn't been in New Fairfield long. I'd started working almost immediately at a job that gave me time to spend with Jim. I had no friends nearby and my family was across the country.

Jim's ex-wife and children would soon take me to court over the house Jim and I had built, and a few pieces of furniture. Jim's divorce decree had given them all of his substantial life insurance.

The only thing he and I had was what we built together. I had nothing to do with their divorce, initiated before we met. I would, however, become the focus of considerable animosity after we married.

The last place I wanted to go when I flew back from Tampa was to the house where he died as I tried to save his life and failed.

I left the lawyer's office and drove to the only other place I knew in town: Chuck's Steakhouse. After a couple of drinks at the bar, I realized I couldn't get up.

"Where have I got to go anyway?" I thought.

42.

I leaned into the corner of the bar, not caring that I couldn't get off the stool.

Suddenly a soft voice at my shoulder said, "How are you tonight?"

It was Harold. I saw the change of expression on his face as I turned to him. The loss of about 15 pounds in the 10 days since Jim's death had taken its toll.

"Are you *okay*?" he asked, looking surprised. "What's happened?"

"You don't want to know," I said. How could I blurt out that I'd just buried my husband? It was still too personal.

"Do you mind if I sit here?" he asked, taking the empty seat to my left.

I nodded, grateful for the companionship. He was as close to a friend as I had there. We didn't say much, although he pressed gently for an explanation.

After a while, I told him. *"My husband died 10 days ago."*

Gently, he covered my hand with his, in stunned silence.

I barely knew this man, yet that small measure of comfort meant more than I could have imagined.

We sat there mostly in silence as I sobered up enough to get off the stool and go home. He asked if he could drive me.

"I'll make it," I said. I was still married, after all.

He asked my last name and where I lived. Not really caring who knew what anymore, I told him.

Somehow, I made it to the house. I walked in the door as the phone started ringing. It was Harold.

For the next five years, it would ring every day like that at least twice.

It was Harold who listened to me as I told him the horror of desperately trying to save Jim's life as he lay dying.

It was Harold who first got me out of the house with, "It's my birthday and I don't want to spend it alone."

It was Harold who helped me deal with issues around a newly constructed home and deconstructed life in New Fairfield where Jim and I had been only a few months.

It was he who folded me into his family during the holidays, suddenly so bereft of joy. Harold's daughters Holly and Debbie, mother Dot, sisters Jane and Annie, brother Gary, and the rest of his family took me into their midst almost as one of their own.

It was Harold who held me as I sobbed, sympathized with what I would endure with Jim's ex-wife and children who seemed to hate me so.

It was he who gave me the courage to face the town over a mishandled property deed that very nearly cost me access to my own property.

It was Harold who held me close in the night, the first man after Jim to do so.

He saved my life by gently urging me to seek medical help, as he pulled me kicking and screaming back into life.

"Sometimes, Kathryn, there are things you can't do by yourself. Maybe this is one of them."

After six months with my head under a pillow, I was dying. But it was *Harold* who reached that small part of me that still wanted to live.

43.

Dr. David Reed was a psychiatrist specializing in grief therapy. I walked into his office in late spring of 1984, about six months after Jim died. I told Reed I didn't want to hear him ask me what I thought, because if I knew, I wouldn't be there.

There are times when grieving people don't know what to think. We need to be told by those who do.

I later learned my anger marked the beginning of healing. He said that depression is "anger turned inward." In time, I would learn to put it where it belonged so I could move on.

After my little speech, Dr. Reed asked me a few questions before issuing orders.

"The fact that you walked into my office on your own tells me you aren't going to kill yourself even though you've been thinking about dying, so I'm not going to hospitalize you. You are clinically depressed. You will be in my office at least twice weekly for the time being. Once the medication I'm prescribing for you lifts the floor of the depression, we're going to start talking. Agreed?"

He's obviously taken my admonition seriously.

David Reed and I spent the next four years sorting me out from the shambles of my life.

With David's gentle but persistent guidance and Harold's love and support, I became stronger than ever.

David was the first person who knew how to get through to me, overcoming time and again the roadblocks I put before him. I'd been hiding so long, I wasn't even sure who I was anymore.

When reduced to your fundamental elements, you have the opportunity to rebuild yourself from the ground up. You can throw out the useless emotional junk collected along the way and end up *better*.

I couldn't know then, of course, that within 10 years both David and Harold would be dead too.

David was killed in a boating accident at 53.

Harold died of a rare and deadly leukemia at 52.

Ten years after Harold and I met at Chuck's Steakhouse, I sat by his bedside as he lay dying, both of us trying to accept the fact of his death, much as he'd helped me accept the gift of my life.

Although Harold and I were no longer together when Albert and I met, I would always love him dearly. He was *family*.

I recalled the night in 2003 when Annie called to tell me her brother was dying. I ran crying out the door just as Albert was returning from a soccer game.

Gently grasping me by the shoulders, Al asked what was wrong.

"I know how much he means to you," holding me close as I sobbed out the story. Pulling back slightly and looking directly into my eyes, he said, "You need to go to him in the hospital. I love you. I trust you. I'll be home when you get back."

I never loved anyone more in my life than I did Al Taubert at that moment.

For the next six months, I spent many hours sitting by Harold's bedside, as Al waited at home with open arms and his great, kind, compassionate heart.

I've *lost* more than most people have ever *had.*

At times I would almost believe that my loving someone marked them for death. I told myself that was ridiculous. But after so many times, I sometimes wondered.

Others sometimes ask what I'm doing to cause people around me to die. They try humor to defuse their discomfort after learning my history. Once, someone jokingly called me a "*black widow.*" That kind of humor fails miserably.

"At least they died happy," I say pointedly, changing the subject. They don't realize how their words hurt.

There was no Harold or David to save me after Al's death. Did God figure I had become strong enough to handle it on my own?

Living with loss is my karma this time around. That which doesn't destroy us makes us stronger.

With what David taught me and the strength gained from being loved by the fine people in my life, I knew I would survive this time.

I had promised Albert I'd be okay. It wouldn't be easy. But I would go on.

44.

I took the pills, following Denise's advice to keep them handy just in case. It started within weeks after Al's passing. In February of 2002, the *heaviness* set in as depression stalked me. Lifting arms and legs soon became a chore as I struggled to put one foot in front of the other, the physical precursor to the emotional meltdown I knew would follow.

I still lived mostly in the room where Albert spent his last days. The cold, empty house once so filled with life, and *us*, had become little more than a beautiful mausoleum.

We designed it ourselves, bringing the outdoors in through every window. He oversaw the outside construction with the contractor. I oversaw the inside, each consulting the other, occasionally deferring to the greater expertise. It had been such fun.

I filled the home with 85 tropical plants and warm, comfortable furnishings. Seeing the tropical foliage against views of winter snow on the trees and fields beyond, was like stepping into another world. Our home on Greenleaf Farms had been filled with warmth and love.

Without Albert, it was nothing more than wood, stone, metal, and tile, merely the place I stored my things.

If it weren't for the animals, there wouldn't have been anything left for me at all. Even the contractor who built our home was gone, dying alone in a motel room of his own demons. They said it was insulin shock. I wasn't so sure.

Our home was the largest and most complex Ron Brier ever built. We had no idea his efforts on our behalf were his attempts to exorcise his own demons. He produced a magnificent home for us. It would be his last.

David Reed taught me to replace old routines with new ones, moving out of the past one small step at a time. I always wanted to learn how to live in the moment. Now I had no choice but to do so.

The antidepressants helped immediately, as they had before. David once said to me that my particular depression was the ideal lock for which Prozac was the key. In a matter of days, the *heaviness* was gone.

45.

Two months after Al's passing, Chris and Cheri invited me to join them in Roxbury for yoga lessons.

I took the 35-minute drive past Newtown High School where Albert had coached.

Driving home the first night, I didn't think much about the street lamp that suddenly flicked off ahead on the highway ramp near the school.

But when it happened four more weeks in succession, I *knew* it was Albert.

We had this funny little ritual with lights. He'd turn off the foyer table lamp and turn on the overhead fluorescents in the adjacent kitchen. "Uses less electricity," he'd say. But I liked coming home to the warm accent light in the foyer, so I'd turn it back on.

We never argued, it was just one of those silly little things married couples do. But after the street lamp incidents, I'd never looked at lights the same way again.

I believe they were the way Albert would send me a message, much like Daddy's parking spaces and pennies appearing on the ground wherever mother went. It happened so often she began walking with her head inclined to the pavement, looking for coins from her beloved husband of 61 years. She found even more as a result.

Lights flickering on and off would happen repeatedly over the years. *Albert was still with me.*

46.

Their soft, sweet cooing seemed to follow me through the years wherever I went. How I loved that sound as a child.

Awakening to their soft *hoo-hoo-ing* from my old bunk at the farm in Texas, I eagerly anticipated another day riding my horse Suds, exploring the woods with Sandra, my best childhood friend. Those were among the happiest times of my childhood, and hers. She would die at 42.

So many people I loved, gone. I never really thought about why those birds were often called "mourning" doves until then.

It was April 2002 and another lovely Connecticut spring just around the corner. For me, the grief was still a cold, dark winter in my heart.

I grieved the loss of so many. I grieved the fact I didn't ask the doctors that one question that will haunt me the rest of my life:

"Why didn't they do a CT scan of his head?"

How long could I live with this pain, guilt and self-recrimination?

It was the only question unasked and unanswered.

It was the one that killed him.

47.

He was one of the biggest people I'd ever seen and in his policeman's uniform, the most intimidating as well. Barely fitting in the booth across the aisle, he was clearly curious about the stranger in *his* town.

"Howdy, ma'am," he growled. One doesn't often hear that in Connecticut. Although "a born-again Yankee," my Texas roots run deep.

"New in town? Name's Charlie," he said, consuming my hand in his firm, yet surprisingly gentle grip. He could snap a bone with that hand if he wished, I surmised. Perhaps he had. But his twinkling eyes and down-home manner put me at ease.

I only passed through the village of Bethel on my way to and from my volunteer work at DAWS. Recently, I'd been stopping at Jacqueline's Restaurant in the town center. Eating breakfast out was one step toward the new life I had to make.

David Reed had said after Jim's death that the best way to start over is by making small changes in old routines that were painful reminders of the past.

It was four months after Al's passing. I could no longer let myself grieve the hours Albert and I enjoyed our wide-ranging breakfast conversations. I had to build new routines, new memories. I had to build a new life.

After a while, Sgt. Charlie Hupp and I began sharing a booth. Another native Texan, Charlie soon introduced me to his good friends Rocky and Pat O'Connor, Eddie Flynn, and his own Marnie. We soon became "The Breakfast Club."

I missed them on the rare days I didn't see them. They welcomed me into their lives, poking holes in my loneliness like Swiss cheese.

I learned to laugh again.

48.

“Hi,” the email began. “I liked what you wrote. I’m a long way from you, but hope to hear from you anyway.”

I’d only meet Steve once, but doing so would set me off on a course that would totally change my life. It amazes me how a single incident can do such a thing. People are like pinballs bouncing off each other and changing course because of it.

Some say God never puts more on us than we can handle. I sometimes wonder if even He forgets once in a while. But I believe we’re here to learn how to do something better and keep coming back until we get it right. I hope I learn it well enough this time not to have to return for a while.

I *have* to believe our suffering serves a purpose. Five months after Albert’s passing, I was reaching out for help.

I had little left of me to give anyone. I was hoping someone, anyone, would just write back. I was drowning in the dark, lonely pit of grief and loss, yet again.

The website had promised everything from friendship to love. Recalling how a similar thing brought me Albert, I hoped perhaps I would at least find a new friend. My friends in Connecticut did the best they could, but they were busy with their own lives, too. I still spent too many hours alone.

Denise and Sheryl dragged me to lunch once a week. They'd get a table in a dark corner so no one could see my tears.

Joanne Cohen would meet me at Rein's Deli, driving from her home in Massachusetts.

Chris and Cheri, Ron Skelton, Charlie DeSantis, Joe and Anne Kugielsky, and others invited me out or helped me with things around the house.

Tim and Barbara O'Connor included me in their Christmas plans, as did my good friend and long-time attorney Charlie Drummey.

Geri and Ed Mills, whom I met through "The Breakfast Club," took me under their wing for chatty dinners at the Stony Hill Inn. Geri would serenade us at the piano bar with her lilting Irish tunes, flaming red hair and Irish eyes a dead give-away on her proud heritage.

Shirley and Rubin Smith's world-class gourmet meals tempted my diminished appetite, as Rube reluctantly answered my appeals to hear how his marketing genius inspired the phenomenon of The Pet Rock and Silver Palate cookbooks.

Weekly, I would take Harold's sister Annie in her handicapped-accessible van to Danbury Mall for shopping and Arby's overstuffed baked potatoes. My problems seemed miniscule compared to Annie's. One day with her put my own life in perspective. Her unending good cheer never failed to inspire me.

Volunteer colleagues at DAWS extended their limitless compassion from the homeless and abandoned animals to me.

I spent afternoons at the shelter working with the dogs. I helped find homes for other "unadoptable" dogs, but hadn't yet been able to find a "forever home" for the Belgian-shepherd mix, Tony.

I spent time with my own wolf dogs Kip and Maggie. The cats were always around to comfort me too.

I was slowly starting to fill the terrible void into which I'd fallen after Albert's passing.

49.

I'd forgotten how good it could feel as my head slipped beneath the waters of the lake. I'd been a couch potato for so long that swimming seemed both alien and familiar. I leaped into another dimension of sensation, swimming slowly across the lagoon.

"You'd better get a wetsuit," Steve had said. "The lake is still cold this time of year."

"Where?" I wrote back.

"A dive shop. You won't need more than a 'mill' or so. Tell them you need a suit for jet-skiing."

"What's a mill?"

"Millimeter. That's how you determine thickness of a wetsuit."

The sign on the counter in Pan Aqua Dive Shop in Brookfield, CT, said "*SCUBA Lessons Starting Next Week.*"

"Can somebody my age learn to dive?" I asked the pleasant looking man behind the counter.

"Sure. As long as you're in good health."

"I used to be a pretty good swimmer, but for some reason, I never thought of diving. I just turned 57. You sure that's not too old?"

"Some of my best divers are older than you are," he smiled. Peter Hearn put me immediately at ease. I told him I'd think about it as I paid for my new wetsuit and left his shop.

Albert had been the athlete in our family. Every day he'd run, walk, bike, play soccer. I'd take Al and Joe Kugielski up the Housatonic River and they'd kayak back.

Ron Skelton would ride over on his bike and off they'd go together.

Jackie would come over for walks in the woods with her Dad. And of course, there was always a soccer game somewhere.

It made me sad thinking how those rituals were over now.

The guys were always willing to help if I needed it.

Albert was gone. Nothing would ever be the same.

I'd not only lost a husband, best friend, and lover. I'd lost an entire family, a lifestyle, and the hundred little routines that had been part of our lives. I'd also lost the only grandchildren I would ever know.

I would never hear from Adam, Dory, or the boys again. My notes to them went unanswered.

My niece Amy gave birth to a son, Angus James Heartsill, a couple weeks after Albert passed away.

Maybe he'd be the surrogate grandchild with whom I could make it work. He'd be proud of his "Great Aunt Kathryn." We'd have fun together like his mother Amy and I did when she was a child.

She once called me her "role model," bringing tears to my eyes.

At Al's memorial service, our friend Tim O'Connor said the best way to memorialize someone you love is to adopt a trait you admired about that person. I admired Albert's ability to maintain balance in his life.

Vigorous physical exercise was a big part of his daily routine. I knew I needed to put more balance into my life, both in nurturing friendships and getting more exercise.

I'd lost count of the times I'd started an exercise program. I simply didn't move enough, nor frankly was I all that interested. I was about as sedentary as they come. Walking the dogs or sitting in a comfortable chair with a good book was about the most exercise I got.

I once asked Albert if he thought I looked fat. After an appraising glance he said, "No. In fact, you could gain 10 or 20 pounds."

So I did.

It just creeped up, a function of *"slow metabolism,"* I'd say. Although I stuffed myself with vitamins and tried to eat mostly right, I never seemed to be able to burn as many calories as I consumed.

Albert once said if I stayed with an exercise program for 6 months, I'd never stop. But he seemed content with me the way I was. Sometimes he'd stop what he was doing and just look at me.

"My beautiful wife," he'd say. "Where did I find you?"

How could I not adore him? It never mattered to him that I wasn't athletic, and probably never would be, or so I thought.

But things were about to take a really big turn.

I didn't have any idea at the time how Steve's urging me back into the water would soon change my life.

50.

"Charlie, where can I go swimming around here besides a pool?"

"Why don't you want to swim in a pool?" he asked.

I'd hear that question a lot over the next few years.

"Because they're too crowded and it's boring making all those turns. Is there a lake around here I can swim in?"

"Yep, but swimming's not allowed."

"Why not?"

"State doesn't wanna' get sued if somebody drowns. Fishin' only. But there's nothin' in it that'll hurt ya' unless you're scared of fish. If somebody was to go out there on weekdays and play it safe, I expect it'd be a great place to swim."

I know I didn't imagine the twinkle in his eye as he bypassed the fact that the "somebody" would also be breaking the law.

That was my introduction to the lake at Huntington State Park between Newtown and Bethel, CT. Three miles from my house, I'd never seen it, buried in the woods as it was. Soon, however, I wouldn't be able to stay out of it. It was seven months after Al passed away.

Clean, clear, fresh water surrounded by tall trees and wonderful rock formations, I was soon lapping it multiple times, waving at fishermen and people picnicking on the shores.

I'd float on my back and look up at the sky to a frequently circling hawk. Steve wrote that the hawk was watching over me. I liked believing that.

I didn't realize what swimming was doing for me until about 6 months after I started. With only a few minutes to make my plane connection to Texas at Chicago's O'Hare Airport, I *jogged* all the way to the other side of the terminal with a heavy carry-on in one hand and a laptop in the other.

Arriving just in time to take my seat, I realized that nothing hurt and I wasn't even out of breath! I couldn't believe the change in me.

My clothes were looser. For the first time in as long as I could remember, I could pop up and down from a deep-knee bend without effort.

Albert had been right. I found a program I'd never quit. It was not only good for my body, but my head. I felt better getting out of the water than when I got in.

At first it took about 45 minutes for that flush of well-being known as "runners' high." In time, it would only require about 10 minutes of swimming for me to experience the endorphin rush that is so pleasantly addictive to athletes.

But I wasn't an athlete. I just loved to swim.

I didn't realize how swimming would influence my future in many other ways as well.

51.

"Mrs. Taubert, my sergeant is really mad at you," said the baby-faced young park ranger.

"He knew you saw him waving for you to come to shore before you swam out to the middle of the lake. I talked him out of fining you. You obviously know how to swim. He's going to let you off with a warning."

I'd been caught by my vehicle. It wasn't too hard to figure out whose it was. I wore my wetsuit while swimming. The SCUBA sticker on the bumper was a dead giveaway. I wasn't a very clever criminal.

"Officer, I know I was wrong. But isn't there anyplace else around here I can swim?"

"Why don't you want to swim in a pool?"

I repeated the story I'd told Charlie. The ranger told me about Lake Kenosia Park in Danbury. If I signed a waiver, they'd probably let me swim as far as I wanted.

It worked out fine, but I'd miss "my lake" in Huntington for the remainder of my life in Connecticut.

The deep green water reflecting the sky; the hawk that "watched over" me; the smooth clean water like warm, clarified butter as I swam laps on bright summer days.

I also missed the dog I saved one day after she tried to "retrieve" me, her mistress shouting from the shore that the old Labrador had a heart condition.

The dog was breathing pretty heavily when she reached me near the middle of the lake. Holding her paws, I swam her to shore. This scenario would repeat itself many times over the years.

"Water dogs" just can't help themselves, I guess.

52.

I started SCUBA lessons that summer of 2002. From the moment I took my first breath through a regulator, I wondered why it had taken me so long!

It occurred to me that the recurrent dream I'd had for so many years was almost prophesy. I was swimming under water, breathing effortlessly, amazed at the colors and the sensation of *flying*.

Albert used to call me "Spooky" when something I imagined came true. Maybe it was just coincidence, but I'd apparently been dreaming about SCUBA diving all my life! I don't know why I hadn't made the connection sooner.

The first time I set up my SCUBA gear and moved it to the side of the pool, I knew it was going to be harder than I thought.

A full tank of compressed air with buoyancy compensator device (BCD), cold water wetsuit and weights can be well over 40 pounds. This would take some getting used to. I was, after all, a recovering couch potato.

For years I hadn't lifted anything bigger than the front end of a big dog, and not without help from the dog. My first attempt to lift the gear almost resulted in throwing my back out of joint. But I quickly learned.

Before long, Sue Grainger, Peter Hearn, Bob Zaloski, and Ed Hansen of Pan Aqua Dive Center would encourage me to continue further SCUBA training.

I took the rescue course shortly after the Labrador retriever incident. Within two months of that training, I had to use it *twice* in real emergencies at Dutch Springs in Eastern Pennsylvania, where we did a lot of SCUBA. Rescue Instructor Ed Hansen told me it was unlikely it would ever happen again. I hoped he was right. But I was amazed at how his training had all come back to me in a flash when I needed it. I felt good about that.

I couldn't believe I was the same woman who so recently would have rather spent her free time sitting in a corner with a book.

What *happened*?

Within a year, I would become a Professional Association of Diving Instructor (PADI) master SCUBA diver.

My first "blue water" dive off Nassau was my first glimpse into the incredible world below. It will remain with me all my life.

As the water rose over my mask, I could simultaneously see the world above and below. "How could we be so close, yet so far?" I thought, gazing into glittering schools of fish, mounds of coral and the rampant colors of another world.

By September 2002, 10 months after Al's passing, I was gaining strength, endurance mentally and physically. I would still cry myself to sleep for a very long time. But that summer saw me putting down the antidepressants once and for all, having discovered "nature's Prozac" in swimming and diving.

I knew I was going to make it.

During the next months, I would continue diving and swimming, meeting "The Breakfast Club" each morning, and volunteering at DAWS in the afternoons.

Also that summer, seven years of litigation over the property in Newtown came to a close, with us winning the battle in the state appellate court, proving you *can* fight city hall and win.

Albert and his friend Ron Goodridge began the lawsuit before his death. With the help of our lawyers and good friends, Charlie Drummey, Irwin Hausman, Mike Ziska, and Kate Herbst of Murtha Cullina, LLC in Hartford, I *finished* it.

People would ask if I would fight city hall again. The emotional cost is at least as great as the financial one, especially on top of everything else with which I was dealing. I don't know if I would or not. But I'm glad I did in yet another case involving a driveway, of all things.

By November 2002, 11 months after Al's passing, I'd also gone from socializing abused dogs to becoming president of Danbury Animal Welfare Society,

Connecticut's largest volunteer-owned and operated animal shelter. DAWS had given me a place to help sublimate my grief. I liked the volunteers and what they stood for. When my new friend and fellow volunteer Donna Esposito agreed to serve as vice president, I agreed to serve as president.

I couldn't explain how I knew I soon might leave Connecticut. I sensed my life there was truly over, and soon it would be time to move on. I didn't have a clue where yet. I knew Donna and I would make a good team, and she'd be there to carry on if I left. I didn't know when I'd leave or where I'd go. But I could feel it coming.

53.

Holidays were hard. During my grief therapy with Dr. David Reed after Jim's death, he told me there was almost something magical about the end of the first year, when one cycle of holidays, birthdays, and anniversaries had passed. The pain doesn't go away. It just gets a little easier to bear.

Christmas season was especially hard, since Albert passed away the day after Christmas. I didn't want to be around during holidays, so I took a dive trip to Cozumel. Riding around the back side of that island in a rented Jeep reminded me of the fun I had when Daddy was teaching me to drive in his old Willys Army surplus Jeep.

Suddenly all those years of worrying about my hair blowing in the wind went out the window. I returned to Connecticut and bought a used Jeep Wrangler. The top was up only when the weather demanded it.

I still couldn't be around family during holidays. It was just too hard to pretend I wasn't hurt when I learned they never even looked at the videotape of Al's memorial service.

"I guess we just couldn't bear to lose him," they said. I bitterly thought how nice it must have been to have had the choice.

I should have been more honest with them. Maybe they would have realized just how much I needed them to be with me, even if only through the videotape of the service.

But they never really knew. I'm not sure they wanted to. After all, I was always the strong one.

54.

Losing a pet to me is like losing a child. I lost two that year. First Dinah, my elderly cat adopted from DAWS long before I became a volunteer there. Then Maggie, the eldest of the three wolf dogs Albert and I adopted when we lived in Connecticut's Litchfield Hills.

I'd seen it coming. Their loss on top of everything else was crushing. But I still had Biz, my formerly feral cat, and Maggie's half-brother Kip. It had been just Maggie and Kip for a while now, their brother Jack dying in his sleep a couple of years before.

Tony at DAWS was still without a "forever home." I guess I knew all along where he belonged.

Bringing him home with me, I was amazed at how well he fit in for one who had spent six of his seven years in a kennel run. He would become Kip's constant companion, as well as mine, when Maggie's time came. It did soon thereafter.

Seven-year-old Tony finally had a home of his own.

55.

I started having friends over for Sunday brunch. The house was getting smaller again, since those first days when Al's absence made it seem cavernous and empty.

I wished I'd had those brunches when Al was alive. He loved having people around, although he came to rely on his own quiet time as much as I did.

I began living in other rooms again. Memories of *us* in each of them weren't quite as painful.

Shortly after we married, I realized Albert had spent little time living alone. He'd gone from his parents' home to college, to the Air Force and flying elbow-to-elbow with other commercial airline pilots before marriage and family. Widowed from his first wife, he moved to an in-law apartment in a home he bought to share with his daughter Jackie and son-in-law.

He loved to read, watch learning and travel channels on T.V., and talk with his friends on the phone.

My need for space gave him license to indulge his own "quiet time" too. But we became so comfortable together that too much space seemed almost punishing.

I'd been in Texas for a couple of days once when he called and said, "Okay, it's time for you to come home now."

It wasn't a command. It was his way of saying he missed me.

At night I'd hear the murmuring of the T.V., the refrigerator door opening and closing, the phone stop ringing as Al quickly answered it, and all the comforting little sounds of his presence as I read myself to sleep.

He once joked it was nice having the T.V. remote to himself. Maybe I helped him find his own kind of solitude. I'd managed that balance between solitude and loneliness much of my life, although not always successfully.

I always needed a lot of solitude. Perhaps it was from growing up with a movement disorder not always easy to manage around people who didn't understand.

Maybe my karma is learning how to live among people in a less detached way. I'll always be somewhat solitary. But I knew I needed to nurture friendships better, the way Albert had.

It wasn't just the sensory-motor issues in Tourette syndrome that caused me to crave solitude.

Never having children of my own, I couldn't contribute much to conversations about family and grandkids. I was more comfortable discussing business. With a once-thriving career, I didn't have a lot in common with most women my generation.

Women most often plan the family social calendar. More often than not, couples seem to invite single men to share events more readily than single women. That may be changing now, but for my generation, single childless women often got left out.

An incident after Jim's death during a grief support group highlighted just how different my life was. An elderly woman who had just lost her husband. Crying softly, "I don't even know how to fill the car with gas."

I realized the chasm between us. In 1983, I was a 37-year-old widow who only a few years before had a thriving business career.

I was light-years ahead of others in that group in my ability to start over. The one-on-one support I received from David and Harold after Jim's death helped me most. Support groups aren't for everyone.

After Al passed away, I knew I was stronger, although at times I didn't want to go on. But now I was moving ahead from living moment-to-moment to thinking ahead.

Life was starting to get interesting in ways I couldn't begin to fathom even a few months before.

56.

It was February 2003, little more than a year after Al passed away. I wanted to volunteer at something that would combine my new passion for swimming with charity.

The *Hudson River Swim* was it.

The Swim Across America was a 15-mile relay down New York's Hudson River to raise money for Memorial Sloan Kettering's cancer research. Billed as a swim for charity and not a race, I thought I would try it.

Swimmers were taken out of the water at rotating intervals, resulting in about six or seven miles of actual swimming between the Tappan Zee and George Washington bridges.

I signed up and started preparing for the event to occur on July 23, 2003.

I sent letters to friends asking for donations.

"*Why don't you want to swim in a pool?*" people asked. But they sent donations anyway.

I trained on the Bethel High School track. I was surprised at how far I could jog. Swimming had given me stamina.

I swam at least three days a week, gradually extending my distance.

I still didn't have a clue how far I was swimming. I went to the Wilton, Connecticut "Y," where I got a few pointers from George Brunstad, who at 70 would later become the oldest person to swim the English Channel.

I'd never be a speed swimmer. I didn't have the slightest hidden desire to beat anybody at anything. But once in the water I could swim forever, especially after that endorphin rush took over.

As the date approached, I could hardly contain myself. Was I really doing this? I couldn't believe this new person was *me*!

The "Newtown Bee" newspaper published an article about my quest in Al's name. Total strangers sent donations.

Hudson River Swim organizers anointed me "Rookie of the Year" because I'd raised so much money.

The day of the event, the starting gun launched us from the ferry into the Hudson just south of the Tappan Zee Bridge.

It didn't take long to realize I was out of my league. Although it wasn't billed as a race, it clearly had become one. Former champion speed swimmers set the pace, leaving me in the froth.

I lost count of the times I was rolled into one of the Zodiac inflatable boats pacing the slowest swimmers. I never got tired. I just wasn't fast enough. Organizers were on a schedule requiring us to be finished before some tanker or another came along.

One asked me if I intended to complete the course after being sloshed back onto the boat for the third or fourth time.

"Of course! I'm not tired, I'm just not fast! I didn't think this was a race," I said.

"Well, it's not supposed to be, but you know how it goes."

I resolved to endure the humiliation of being hauled out of the water at regular intervals just to be dumped back in for the next mile.

I think I was the last one to cross the finish line. But then, I was also the second oldest at 57, who not even two years before had been the quintessential couch potato. Now I was swimming in a 15-mile relay down the Hudson River!

I could outlast anybody in the water as long as I didn't have to go anywhere fast. I swam the entire distance. A year and a half after Al's passing, I'd become an *athlete*!

The post-event ritual at the end of the 15 miles saw many of the 65 swimmers tossing off their bathing suits and jumping into the water under the George Washington Bridge.

I was floating on my back (*in* my suit) looking up at a tiny human figure waving down from that amazing bridge. Suddenly it occurred to me that it was almost 25 years to the day I'd first crossed it, relocating from Texas to Connecticut.

It was then I knew it was time to leave.

If I was really going to move on, I'd have to leave my beloved Connecticut and my old life behind.

Some part of me hurt deeply at the thought. It had been home for so long. My life there ended with Albert's passing and I couldn't live life through my friends, as much as I'd miss them.

I needed a place where the person I was becoming could continue evolving. I'd never really leave the past behind until I found out who she would become.

But I knew I would miss Connecticut for the rest of my life.

57.

"I've got some good news and some bad news," Jim Osborne said in November of 2003 as he picked me up at the hotel in Fort Myers, Florida.

"I've found a place that meets 19 of your 20 criteria."

"I guess I already know what the bad news is," I replied, shocked that he'd found one that so nearly met my desires.

"You're going to have to pay more," he grinned.

"Show me everything else you've got first," I said.

And off I went with the realtor to whom I'd emailed a list of things I was hoping to find in a new home.

Instructing Osborne to get as close as he could to meeting the criteria, I never expected he would be that successful!

It was my second trip to Florida. The first had been in August 2003, three weeks after the Hudson River Swim. At that time all I knew was that I wanted to go to a place where folks were grateful for a cloudy day. The prior winter convinced me I didn't want to remain in the Northeast for another one. I wanted to be able to swim or dive every day if I chose.

Jim Holbrook once talked about retiring to the Carolinas, so three weeks after the Hudson River Swim,

I pointed the Jeep in that direction. I quickly decided it wasn't far enough south.

Continuing onto Florida, I knew I was getting closer to what I sought.

I spent a week at a 55-and-over community near Ocala, obtained a cavern diving certification in Ginnie Springs, and visited Jim's brother Tom Holbrook and his wife Sandy in Tampa.

Strolling through the common room of the community where I was staying brought me face to face with a sea of gray hair bent over bingo. I wasn't ready for bingo yet, and there weren't any SCUBA clubs there. I was "only" 57. I drove back to Connecticut vowing to see more of Florida as soon as possible.

My trip back to Fort Myers in November was breakfast clubber Pat O'Connor's suggestion. I figured if I was going to move, I was going to go as far south as I could, short of the Florida Keys. I didn't want to live in the Keys because of the potential for hurricane damage.

I searched the Internet for information about the Fort Myers/Naples area, including the hurricane statistics. Growing up in "hurricane alley" of Galveston Island, I was determined to go to a place where I wouldn't have to worry as much about those monsters. The area near both Fort Myers and Naples seemed to fit the bill.

I found Jim Osborne's realty online, sent my criteria, and flew back to meet him in Fort Myers in November.

It didn't matter that I didn't know a soul in Southwest Florida. I'd moved so many times I could almost do it blindfolded. There was something exciting about it. A chance to start fresh, find out what was next. I'd healed by this time enough to know I was going to be okay. But I still had a long way to go.

58.

The Fort Myers-Naples area appealed to me right way. I asked a local dive shop operator why he had his shop on Florida's West Coast if, as I'd heard, the *diving* was better on the east coast.

"Because the *living's* better on the west coast," he said. That was all I needed to hear.

There was also enough to do in the area to keep me busy when I wasn't in the water. I had no idea at the time I'd also step back 30 years and turn an old dream into a new career.

Our last stop was next to the development Osborne first mentioned. I saw a model home I really liked. Jim said the builder was also constructing homes in the place I'd told him to save for last.

From the moment we drove through the gates of Miromar Lakes Beach and Golf Club, I was hooked. That big, beautiful, blue-green fresh water lake had my name all over it!

"Will they let me swim in that lake?" I asked.

"Why don't you want to swim in a pool?"

Repeating the same story I'd told countless others by now, he said we'd ask.

"If they do, we may just have a deal," I said.

I hadn't even looked at the property yet.

On December 31, 2003, I closed the deal for new construction to begin March of 2004. It was two years since Albert had *died.*

"*Died.*" I was finally able to say that word.

"Passed on" seems less *final*. But there's also a measure of denial in it. Denise once told me that "denial is a developmental state."

Some people get through the grieving process faster than others. But there are no timetables, no deadlines, no hard and fast rules.

David Reed had said that grief from sudden, unexpected loss as I'd experienced with Jim's death is often harder and lasts longer than grief from an "extending dying." Having now experienced both, I knew what he meant.

David also said that after six months, if the bereaved isn't beginning to "get her head out from under her pillow," she may need therapy and possibly medication, as I had.

David's help after Jim's death had given me strength to deal with Albert's loss as well.

He would never know how important his help would be to me in years ahead. Long after Dr. David Reed died, I was still benefitting from his counsel.

No one has the final word on when healing should occur, or how. It happens when it happens. Sometimes we need help getting there. But the schedule is determined by no one else but us.

59.

By two years after Al's death, having become both a PADI master SCUBA diver and Divemaster, the first professional level of SCUBA, I was helping PANAQUA instructors with new diver classes.

I also obtained a Handicapped SCUBA Association (HSA) dive buddy certification to be able to dive with the disabled. HSA Instructor Stewart Snyder paid me a tremendous compliment by saying he thought I'd been diving "many years." I may be a klutz on dry land, but water has always been my element.

I'd also achieved a Red Cross Water Safety Instructor's certification (WSI) to teach swimming lessons. While pursuing my PADI Divemaster certification, I was helping with swimming instruction at the Danbury YMCA for the experience.

By that time, I knew where I was going, and when. I had a *plan* again. I'd still have many tearful moments of loneliness and grief, but I was building a new life.

But it was still a far cry from the one I'd lost.

I was getting ready to relocate again. The first thing I did was sit down on the basement floor and cry.

Almost 5,000 square feet of *stuff:* Al's, mine, his late wife's, Jim's, our parents, Al's kids, and ours.

There were 65 boxes of papers, books, and memorabilia in the basement alone.

I had two months to clear it out, having sold the house on Greenleaf Farms within two days of listing. I didn't think it would sell *that* fast.

Recalling David Reed's mantra of one minute, one day, one week at a time, I progressed through one box, drawer, cabinet, closet, room, and *floor* at a time.

I made piles for family, DAWS tag sale, Goodwill, consignment, storage for Florida, and the stuff I'd need for the 7 months I would be "homeless" while the new house in Miromar Lakes was under construction.

I made almost daily runs to the town dump with the Jeep filled with stuff that didn't belong in any of the other piles.

The week before I moved out of the house, I hired a 15-yard capacity dumpster, invited friends over for pizza, told them to take whatever they wished from what was left, and then help me fill the dumpster with the rest.

On April 7, 2004, I left Greenleaf Farms for the last time. It was 10 years to the day Al and I had moved into our dream home.

Tearfully, I drove down the long driveway toward my new future, knowing I'd never return. That part of my life was over.

PART III

AUGUST 2004 - JUNE 2009

60.

In August 2004, the Jeep was packed, the dogs were fed. I'd said goodbye to all my friends. Ron Skelton had taken Biz in temporarily after I'd left Greenleaf Farms. Kip and Tony and been living with me at Chris and Cheri's in Bethlehem, Connecticut, since I sold the house on Greenleaf Farms in April.

Instead of remaining in Connecticut until the house in Florida was finished in October as planned, I suddenly decided to move in August. I'd live in a Florida rental near my new home under construction. My excuse for leaving earlier than planned was to be near the house during its finishing stages. Only partly true, I really needed to get on with leaving the still-intense pain behind.

It was early morning. Chris and Cheri had already left for work, having said our goodbyes the night before. I tearfully hugged the dogs, got in the Jeep, and headed south through the beautiful Connecticut countryside.

Driving from Bethlehem to Danbury through New York's Westchester County and across the George Washington Bridge to New Jersey and beyond, I felt I was leaving the best part of my life behind. I was roiling with mixed emotions.

I was sad at leaving my adopted state, my good friends, my animals, and all that I had known there. Yet I was excited to finally be moving on. I would return to get the animals soon after moving into Miromar Lakes sometime in November, four months hence.

At once relieved and broken-hearted, I knew Florida was the place that would further help me heal.

61.

Writing had always been the best way to deal with my feelings. As a child I struggled with motor dysgraphia as I poured my heart out with pen and paper. There were no computers then. The clunky typewriters of the day weren't much easier for me than wielding a pen either.

I'd turn my feelings into poems and stories in the best way a lonely child could.

I recall standing before my young schoolmates as I finished reading a poem I'd written for English class.

They just sat staring at me as I finished. It must have been awful! I'd just bared my soul and all they did was sit and stare! "*The Forest Is My Home*" was a strange subject for a little girl who lived on a sandbar in the Gulf of Mexico.

Maybe I'd bitten off more than I could chew.

Clearing her throat, "That was very good, Kathryn," our teacher said.

I quickly took my chair with a sigh of relief.

Maybe she was just being kind, I thought. But the almost furtive glances of my schoolmates held no criticism. It was as though they were looking at me for the first time.

As a shy girl who could barely get up the courage to smile at a boy upon whom she had a crush, I didn't know who I was any more than anybody else did. Some years later, an English composition teacher expressed disappointment when I dropped her class for another. "You have a talent for writing. I hate to see you give this up."

Composition came easily to me. It was getting it down on paper that was difficult, with my handwriting problems. I focused so much on the mechanical difficulty of writing that it never really occurred to me I had a talent for actually putting words together.

Decades later, the advent of the computer keyboard and word processing software liberated me.

Motor dysgraphia didn't even have a name when I was a child, much less any sort of remedial therapy. Now we know it's not an uncommon condition in people with Tourette syndrome, although not limited to us.

I suppose it's one reason I always loved music with lyrics that told "stories." Those old tunes seem to be able to say what I tried so hard to write but couldn't because of the physical discomfort of dysgraphia.

The computer opened doors to me I didn't even know were closed.

Suddenly, all those simmering thoughts, feelings, dreams, memories, and observations were loosed from the constraints of my handwriting disability.

Even though I couldn't wield pen or pencil well, I would eventually type 100 words a minute on the keyboard.

As a child, I would retreat to the woods at the farm from the sometimes difficult life growing up with undiagnosed Tourette syndrome. That poem I'd written for my class was prophetic. I had no conception that one day I would live "in the woods," just like I wanted to do.

I would always be more at home walking among tall trees under a full moon than I ever would in the middle of a city.

When Albert joined me there, I knew I'd found a kindred spirit. Those moonlight walks with him and our dogs were just another aspect of my life that died with him.

The lonely child was a contented woman with the man she adored.

When Al died, the idea of a book began to form. But how could I write about a past I needed to leave behind? That past would be the crux of such a book. Maybe it would help others going through the same things. Everyone grieves the loss of loved ones eventually. I certainly had. More than once.

I didn't have the emotional energy or self-discipline to write a book then. I had no idea how significant writing would become in my new life.

62.

My research prior to moving told me a major hurricane hadn't struck that part of Florida since 1960. But a week after I arrived, Hurricane Charley struck with a vengeance.

Growing up in Galveston, I understood the horror of hurricanes perhaps more than most.

The devastation wrought by Hurricane Charley spurred me to write about it in a series of emails to friends.

For Galveston natives, hurricanes take on mythic proportions. Charley, like many others, seemed *alive*. I always had a tendency to personify Nature. She had, after all, been my lifelong source of solace and comfort, even in her fury.

Hurricanes do awful things to people. But I understood them. It was Nature's way of replenishing aquifers, cleansing coastlines, renewing "dead zones." There was more malice in our species than would ever exist in a hurricane. I just didn't want to get in another one's way.

In Charley's aftermath, I worked as a Red Cross volunteer in a mass casualty shelter near my new home. I wrote about my experiences. I didn't know at the time my emails would make their way across the continent to someone I'd never met, but for whom I would learn to care deeply.

I'd arrived in Florida under typically beautiful sunny skies to find all hell breaking loose a week later. The irony of getting hit by a major storm after having moved to a place that hadn't had one in more than 40 years wasn't lost on me.

I hoped Charley wasn't an "omen." But it wouldn't be the first hurricane-borne tragedy with which I'd have to deal in the coming years.

The next one would be far more devastating.

63.

To: Kathryn
From: Jim Collison
I hope you don't mind my writing to you. Our mutual friend Troy Minton forwarded your emails about the hurricane. He thought I'd be interested since I'm also a writer. Reading your piece, I felt as though I knew you. I wanted tell you how much I enjoyed them. Don't feel the need to reply if it makes you uncomfortable.

Out of the blue, Jim Collison entered my life. Of course I wrote back, since Troy had been a dear friend since college. If he thought enough of this Jim to forward my emails to him, he must be okay.

Thus began an online relationship that would last for years. Jim wasn't merely a writer. He'd been a successful photojournalist with work on display at the Smithsonian Institution. He'd flown his own plane all over the world, photographing and writing about exotic places, people, and events.

Retired and recovering from a serious auto accident, he was living in Marin County, California, just above San Francisco's Bay Area Bridge. Doctors couldn't say if or when he would heal from the balance injury he'd suffered in the accident. His vehicle had been "T-boned" by another, causing a closed-head injury that left him with persistent dizziness and vertigo.

Email exchanges evolved to phone calls. Jim was a year younger than Albert, and born in the same New York town. Living on opposite sides of the continent, I knew we'd probably never meet, but our friendship grew in spite of it.

The similarities between Jim Collison and Albert went beyond age and origins.

"I'd never saddle you with my problems, Kathryn," he said a year or so after we'd grown closer through our communications.

"I beat cancer once, but this vertigo has pretty much knocked me off my game. Our connection is important to me, though. I look forward to our talks."

He was right. I didn't think I could endure falling for somebody only to lose him again. Especially someone who reminded me so much of Albert.

Jim encouraged me to talk about Albert and my life with him. People don't always know what to say when someone dies, so often say nothing.

They don't realize the bereaved *need* to talk about their lost loved ones. Those who have passed on help make us who we are. They'll *always* be with us even as others' lives go on.

Jim seem to understand that and to enjoy hearing about Al. Maybe it was because they had so much in common.

Over the next few years he and I would be in and out of each other's lives. He was always there somewhere, however.

Jim was the stranger who wasn't: the faceless voice on the phone deep in the night, listening, consoling, and encouraging. He told me of his past, his hopes and dreams, while encouraging my own. He was a kindred spirit I'd never meet until it was too late.

64.

I moved into the new house in Miromar Lakes on October 20, 2004, and prepared to bring Biz and Kip back to Florida.

I missed my animals terribly. It was autumn in New England and the beginning of what I'd come to think of as the *dying season.*

I lost Jim just before Thanksgiving. Albert died the day after Christmas. It was turning cold in Connecticut and the trees were getting bare. I didn't want to go back.

Originally I'd planned to drive Kip to Florida before flying back to retrieve Biz.

Once in Connecticut, however, I couldn't bear to leave either of them behind again.

So I covered the inside of the car with plastic bags and duct tape, doubling the width of the back seat by stuffing blankets on the floorboard. I loaded Kip's 120 or so pounds in the backseat.

I put Biz in his carrier in the front and left for Florida in early November 2004.

Thirteen-year-old Kip was nearing the end of his life. Increasingly feeble, he needed special care in his last days.

My heart broke as I left Tony behind that early August morning, watching through the fence as Kip and I left him. I had hoped to go back for Tony, but soon I realized he wouldn't adjust to life well in Florida.

Tony needed other dogs, lots of space to run, and cold weather. The Florida heat and humidity would be hard enough on Kip with his multi-layered wolf's coat. Kip didn't have long to live. Tony would suffer the heat, being unable to roam free, and eventually the loss of his buddy Kip as well.

I wouldn't get over leaving Tony in Connecticut for many years. I knew he'd have a good home with Chris and Cheri, their dogs, cats, and horses. He'd never be confined to a kennel again. He'd have acres to run and play.

I recalled the day I brought him home to Greenleaf Farms. He bounded out of the DAWS kennel into my car as though he knew he was leaving kennel shelter life forever. I couldn't bear the thought of him being restricted on my Florida "lanai" with no place for him to roam.

Almost six years later, at 13 and in his last days, I would see Tony again in a tearful reunion that convinced me once and for all, dogs *do* remember.

Kip, Biz, and I arrived in Fort Myers near midnight two days after we left Connecticut. One night with them in a motel during the trip convinced me we weren't going to spend another that way. None of us slept. So the next day we drove straight through from Virginia to Florida.

Three miles from our new home in Miromar Lakes, we got pulled over by a cop. Shining his light in my face and inquiring about my condition, he turned his light first to Biz's carrier in the front seat, and then to the very large *wolf* staring at him from the backseat.

"Are you okay, ma'am?"

"Yes sir. I'm just really tired. I'm just arriving from Connecticut, and only a few miles from my new home. I've been driving since 5 a.m."

"You were driving very slowly and weaving the car."

After a detailed Q&A, he realized I wasn't inebriated and told me to "go home and get a good night's sleep."

He never took his flashlight off Kip.

He never asked. I never said.

I smiled groggily to myself as I thought of the tales told that night in the barracks when that nice young Fort Myers police officer got off duty.

Kip was just another big, loveable, friendly "dog" to me and anyone else in his world.

But *Rudyard Kipling* looked every inch of his three-quarters Arctic wolf heritage.

65.

We spend the first part of our lives acquiring stuff and the last part trying to get rid of it.

I had about half as much space as I did in Connecticut. I wanted to simplify my life.

I lived for seven months with the belongings that just fit into the back of my Jeep. Having put everything else in storage, I felt an unexpected freedom. Not being tied down with so much *stuff* was liberating.

I wondered what was in those boxes that I hadn't needed all those months that the movers were bringing into my new home! I gave three pick-up truck loads of things away to the construction supervisor's church garage sale.

Carl Weathers was a born-again Christian and a giant of a man. One day he told me he'd been "saved by Jesus" from a life of drugs and petty crime. He invited me to attend church with his wife and family. My own spiritual beliefs ran more toward some combination of Western and Eastern mysticism. I'm not especially religious, but I am deeply spiritual.

Although reared as a Methodist-Episcopalian, I hadn't attended church regularly since I was a child.

One day shortly before Carl and his crew completed building my new home, he quietly told me how much he and his wife liked me. They hoped I would be able to join them in Heaven, but they feared I was going to

Hell if I didn't immediately "accept Jesus." He said it so casually and calmly that at first it didn't sink in that I'd just been told I was going to Hell!

I told him I hoped he was wrong about my ultimate fate, trying to lighten it up. I didn't know how to say although reared Christian, my spiritual beliefs had become an amalgam of many faiths. I'm probably mostly some combination of Buddhist and Druid.

Carl had a good sense of humor, but I wasn't sure he'd find that funny. I thanked him for his concern for my soul and told him I'd give it serious thought.

Carl was a good man who built a beautiful home. I hoped he was wrong and that we'll all end up in the same heavenly place.

That exchange reminded me, however, that life in Florida was going to be different than what I'd grown used to in the greater New York City area.

Turns out my concerns weren't particularly justified. Florida has its own kind of "melting pot."

66.

After being basically "homeless" for the preceding seven months of 2004, I was glad to have a home of my own again.

I couldn't believe I actually lived in such a place! It was a full-scale resort community with amenities like those found in the most exotic European seaside resorts. The aquamarine lake was just steps from my front door. I could swim every single day!

Shortly after moving in, my new next-door neighbors Liz and Les Davidson invited me to a small dinner party. As one of Miromar's few single women, I was sure I'd be a source of curiosity and speculation. I'd be more *visible* here than in Connecticut. My Florida "villa" was no more than about 15 feet away from my neighbors.

I was ready to let somebody else take care of the lawn and shrubs for a while. Part of the deal here was exactly that, so yards were a lot smaller than what I had in Connecticut.

Living in rural Connecticut for so long, being so close to others would take some getting used to.

Putting myself "out there" a bit more was part of the promise I made to myself. I hadn't exactly been *invisible* in Connecticut, with my volunteer activities. But I had lived a relatively quiet, somewhat inconspicuous lifestyle. Being home at the end of each day with Albert had always been the best part of my day.

I was now trying to follow Al's example and create more balance in my life.

Albert was probably the sanest person I ever met. He sallied easily among friends and strangers alike, never showing the slightest discomfort.

He soon realized my anxiety just before we'd attend some sort of public function was merely nervousness about being in a room full of people. Once I was there I was okay.

I'm not as naturally gregarious as people think. On some level, I'm still that "ticcy" child trying to hide.

I admired Albert's ability to move around the room chatting and laughing without discomfort. I was content to observe from the edge of the room. I could stay in one spot and *appear* sociable as though I really were at ease. Everyone else was generally so busy circulating they'd get around to me eventually.

I was always glad to get home. "Sensory overload" required a retreat to quiet places for me to recharge.

Dr. Donald Cohen of the Yale Child Study Center once likened the sensitivity of people with Tourette syndrome to that which produces the *flocking of birds in flight*. Some think we're more acutely *aware* of our surroundings. As far as I know, no one has done any research on this. It's mostly anecdotal. There's no money in it. Most research seems designed to find drugs or "cures."

Most of us just want to get on with life. Few but only the most severe cases of Tourette syndrome require medications. I don't take it because the side effects are generally awful. Most people don't have any idea I have TS anyway. There is evidence that we may have adaptive strengths in mental processing and fast, goal-directed movements. But until someone discovers a way to make money off helping people with Tourette syndrome understand what they may do well or better, there won't be any more research on it.

Most people I know with TS seem to have a heightened sensitivity to sensory input that can be very tiring. Too much noise is especially distressing for me, especially if combined with an unending assault of sights and scents.

Returning to our quiet home after a noisy, crowded public gathering was a welcome relief to me.

Albert not only understood that, I think he relied on it for the "quiet time" it allowed him too.

But he was gone now. This was my new life. I had to make accommodations. Diving headlong into a room full of strangers was among them.

67.

Liz greeted me at the door with her characteristic warmth.

"How are you, dahling. Come in!" she said in her New Jersey accent.

I think that's one reason I felt so comfortable with the Davidsons. Their accent was more like what I was used to in the northeast.

Stepping into the room, I soon heard a calm "Welcome to da' 'hood!"

Ken Smrstik's South Chicago greeting sounded almost like something I'd hear in New York!

I couldn't believe it. Southwest Florida was proving more of a melting pot than I'd imagined. Soon I would learn most people here were from somewhere else.

Including me.

68.

Biz and Kip were managing well. Kip stayed mostly on his 6-foot by 4-foot pillow under the lanai ceiling fan. He went everywhere with me in the back of the Jeep. He was too old to jump anymore, so I had to lift him.

He loved our trips to McDonald's. After the initial shock of seeing a *wolf* riding around in the back of a Jeep, the young servers in the drive-through window soon looked forward to seeing me toss the sausage over my shoulder directly into Kip's waiting maw.

Kip was without canine companionship for the first time in his life. He still had Biz and me, but I couldn't leave him alone for very long with his acute separation anxiety.

Biz and I were now all old Kip had. The photo I have of Kip as a cub snuggled in Al's lap was among my favorites. Kip had craved physical closeness from the day we brought him and his brother Jack home. His 13 years of loyalty earned him as much comfort as I could provide.

I found temporary quarters for him with volunteer Deanna Deppen of Naples' Shy Wolf Sanctuary Education and Experience Center. When I traveled to Texas to see mother, Deanna kept Kip in her large fenced backyard with her own wolf-dogs.

Kip survived six more months after moving to Florida. The night I returned from a Texas trip, Deanna found him under a tree, as though asleep. It was exactly the way Jack, his littermate and life-long companion, had died.

I was down to one animal companion for the first time in 25 years. Biz would adjust easily to life on the lanai, once I covered it with 200 or so tropical plants.

For the first time in the three years since Albert died, I would spend holidays in Texas with family. I had finally left behind the hurt and bitterness I'd felt at learning they hadn't watched the videotape of Al's service.

People do the best they can with the tools they have. Some have more tools than others.

Maybe I am the strongest of them after all.

69.

I started swimming in Miromar's Lake Como soon after arriving in Florida. There were no rules against it, although the oft-asked question, "Why don't you swim in a pool?"

That was soon accompanied by, "Aren't you afraid of the alligators?"

I studied animal behavior all my life, and had worked as a professional animal trainer with Sea Arama. I'd learned that most animals, including alligators, are creatures of habit. If one understands their behavior and judiciously avoids provoking confrontation, one is generally safe. The key is understanding what provokes them.

More people are killed by falling coconuts every year than alligators.

Nevertheless, I wouldn't swim in the lake between dusk and dawn, nor anywhere near the swampy reeds during mating and nesting season.

Miromar's "lakes" are actually a former limestone quarry. It's a closed system of clean, fresh, filtered water. There is alligator habitat in the rear sections. But the front lake had been mostly cleared of it and replaced with boat docks and white sand beaches.

Once in a while a small 'gator encroaches, but they're more afraid of us than we are them. I judiciously stayed away from areas where they might hide.

Alligators don't particularly like being around people. In any Florida body of water there's always the chance of an alligator, but I felt secure in Lake Como.

I'd grown up swimming in Clear Lake near Houston where the 'gators kept to their side of the lake and humans kept to theirs.

I didn't see much difference between swimming near alligator habitat now than I did 40 years ago. There were far more humans now, and far too many have virtually no familiarity with animal behavior. Fear rules where ignorance prevails.

Alligators are opportunistic feeders, but they don't seek out fully grown humans to eat. We get bitten because we provoke confrontations, unintentionally or otherwise. Small children and pet dogs are at greater risk than fully grown humans.

Erring on the side of caution, I'd closely monitor the rare Florida encounters just to make sure the 'gators were still observing the same rules!

Lake Como was perfect for me. While other residents boated, skied, or fished, I would be the only one to swim in it for some time yet. That would soon change in a really big way!

I began attending Lake Committee meetings. No one had really thought much about SCUBA or swimming in the lakes yet. I hoped to insure that they would be included in the list of lake activities.

Biz soon staked out various places on the lanai among the few plants I'd hauled from Connecticut.

I got some odd looks from state troopers as they passed me in the Jeep during the trip from Connecticut. It never occurred to me I might be violating some sort of law by transporting a bunch of plants across state lines. The Jeep resembled a mobile nursery, but I wasn't stopped.

My lanai dwarfed them. Soon I added large pots of gardenia, hibiscus, and starflower trees. Next came ferns, bromeliads, and many others surrounding burbling fountains here and there. I discovered hordes of small creatures had hitchhiked in among them.

Chameleons, anoles, a stray katydid or two. Eventually frogs, and of course, the occasional black racer snake. It became a veritable little jungle out there. Biz loved it.

I thought he'd miss the big woods in which he'd grown up, but he seemed content on our lanai "jungle." He was getting old too. Never having seen an alligator in his life, he'd be far more interesting to them as a snack than I would have been.

I had to get used to the occasional tailless lizard or petrified frog under the couch. I left the sliders open from the great room onto the lanai much of the time.

The critters at Miromar were smaller than those of the Connecticut woods. There were, however, incursions that called for certain accommodations. I drew a line at the small snakes with which Biz occasionally "gifted" me.

He mostly dropped live lizards at my feet. I'd catch them as he sat by purring. Petting him for his thoughtfulness, I deposited the hapless creatures back among the plants. I wondered if he ever got frustrated because I never *ate* one of his gifts. Maybe he just thought humans were stupid.

Sometimes, I think we are.

The warm, jasmine-scented air and swaying palms were so unlike November in Connecticut. I missed my home there, but I was relieved to be in Florida. It was where I wanted to be, as Miromar's slogan promised.

I'd unpacked all but a few remaining boxes. The house was beautiful. It had glass sliding doors all across the back overlooking a manicured golf course, sable palms, and fragrant, night-blooming jasmine and native grasses covered in a purple haze of bloom.

My lanai soon blossomed all the time with tropical colors. I remembered looking through our windows on Greenleaf Farms past similar plants onto the outdoor world of ice and snow. The pink bromeliad I bought for Albert during his surgery with Dr. Olsson had come with me to Florida. It was thriving and producing so many offshoots that before long I had multiple pots of them.

It never occurred to me only a year or two before that I would one day live in Florida. I didn't miss the gray skies and cold of the northeastern winters one bit.

I wondered how I had lived for three years in the sometimes minus 55-degree weather of Rochester, N.Y., when married to Jim. I never, ever imagined I'd end up 25 years later in the "coconut zone" of Florida.

Moving more than 25 times, living in five states, thriving in several careers and burying two husbands taught me to adapt if nothing else.

I would always miss the 10 days of a Connecticut spring when the world goes from gray to green. There is little as lovely as southern New England when it blooms again.

I was building new memories. I never imagined that soon one old memory would become an exciting new reality.

70.

A few weeks after moving to Miromar Lakes, I started exploring the region. Venturing into Naples one night, I found hundreds of people wandering in and out of the tony stores and sidewalk cafés of Fifth Avenue South. Street musicians performed under balmy night skies. Floral scented air overlay the sights and sounds of this former fishing village turned upscale tourist and retirement haven nestled at the edge of the Florida Everglades. It was beautiful.

Sitting on a bench near the Sugden Theatre, I soon heard faint, compelling strains of a lovely old standard wafting through outdoor speakers of a nearby restaurant. It was the kind of music I'd performed 30 years ago.

I peeked in the door to see a tall, light-skinned African-American musician at a baby grand piano in the corner of the bar.

Taking a seat, I returned his acknowledgment and ordered a drink.

"Are you a vocalist?" he said not long after.

"I was a long time ago," I replied, wondering how he could have known. I hadn't realized he could hear me softly humming along to his playing.

"You still got the pipes, baby," he replied. "Wanna' do a tune?"

“I don’t even remember the keys,” I said, still mystified.

“I can play in *your* key,” he said confidently.

I thought he resembled actor Morgan Freeman wearing a black beret.

“It’s been too long. I’ll just sit here and listen."

Nodding quietly, he went back to playing, singing the occasional tune in a smooth baritone.

People soon filled the bar with laughter and clinking glasses. Truluck’s Steak and Seafood Restaurant was a popular local nightspot. Smooth jazz musician Claude Rhea had apparently helped make it so.

Claude was Naples’ own “Mr. Music.” His role in my life would soon seem like something right out of a movie.

71.

It was the Christmas season of 2004. I'd been in Florida since August. I knew my dear little mother was struggling with advancing infirmity. Now living a mere two hours from her by plane, I could spend more time with her, and did so as often as I could.

My parents, Lee and Dorothy McDonald, were two of the nicest people I ever met. Mother gave us roots. Daddy gave us wings. We didn't have much money, but my two sisters and I had everything we needed and almost everything we wanted. Somehow our parents made it work. It wasn't always easy for them, as I would later learn. Daddy worked two jobs. Money was tight and their three growing daughters hoped to attend college.

During regular hours, daddy was a cotton-inspector for the Western Weighing and Inspection Bureau. At the time, Galveston exported 40 percent of the nation's cotton. It was my dad's job to make sure the cotton shipments arrived undamaged by railroad car before being loaded onto ships in Galveston's harbor. He spent most of his days outside, pretty much his own boss. My dad would have been miserable in an office job. He loved the outdoors.

During evenings and weekends, daddy and a friend would put up television antennas and fix TV's. One day mother saw daddy climbing on a neighbor's steep, gabled roof and made him promise never to do it again. He was getting on in years. She made up the slack in income by going back to work in a hospital medical records department when I entered seventh grade. Up until that time she had been a stay-at-home mom. We lived a pretty traditional, 50's-era lifestyle.

Almost every weekend during my childhood, my parents would pack us up for the family farm my grandfather bought in the early 1900's. It was 100 acres of beautiful property on Clear Lake, midway between League City and Kemah, TX. I would spend some of the happiest moments of my childhood at "The Country."

My grandfather died before realizing his dream of retiring to it, but the farm remained in our family until about 1973. At the time my grandfather bought it, the farm was the only "developed" property on the south side of Clear Lake, with two farm houses, a barn, chicken coop and utility sheds.

At the time we sold it more than 70 years later, it was the only *un*developed property on the south side of the lake, almost directly across from what had become Houston's Johnson Space Craft Center.

I remember the day it was sold. I had grown up on that property with my horses, and the cattle, chickens, and pigs Chester had on the place. Chester Holland leased the surface rights, since our family had given up trying to raise anything but kids on the place.

I never recall Chester not being there. It seemed as though he never aged. The first and only time I saw him without his old brown hat, I noticed he had tightly curled graying hair cut close to his head. By day,

Chester Holland was a supervisor at one of the Texas City oil refineries. That was a good job in those days, especially for a black man in the 50's and 60's.

Chester will forever remain in my heart for the kindness he showed when one of our horses died.

Burning up with a fever from the flu, he dragged himself out of his sick bed to dig a hole big enough to bury Sally on our property, rather than call someone to haul her off to "the glue factory," as we called it. He later told my dad he didn't want me to have to remember her that way. I was about 10 years old. That was an early lesson in race relations I never forgot. Kindness and compassion know no color.

I hated to see the farm get sold in the 70's, knowing that it would soon be covered with luxury homes on the prime, lakeside property. "The Country" of my childhood would soon be no more.

My dad was forced by company policy to retire from W.W.I.B. at age 65. A few weeks later, however, he went back to work as a bailiff in Galveston County's criminal court system, where he served the Halls of Justice until he was 87 years old.

For years after his death in 1996 at almost 90, mother received notes from "daddy's judge" and his wife saying how much they missed him. "A real devoted family man," the judge once wrote. He was, indeed.

Mother was the youngest of five children. Her English-born father immigrated to the USA after acquiring malaria in his travels by ship through South America. Settling in Waco, Texas, he and my grandmother supported their family from his wages as a carpenter and coffin-maker.

After high school, young Dorothy left Waco to live with an older sister in Galveston. There she met my father, the eldest son of a prominent Galveston family. Mother always thought herself "timid." She once referred to herself as "not very interesting."

Dorothy McDonald was the best mother any little girl could ever have had, and the perfect counterpart and companion for Lee.

She was far more interesting that she would ever believe, and stronger than most could imagine.

She was almost apologetic when I told her I was coming to see her, shortly after moving to Florida in 2004.

"I know you're busy Kathryn. But I always love to see you." I couldn't convince her I was *never* too busy for her.

Being in Galveston was still difficult three years after Albert had died. He and I had a history there, unlike Florida.

I'd grieve alone during my dawn walks along Galveston's Seawall Boulevard across from mother's retirement community.

During one such walk, the street lamp at the corner of the boulevard and the building where mother lived suddenly flickered in that mystical way they'd been doing since Albert died.

Turning to look, I saw a tall, *familiar* figure standing beneath the light just as it flickered off.

I'd been cautioned about walking alone on the beach at that hour. But unable to resist looking over my shoulder as I walked away, the figure was suddenly *gone*.

I walked closer to see where he'd disappeared. It would have been impossible in that location as open as it was.

It was Albert.

72.

It was February 2005 and the height of "season" in Southwest Florida, when the population more than doubles with part-time residents and tourists.

I hadn't been to Truluck's restaurant since November. I'd been getting settled in my lovely new home, swimming, diving with the Eagle Ray Dive Club in Bonita Springs, and getting to know the area nearer my home.

I had avoided going back to Truluck's. Some part of me still felt *loss* after leaving music decades ago. Music had been a healing influence on me when I had sung professionally for a few years.

I was 24 at the time. I'd exhausted every other place looking for work in the small college town to which I'd fled after leaving my first husband, Paul Fuhrhop, for the *first* time in 1970, after two years of marriage. I left Galveston for Nacogdoches, intending to go back to college.

I hoped to find a job to support myself and make money for school. I walked into a local motel and asked the proprietor if they needed a desk clerk.

"Ever worked in a motel before?"

"Yes, ma'am. I used to sing at the Flagship Resort Hotel in Galveston."

"Go see my husband in the club. We're thinking about hiring a singing waitress."

With no money, no job, no other prospects and a sinking heart, I walked across the parking lot to the restaurant. I'd never waited a table in my life. But I had no place else to go.

"Go introduce yourself to Steve Wayne and see if he'll let you sing," the man said.

Three hours later, I had a job, two new friends, and a whole new plan. I soon left East Texas for the Dallas city lights, as part of *The Steve Wayne Trio*.

And all I had to do was sing.

73.

Steve's Native American ex-wife had disappeared with their infant son back to the reservation not long before. He didn't have a clue how to find them.

George's fiancé died in an auto accident shortly before their wedding.

I had left my marriage, shattered over the loss of what I'd naively believed would be the first and last one I'd ever have.

The three of us made incredible music together, with Steve's arrangements of the old standards so popular in dinner clubs of the 40's, 50's, and 60's.

He was a career musician with a friend in East Texas who'd given him a place to stay while healing from the loss of his family. A musical prodigy from the age of 6, Steve played the Gulbransen organ and piano. He also sang and wrote musical arrangements, having worked with some of the biggest names in the business. Spending years as part of the Air Force "Men of Note," he also toured the country with a succession of bands.

George played guitar, bass, mandolin, and banjo. He I were just along for the ride until we found ourselves again. George said if he didn't make it "big" within 10 years, he would go back to his family's trucking company in Oakland, California. I would often wonder if he ever did.

The three of us sublimated our pain on the bandstand six nights a week. We thought ahead only so far as our next set, gig, and meal. It never occurred to me this would be only the first of many times I would have to start my life over again.

74.

Before long, *The Steve Wayne Trio* was picked up by a major entertainment booking agency that scheduled us for gigs in Michigan, and then New York.

Just before we left Dallas for Michigan, I left the *Steve Wayne Trio* to *remarry* my ex-husband Paul Fuhrhop.

Two years later in 1972, he and I would divorce again. By that time, however, I'd found another calling with The March of Dimes, with whom I'd eventually relocate to Mamaroneck, New York.

I had often wondered in the intervening years what might have happened had I not left music. But I had no regrets. The direction I'd taken was best. When Paul and I split the second time, we did so as friends, which we would remain. There was no bitterness between us.

There were things about the music business that I hadn't liked at that time anyway. Always being in the public eye and having to stay up late at night among them. A morning person, I always felt sleep-deprived after working so late.

I was never entirely comfortable in the public eye. Maybe it was growing up with Tourette syndrome. There were times as a child when I all I wanted was to just disappear into the woodwork.

Leaving *The Steve Wayne Trio* in 1971 was the second time I left music. The first was in 1967 when I left *The Johnny Garcia Trio* at Galveston's premier resort, the

Flagship Hotel, to return to college. It had been an exciting year. I was training sea lions and bottle-nosed dolphins at Sea Arama Marineworld during the day. Sea Arama was one of only about three marine aquariums in the continental United States at that time with dolphin shows.

There weren't that many qualified sea lion and dolphin trainers looking for jobs in the mid-60's. Majoring in biology and pre-veterinary medicine, I went to work at Sea Arama the summer after my second year in college. I ended up getting hired as Sea Arama's first official sea lion trainer and among the first, if not *the* first, female dolphin trainer in the continental USA.

After scrubbing the smell of fish out of my hair and using copious amounts of wintergreen oil to rid my skin of the scent, I'd go to work singing in the evenings at the Flagship Hotel.

It was 1966. Pianist Johnny Garcia had seen an article in the newspaper about my training sea lions at Sea Arama. He told one of the guys that worked there to tell me to come do a tune or two with his band.

I first met Johnny and his band two years before when they were performing at a high school graduation party I attended. I mustered up the courage to ask him if I could sing a song with them. I don't recall the song but I know it was one of the "old standards" I'd learned over the years listening to the radio.

While all my friends were rocking and rolling with Elvis, I was remembering everything Ella Fitzgerald,

Rosemary Clooney, Julie London, and Edie Gorme ever did. On that night in 1964, at 18 years old, I did something that surprised everyone, including me. I sang with a real band for the first time in my life!

Johnny remembered me two years later when he saw the newspaper article and invited me to the Flagship. I couldn't resist. One night I went to the Flagship's Pennant Club where they were playing and did a couple of songs with them.

Shortly thereafter, Johnny offered me a job. Family friend Bill Cherry, well-known Galveston businessman, published writer, and former musician himself, helped me negotiate the deal.

Soon I was performing nightly with The Johnny Garcia Trio after working all day at Sea Arama training sea lions and bottle-nosed dolphins!

I was 20 years old. Although it was glamorous and exciting, it was a little too much "visibility" for me.

Johnny Garcia, Oscar Ochoa (bassist, vocalist), and Chano Rodriquez introduced me to the world of professional music. I learned a great deal from them. Sadly, they're all gone now, Johnny the last to pass away. He died in his 80's of kidney failure in California where he and his wife Melba had relocated not long after I went back to college.

Johnny was the consummate gentleman, musician, and friend. He had class as well as musical skill. He spent time working on the original "Love Boat" cruise ship after moving to California. He could play anything in any key. He helped me build a "book" of tunes I still have.

In 1967, I went back to college after a year and a half of this exciting lifestyle. Not long after, in 1968, I married Paul for the first time. Life, for a while, was well outside the public eye.

I dabbled in music in Connecticut and New York during the 80's after Jim passed away and before meeting Albert. Mostly I just sang in the shower. I was one of those people in the adjacent vehicle you laugh at as they sing all by themselves.

Musicians may leave the business, but never the music. It's part of our DNA.

For love, I had left music and the opportunity to sing in the swank dinner clubs of the Midwest and New York. Over the years I would have unanswered questions about leaving, but no regrets. I would subsequently leave two thriving business careers for the same reason.

I never really wanted so much attention in spite of the fact I seemed to find myself in positions where it came readily. I would discover something I enjoyed doing and before long I'd be thrust into the public eye or promoted to a position of greater visibility.

For a while, I'd enjoy it. But eventually it would catch up to me. All I really wanted was a relatively quiet life doing something I enjoyed with someone I loved. And if possible, I wanted it to be somewhere near the cool green solace of the woods.

75.

Claude Rhea's invitation to sing stuck with me. Twice before I stepped up to a bandstand to "do a tune," and ended up with a job.

But no one resumes a career in music at my age, especially a "girl singer." I was certainly no longer a "girl."

I'd given up playing violin, cello, and piano at age 10, and the bulk of my experience as a singer was 30 years past.

I never imagined singing professionally again. But the emotional outlet was compelling.

I had no idea part of my healing would again include music.

I couldn't forget the way Claude had played those old standards. I didn't even know if he was still at Truluck's on the night, five months later, when I decided to go back.

"Where you been, baby?" he said as I took a seat at the piano bar.

"You remember me?" I stammered.

"You're the songbird who was in here a while back. Ready to do a tune?"

"No," I smiled. I reminded myself it was part of the gig to make single women patrons feel at ease.

Over the next few weeks, I returned several more times, making friends from among the regulars. We started meeting on Thursday nights at the piano bar. Claude's talent on the piano was everything I'd remembered and more.

Neither of us had any idea the role he was about to play in my life.

76.

I'd just taken a seat at the piano bar when a diminutive fashionista in a wide-brimmed hat turned to me with what I would soon learn was her characteristic greeting.

"Hello, pussycat," she said from within an ocean of colorful costume jewelry, henna red hair framing a youthful face.

"Haven't seen you here before! I'm Lila," she said, lifting her drink much as royalty would a scepter.

"I love your jewelry," I said, thinking how she resembled an 80-something Shirley MacLaine.

Strands of beads and pearls, rings the size of head lamps and half-dollar sized earrings, Lila was dressed to kill. Thinking not many women could successfully combine so many different colors, patterns, and styles in one ensemble, I soon learned Lila Astroff was, indeed, unique.

"Dahling," she said in an unmistakable New York accent, "most women look in the mirror and say, 'You got on too much jewelry,' while I say, 'Add another piece!"

I liked her immediately.

Noting the pin on her jacket with "Queen Mother" in blazing rhinestones, it was easy to surmise how she acquired the nickname. The hat alone suggested this was no ordinary doyenne out for an occasional night on the town.

Lila was the quintessential Manhattan party girl straight out of the golden age of late night speakeasies and high-society club hopping till the wee hours. Although in her 80's, she didn't even get started till around 9 p.m., when most of her generation were long asleep.

A handsome, successful man in his 40's, Ron Yohe was as charming and funny as he was caring. Having met Lila and her late husband Everett not long after their arrival in Naples, Ron had been Lila's close friend, confidant, and caretaker since her husband's death. His friendship would also light up my own life in ways that only a man without any designs on me as a woman could.

Ron had lost his own husband and partner of many years. It seemed there were a number of us hiding our pain with music.

While I was hiding mine singing silently along with Claude, Lila, widowed not long before, also was hiding hers behind a façade of ceaseless good cheer and sometimes bawdy good humor.

She was, perhaps, even lonelier than I.

Soon the three of us would meet on Thursday nights at Pazzo's in Naples for a drink and dinner before going to Truluck's.

She would later say she was my number one fan. But I had rapidly become hers! With a wit sharp enough to add “Zorro” to her rhinestone monikers, she was a fixture in the upscale restaurants and bars of Naples’ tony Fifth Avenue South.

I once told her how she reminded me of a cross between Mae West and former New Yorker, U.S. Representative, and social activist Bella Abzug. Without a moment’s hesitation, Lila retorted, “Yeah, but I got bettah hats!”

Bartenders and wait staff knew her by name, finding the best seats for her. She preferred sitting at the bar where she could be in the middle of everything and everyone.

“I met most of my friends in bars,” she said, dropping the “r” and adding an “h.”

Patrons old and new left her with a handful of business cards in hopes she would include them on her list of potential companions for nights out on the town. There was no shortage of friends in those days wanting to bask in the glow of her joie de vivre. You couldn’t help but feel good around her.

Scarlet nails wrapped around a vodka rocks with one hand, waving over friends, wait staff, and total strangers with the other, Naples’ own “Queen Mother” held court with dozens of her adoring subjects.

Including me.We had no idea at the time that those Thursday nights would be among the best we’d ever have together.

77.

It was around the end of April when Claude shoved the microphone in my face and demanded that I sing.

I was still politely declining his invitation, but on that night, I didn't know whether to be intimidated or relieved.

I hesitantly took it from his hand as he nodded his approval and asked me what I was going to sing.

"I'll do 'Funny Valentine,' but I don't remember the key."

"I can play *your* key," he said, echoing the first night we met.

I would soon learn that Claude Rhea could play just about anything in *any* key, having begun playing the piano professionally in Savannah, Georgia, at 15 years old.

This self-taught musician would eventually work with some of the finest smooth jazz musicians in the business. But he too, was covering up pain with music.

"Sing a few bars," he ordered while he quickly assessed the key.

It was like I never stopped. Something inside of me *just let go*.

Looking quietly at me as the tune ended, he *knew*. Only another musician who had been there would.

For every feeling there's a lyric. For every experience, a song.

It was 2005. I was 59 years old. Claude hired me on the spot.

78.

It was exciting and glamorous. At once anxious and fulfilled, I was again propelled into the public eye in spite of my aversion to it.

Most people don't think I'm as shy as I am. Sometimes I thought I *must* be a closet exhibitionist engaged in a constant struggle with myself to "get out." But *visibility* is a two-edge sword. I was both drawn to and repelled by it.

Soon Claude and I were working at private parties in exclusive Old Naples, as well as Truluck's. He became my friend as well as mentor.

Music was a place to put the lingering pain of losing those we loved most in the world. Claude had lost his beloved Lucille, the late wife from whom he was divorced but nevertheless still loved dearly. Not long after, the jazz club built around him in Atlanta burned to the ground. He moved to Naples to start over.

Albert was in every sad song I sang.

Lila momentarily escaped her loneliness surrounded by her with adoring minions in the upscale restaurants and bars of glitzy Naples.

Ron lost himself in his work while transferring his love for his lost partner, Brent, to those of us struggling with our own bereavements.

We were living one day at a time, never knowing or thinking about what the future held. Just getting past the *past* was good enough.

79.

People sometimes thought ours was a romantic relationship. It was easy to understand why, considering the musical chemistry between Claude and I. But the intimacies we shared were far more complex and enduring.

Women loved Claude. They often asked me if we were "together." Sometimes it was easier to let them think it, stopping the advances of those more interested in what we did than who we were.

The music business can make you a little cynical about relationships.

"We're just good friends," we'd say.

Claude sometimes had a hard time resisting all that attention. He liked the ladies too. I knew, however, the one whom he really loved. I believe Mary Lee Criner and Claude would have been together for the long-haul, if only they'd had the chance.

I only met Mary Lee twice. She rarely came to his gigs, preferring to remain in the background of Claude's life. She was quiet, sweet, and obviously very much in love with him. He adored her in his own way, of that I was certain.

Mary Lee would later tell me I had been her only *real* competition. When I hurriedly tried to explain our relationship, she just smiled.

"I know that, Kathy," she said. "But Claude loved you in a way he didn't love anyone else. He was so proud of you."

During the year and a half Claude Rhea and I worked regularly together, I rebuilt my repertoire and fine-tuned my "chops." I found a vocal confidence I didn't have in youth. Life experience no doubt helped.

I was meeting many people and putting my life back together in many ways. With Claude's patient mentoring, I was thriving in music. He rarely told me what to do. He'd smile when I did it well and give me that wry look when I didn't. He never groused or complained. He taught by example and gentle nudging.

One night a patron brought his little boy to hear us, saying his child wanted to play the piano and sing someday too. The little guy hesitantly offered me a cocktail napkin and a pen. It was the first autograph anybody had ever asked of me.

At that moment, little was as important as seeing that shy little boy smile. I hoped he found himself in music someday too.

80.

I could hear her shortness of breath as she struggled to speak. It was July 2007 when I got on a plane to attend the bedside of my sweet little "Mamma" in Texas.

She was dying.

She worked so hard to make a new life for herself after Daddy died. She still had the little red plastic Valentine's Day heart with a note he'd written shortly before his death in 1996. Nestled in a little silver box on her dressing table, it was a constant reminder of their 61 years together.

"*One More Time,*" he'd written in his angular hand. That said it all.

How I loved them both, and envied them all those years together. I'd been so blessed to have them as my parents.

I always told Mamma she could live with me. "I don't want to be a burden to my children, Kathryn," she'd say. I couldn't convince her that she'd never be a burden to me.

She'd moved to Galveston Island's Edgewater Retirement Community near her home, family, and friends of 70 years.

On this day as she lay dying in the hospital's cardiac intensive care unit, I again asked her if she wanted to come live with me.

With the barest of nods, her still lovely pale blue eyes, now watery with age and failing health held the answer. Somehow, I'd make it happen.

The doctor said she could travel as long as she could sit up and transfer to a chair. It would be difficult.

She needed round-the-clock oxygen and was barely able to get out of bed. Hospice encouraged the move.

She saw my life as exotic and exciting. Perhaps it would give her something to look forward to. She was always proud of me. Her children's smallest accomplishments were her greatest pleasures.

She and my Dad made me feel as though there was nothing I couldn't do. I promised myself her last days would be as good as I could make them.

It was a frantic race against time. Arranging airline transport with oxygen tanks in the post-9/11 world; disposing of her apartment and possessions; getting to and from airports; preparing a room in my Florida home; making arrangements with Florida hospice for her care in my home were overlaid with the possibility the move itself could kill her.

Florida friends Chuck Harrison and Martha Gill helped convert the guest room in my home into a hospital room before we arrived.

My sisters Dorothy and Mary and niece Amy emptied mother's two-bedroom apartment at Edgewater and disposed of her furniture.

We packed and shipped some of her clothes and personal effects to Florida as I made travel arrangements for her move.

Other Edgewater residents often told me how she had been the first to befriend them when they moved into the retirement community. Recalling her own anxiety about moving to it seven years prior, she had shyly created a new life for herself. Her empathy for others in the same situation had endeared her to so many who came later.

As the unofficial greeter of new residents, "floor monitor," and long-time Galveston resident, she blossomed from a quietly retiring wife and mother living in the shadows of her husband and daughters into a retirement home doyenne.

Now at death's door, she was leaving behind everything she knew for the last time. Or so we thought.

We arranged a "going away" celebration the day we left, renting a stretch limo for the novelty, comfort, and safety. Mother had never been in one before. Virtually every resident and employee who was able to do so came to her going-away party.

But mother wasn't quite ready to let go yet.

The trip seemed twice as long as it was. I lost about five years when the pilot told us midway the weather might force a change of destinations. Thankfully it cleared enough to allow us to land in Fort Myers. My home was only 10 minutes from the airport. The time getting her from airplane to bed in my house seemed far longer than it was. But we made it.

The day after arriving in Florida, she was sitting up in the recliner with Biz on her lap! Although the hospice nurse's assessment of mother's condition was cautious, it was almost as though old Biz knew better. He would become part of her amazing recovery.

At least for a while.

81.

Mother's health after arriving in Florida improved to the point she could remain off oxygen for a few hours at a time, accompany me on short excursions, and raid the refrigerator in the middle of the night.

Although further improvement in her condition was unlikely, she at least had a new lease on life.

We spent several months getting her medications, rest and diet regulated. We also were having fun. As well as she'd adjusted to living at Edgewater, there was simply nothing that did her more good than living with family.

Every day was a new challenge for me. I lived in a quiet neighborhood. There were only about a third of us who were year-round residents. Mother was housebound without me.

Most afternoons I'd take her out for an early dinner, oxygen tank in tow. How she loved to eat, people-watching with her lovely old head turning this way and that as someone new walked by.

I burned into memory the image of her sitting behind a platter of nachos almost as wide as she was. She finished almost the entire thing!

She loved riding with the top down in the little convertible I'd purchased after moving to Florida. With sun visor planted firmly on her forehead and large-lensed sunglasses half covering her face, my sporty little Mamma was having the time of her life!

Still working with Claude, I employed a private sitter and hospice volunteer to stay with mother when I wasn't home. But I was determined to add something new to her life.

"Mamma, what's one thing you wish you could do you never did?"

Pondering the question a moment, she told me she had always wanted to be able to go into a "nice bar," have a drink, meet people, and listen to the music without worrying about not having an escort! In her day, women didn't do such things.

She hadn't met Lila yet. But that would soon change.

I hired an aide to go with us a few weeks later when I thought mother strong enough. The best photo I ever missed was of Lila and mother sitting side-by-side at the piano bar, dressed to kill, cocktails in hand, chattering happily away.

Mother said later how much she envied Lila's ability to be so outgoing. The quintessential New Yorker, Lila spent most of her life living the Manhattan dream. The daughter of a well-to-do couple from whom she inherited her love of the night-life, Lila had grown up in relative privilege during the hey-day of New York City's recovery from prohibition.

Lila told me she envied my mother's lifestyle. Mother was the fifth and youngest child of a poor carpenter and homemaker, married 61 years to the only man she ever loved. With three daughters, countless pets, a quiet life in a relatively small Texas town, Dorothy Catherine Cain McDonald was the quintessential 50's-era homemaker.

But for that moment, 85-year-old *Lila* and 93-year-old *Dorothy* were just two "girls" out on the town. I knew it couldn't last. But mother would have a few more such evenings during which an old fantasy was reality.

We had that in common too.

82.

I often said that Claude was the only person who called me "Kathy" and lived to tell about it. I had ditched that nickname decades ago after having lost "Kathryn" because a junior high school teacher couldn't deal with two of them in the same room. I took back my *real* name shortly after high school.

Somehow, I didn't mind it so much when Claude called me "Kathy." I tried correcting him, but I think it meant something that he was the only one to get away with it.

I later learned from his son Farod how proud Claude was to have "discovered" me. During the dark days thereafter when Farod called me "Kathy," I felt as though Claude had bequeathed the right to his family. It was okay, because it reminded me of the wonderful man who had become my *brother*.

"Kathy, you need to do a CD," Claude said one night.

"I never liked hearing myself sing, Claude."

"You gotta' second chance now, Songbird. Do it."

I avoided thinking much about it. After all, I was 60 years old! *Nobody* resumes a singing career at that age much less records a CD!

Never ever say "Never ever."

I didn't have time anyway. There was also something new on the horizon. Mother wanted to go back to Texas!

83.

I could go anywhere at any time. But mother was confined to the house without me. She recovered well enough to miss her friends and the rest of the family in Galveston. I couldn't blame her. She was lonely.

It had become a constant topic of conversation. Ambivalent, she wanted to remain with me and return to Texas. She was still in hospice care in spite of her amazing recovery. Her condition was still precarious.

Her heart was still failing, although more slowly. Returning to Galveston would be difficult. She'd have to live in skilled nursing instead of an apartment in the independent wing of Edgewater. It would be the reverse drill of bringing her to Florida. It exhausted me thinking about it.

I tried to tell her that things would be different if she went back. I never came right out and told her she was dying. I don't believe she would have believed it anyway. I had learned from Albert that the patient will let you know what they want to know and when.

I didn't tell her the end of her life was nearer than she thought.

In spite of having stepped back a bit from death's door, she was still 93 years old with a failing heart.

She used to tell people to "get hospice" because they had taken such good care of her.

“Why doesn’t everyone use them?” she asked. I don’t think mother truly realized what having hospice care truly *meant*.

I explained to her that hospice wasn’t generally employed until very near the end of one’s life.

Thinking quietly a moment, she accepted that answer and moved onto something else.

Our roles had truly become reversed. She was like the child I had once been, satisfied with the simplest answers to sometimes difficult questions.

Although she often claimed that she was “ready to go,” part of her was too much a survivor to quit yet. Like Albert, she kept on going, one day at a time.

It was always a struggle to know how much information was too much, or not enough. Too much can destroy the will to live. Too little risks taking dangerous chances.

I urged her to mull it over through the holidays, hoping she would change her mind. But she didn’t.

84.

Claude and I were taking a break on the porch of the club.

"Kathy, men always ask me about you," he said. "You gotta' way that makes them hesitate to approach you."

"That's not the first time I've been told that," I replied. I didn't need to explain why I didn't really want to change it.

He already *knew*.

A few patrons followed us outside to chat. People usually get chattier when they drink. It was, after all, a *bar*.

It was hard to attend to them that night. I just smiled and pretended.

Claude took long drags on his cigarette and just listened. A quick glance in my direction said he knew exactly what I was thinking. He learned long ago to deal with this part of the business.

Growing up with a white father, African-American mother, and full-blooded Cherokee Indian grandmother had taught him patience.

"I didn't really know where I belonged until I discovered piano. Mamma bought it for my sister, but when I sat down and started playin', it became mine."

He was working with seasoned jazz musicians before he was of legal age to play in the clubs. Honing his craft in smoky bars and "gentlemen's clubs," he eventually performed his way into some of the best places in Georgia. He was the first African-American entertainer to play for the governor in the Georgia statehouse. His credentials were impressive, but he never bragged.

One day he gave me a book that said it all. "***Sights and Sounds of Savannah Jazz"*** by Julius "Boo" Hornstein featured an entire chapter on Claude Rhea!

He was famous! I couldn't believe no one around here seemed to know of all his accomplishments. I'd soon find that more common than not among the local musicians.

Moving around the table to avoid the cigarette smoke, I soon excused myself from the conversation and went back inside.

My mind drifted back to cool Connecticut summer evenings, sitting on the deck with Albert, our pets lounging nearby.

Talking about anything and everything or sitting quietly in the deepening night, we drifted contentedly on the gentle currents of our quiet, privileged life.

At that moment, I'd have given 20 years of my own life and everything I had to have him back.

85.

I didn't like the way Claude was getting treated. It reinforced another reason I'd left music earlier. The business was even less musician-friendly now.

Claude had just played an hour-and-a-half set, instead of the usual 40 minutes on and 20 off. Musicians need their breaks. I've often said that four hours on the bandstand is the equivalent of eight working in an office. I know because I've done both.

But if customers were really into the music, Claude would keep playing. That night, they were.

He finally stepped outside for a break. Within minutes, the assistant manager at the time stood in the door, stabbing his watch with a finger and staring at Claude.

The night before that same guy actually *sniffed* the coffee cup into which Claude had secreted a shot of brandy, chastising him as though he were a wayward child.

"You know you're not supposed to drink on the job."

That was almost punitive to a working musician for whom there were no other benefits whatsoever.

I never saw Claude drink too much. Sometimes, a shot or two helped relax him, especially when he was asked to sing, which he didn't particularly like.

"The piano is my instrument," he would say. "Kathy's the songbird."

Everyone loved his singing and our duets.

His rousing "Red Rooster" was so popular that regulars started bringing him ceramic roosters to sit atop the piano.

It seemed to me, however, that musicians got even less respect from employers presently than 30 years ago.

Claude nodded quietly when I told him a few weeks later I wasn't returning. I could see the handwriting on the wall. He was about to quit as well. He wouldn't have trouble finding a new gig. He'd put jazz on the map in Naples.

By this time, I was also working regularly with my own group, *AllThatJazz*.

I was also very worried about mother. She didn't realize how different going back to Texas would be. I knew the trip back would be another juggernaut and once there, I'd be unable to bring her back to Florida.

She had fallen several times, thankfully not breaking anything. She still needed round-the-clock monitoring. Even with outside help, it required a lot on my part. But I wanted her to live out her life in a family home.

One day I found her struggling to open a pop-top can for lunch. Her old fingers had grown weak with age and infirmity, so she unsuccessfully stabbed at it with a knife until eventually giving up. I felt so sorry for her. She had merely wanted to feed herself.

I didn't always sleep well, hearing her every move or change in breathing on the baby monitors between our rooms. At times she'd try to get up in the middle of the night, fall, or soil her bedclothes. She always felt so badly about it, more worried about me than herself.

I never regretted having her with me. But I was concerned about her emotional state. She seemed increasingly lonely for other family members and friends. I couldn't convince her that going back to Edgewater wouldn't be the same.

She'd lie in her bed looking out the window. She told me she looked forward to seeing Miromar's community patrol car pass by as one of the few signs of life in our quiet neighborhood.

A few days in an adult daycare depressed her. Most of the people there were dependents of hard-working families who were gone all day and needed a place for their loved one to stay. Although a pleasant enough place, mother had little in common with anyone there, nor they with her.

Attempts to get her together with a couple of other elderly women living with neighbors nearby weren't fruitful. They were all just too old and sick to start over again.

Between worries over mother's mental state and my increasing awareness of music's more unpleasant aspects, I needed a distraction.

86.

Shortly after moving to Florida, I convinced Miromar's management to have a charity swimming event. Once again, I hoped to combine my love of swimming with charity.

Miromar had never done anything like the Hudson River swim, but management agreed to give it a try. We'd use both Lake Como and the community pool for those uneasy about swimming in open water.

The Florida Lions Camp would be the recipient of any funds raised, largely due to Miromar resident Chuck Risch's involvement with the Lions.

Chuck was rendered quadriplegic in a water skiing accident shortly after retiring to Miromar. He'd been an experimental automotive design engineer. I soon learned this man could accomplish more from his wheelchair than most of us could with two fully functioning arms and legs.

Just before the inaugural *Gulf Coast Charity Swim*, Chuck asked if there was any reason why a disabled person couldn't participate.

I had an idea where he was going with that question. This man's determination put most people to shame.

As a Handicapped Scuba Association International dive buddy, I was trained to be in the water with the disabled before. Chuck had been a swimmer, expert water skier and SCUBA diver prior to his disabling injury.

“What did you have in mind?” I asked hopefully.

Sure enough, Chuck Risch wanted to swim in the event.

87.

Chuck rolled his wheelchair down the ramp into the pool before we eased him onto the float. I placed dive fins on his feet, gently moving his legs as though finning.

He had just enough mobility to move his legs slightly. Soon he asked to have the float removed from beneath him.

The first *Gulf Coast Charity Swim* on July 8, 2006, at Miromar Lakes Beach and Golf Club was a resounding success.

Chuck Risch "swam" four laps in the pool on his back, two friends guiding him from either side.

He raised the second highest amount of money in the entire event! That and subsequent charity swims raised enough money to put each of 145 disabled kids through a week of summer camp.

I swam six miles non-stop for the fun of it. As event chair, I disqualified myself from prizes.

Swimming long distances was now routine for me. I didn't want this event to become a competition for speed or distance.

It was ironic that I had become the one to "beat" in a long-distance swimming event! Only a few short years before, I'd been the rookie being rolled onto the boat at the end of each lap to keep from holding up the entire event!

I got out of the water now not because I was last in the queue, but because everyone else was tired out!

Never ever say "Never ever."

The Gulf Coast Charity Swim (GCCS) eventually led Miromar Lakes to host the USA Swimming Association's national trials.

Gregg Cross of USA Swimming had been among the organizers of the "GCCS." Asking me one day if I thought Miromar would go for hosting the USA Swimming event, I felt certain Miromar's management would be interested. The GCCS had proven that Lake Como was an ideal place for such an event. I encouraged Gregg to pursue the idea.

In October 2007, top USA and Canadian men's and women's swimmers competed in Miromar's Lake Como for a space at the first international Olympics Open Water Swimming competition in Bejiing, China.

Conditions in Miromar's Lake Como were almost identical to what the Bejiing Olympians would face.

That too, was spectacularly successful, putting Miromar Lakes Beach and Golf Club on the map as a world-class swimming venue.

The day before the event, I donned my mask, skin, and fins and swam the course from which those athletes would attempt to secure their place in open water swimming history.

The distance I swam non-stop for two hours, wearing my SCUBA fins, would be doubled by those young athletes in their bare *feet* the following day. It gave me an even greater appreciation for the extraordinary dedication of these young sportsmen and women.

Swimming the course that could propel a young athlete into world sports history the very next day was an amazing moment for me. To be that close to such a feat was a far cry from the couch-potato I had been only a few short years before.

I was amazed and humbled.

88.

I was now diving regularly with my new friends of the Eagle Ray Dive Club. Jolene and Chris Dixon owned and operated the Eagle Ray Dive Shop in Bonita Springs, Florida. We had become good friends since I joined the club, making dive trips to the Caribbean, Mexico, Dutch West Indies, and Central America, among others. It was a great bunch of people with whom I'd have many wonderful times. We'd meet monthly to review Chris's world-class photos of our dive trips, eat, and just generally have a good time.

Warm water diving had spoiled me. After the routinely cold-water diving in the northeast, I hung up my heavy wetsuit, vowing never to wear it again. Peter Hearn and his staff at Pan Aqua Diving in Connecticut had trained me well. But dropping the 7 ml wetsuit, hood, and gloves along with at least 10 pounds of the weights required to help descend in that getup felt wonderful. I went from feeling like a "Michelin Woman" in my SCUBA gear to a far sleeker and more comfortable fish in the water.

There were many times I wished I could share things like this with Albert. I was beginning to struggle to recall his handsome profile as he lay in peaceful repose next to me in those early morning hours. It made me sad to remember it.

Al had never heard me sing the old tunes I was performing with Claude and *AllThatJazz*. He knew I'd once been a singer. Shortly before he died he gave me a boxed set of the old standards, knowing how much I loved them still.

He never saw me swim like I was doing now. He didn't have a clue any more than I did that I would become an open water endurance swimmer, regularly swimming five or more miles weekly, or that I'd become a professional-level SCUBA diver as well.

I had always been involved in volunteer work when he was alive, but he never knew how right he had been when he told me once I found the "right" athletic activity for me, I'd never quit.

Little was as important to me during our life together as being Al Taubert's wife and partner. I was so proud of him. I was content to remain quietly by his side as his bright light shined over me and everyone else around him. I didn't really need anything else. I could have remained that way the rest of my life.

For all that was happening to me now, every day I still missed what he and I had together.

89.

Claude and I still worked together from time to time and spoke at least weekly when we weren't. From time to time I'd hire him for my own gigs.

I booked a contract for *AllThatJazz* at Miromar Lakes Blue Water Grill. Eventually we regularly performed at Miromar's brand new, award-winning Beach Clubhouse.

Claude was still urging me to "do a CD." Maybe he was right.

Mother would enjoy it. She couldn't go to my gigs anymore. Crowds overwhelmed her. She couldn't see from her wheelchair, and the anxiety caused her to have more difficulty breathing. If I recorded a CD, she could listen all she wanted without leaving the house.

But if I recorded, I'd have to listen to myself sing!

Steve Wayne once said, "Most people in that room out there can't hear what you can." If I screwed up, he said, just ignore it and keep on singing.

Maybe he had been right after all. I didn't like hearing myself, but I decided to do it anyway. I'd record my first CD.

90.

The three of us had tears in our eyes by the end of the tune.

I was surprised when Rick Howard asked me if I knew the haunting Brazilian ballad by Antonio Carlos Jobim and Gene Lees. I never understood why one of the most beautiful of Jobim's collaborations hadn't achieved greater success in the USA.

Rick loved the tune almost as much as I. He and his wife Lisa came over to work out the arrangement for the CD. "*Someone To Light Up My Life*" would be the first song I'd record.

I first heard it shortly before meeting Albert, subsequently associating it with him. This would be one of those songs I'd always remember where I was when first hearing it.

Eventually I'd find that guitarist-singer-composer Rick Howard knew just about every lovely Latin tune there was. He'd even written a few of his own!

Rick was a musician's musician. He played guitar, bass, composed, arranged, produced, sang, and dished up a constant stream of clever banter on the bandstand. After years in the coveted role of New York studio musician, Rick, Lisa, and their sweet little dog "Lallie Anne" got tired of the cold and moved to Florida. I met Rick at a jam session when I was still working at Truluck's with Claude.

One night my friend Michael Miller invited me to join him at a small Naples café for their weekly "jam session." This time I didn't hesitate when asked to sing a tune.

Before long I was sitting in regularly with Rick and others. It wasn't long before I'd start booking some of those same musicians, especially Rick, for my own gigs as well.

My first *AllThatJazz* gig was with Claude at Miromar Lakes Blue Water Grill. I'll never forget my anxiety prior to our "debut" there.

These were my neighbors! If I screwed up, I'd have to endure the embarrassment every time I saw them in "the hood."

After the event, I lay wide awake, amazed it had gone so well. With Claude's support, it was a piece of cake.

Was I really good enough that accomplished professional musicians and recording artists like Claude Rhea and Rick Howard would want to collaborate on a CD with *me*?

I hadn't heard my own voice outside a reverberating shower stall in 30 years. I hadn't liked what I heard then.

But Claude's gentle persistence convinced me. It would be nice someday when I was a doddering old woman to listen to it while "remembering the day."

Maybe my great-nephew Angus would be proud of his old Aunt Kathryn too. “She’s a singer you know,” he’d later tell a teacher when I arrived at his school.

I didn’t get to see him much since his mother and father were divorcing. I was sad about that. They’d started off so well.

In time, circumstances would permit me to have Angus back in my life. I wanted him to know his mother’s side of the family in ways that would assure him just how much he was loved by all of us, even though his parents were no longer together.

91.

I'd sat in on a few jam sessions with the extraordinarily talented Stu Shelton, eventually hiring him a few times for my own gigs. Stu was an amazing jazz pianist, among the busiest working musicians in the area. He also had his own recording studio in Naples.

I barely read a note of music, didn't understand music theory, or speak the language. I never had any real voice training. But I was working regularly and getting a lot of press.

Rick, Stu, and Claude would eventually collaborate on our arrangements for the CD, speaking in what sounded like a foreign language as they did so.

Genius is when somebody makes something difficult look easy. These guys were geniuses in my book. Most people don't have the slightest *clue* what musicians endure while learning their craft. The really good ones make it look easy.

When they spoke in chords and progressions, I'd just sit and listen, totally in the dark. They'd forgotten more about music than I'd ever know.

But if I could hear it, I could sing it.

Once I learned that, Claude's telling me my "big ears" had nothing to do with anatomy and everything to do with music, I forgave myself for not knowing more theory. I just focused on what I *did* know.

I could hear chords and progressions, even though I couldn't identify them.

I could harmonize, although I couldn't say what notes I was singing.

I could improvise, sing "scat," and phrase a song in a way that "felt right," and people seem to appreciate.

I could memorize lyrics after only a few times hearing them.

I could write them too.

Had I stayed with music, I'd have resumed piano lessons and learned the "language" of music. It was too late for me to achieve their proficiency with an instrument. But I was determined to do my part to help make this CD something about which we could all be proud.

These guys didn't seem to mind that I didn't understand their language. I know they were amused at times. One day Rick instructed me to end a recording with a certain chord progression. Smiling at my confusion, he just smiled and said, "Don't worry. You'll hear it." I did.

I never expected my CD to be anything more than a vanity production and a chance to record some great tunes with some of the best musicians I'd ever heard.

I had no idea it would become that, and more.

92.

I was surprised listening to the first cut of "*Someone To Light Up My Life*."

Was that *me?*

It sounded better than I'd hoped, but it highlighted things I didn't like about my singing.

Sometimes I could hear my Texas drawl, not entirely diminished by decades in the northeast. I'd always been distracted by a singer's dialect and vowed never to sing with one of my own from that point forward.

It was harder than I thought. I'd ask Stu to let me "punch in" a replacement to "get the Texas out." I was proud of my origins, but the dialect didn't go with the music. I soon discovered how important recording was to improving one's performance.

Sometimes I thought my vibrato overdone, or enunciation unclear. I learned to control my voice better, when to hold a note and when to let go.

Sometimes the tempo was too slow or too fast, or my phrasing not quite right. Had I not recorded, I'd never have known.

Claude was right. Was part of his insistence that I "do a CD" to help me improve as well as document what I could do? He never said.

I was pleased at the outcome, and not a little amazed.

93.

My first CD, "*Where Can I Go Without You?*" was released in November 2007.

I recorded 10 tunes with Claude on piano, Rick on guitar and vocal duets, Stu on piano, and two other fine musicians, Bob Zotolla and Jerry Sawicki, on trumpet and sax.

At 61 years old, I'd recorded my first CD!

"*Someone to Light up My Life*" and "*Tres Palabras*" were eventually selected for regular radio airplay on my favorite local station, WAVV 101.FM, of Naples/Marco Island. This is a real coup for any working musician.

"*When October Goes*" was also special to me. I'd first heard it in 1984, the year after Jim died. I promised myself if ever I had another chance to record, this would be first on the album. I never ever expected it to be.

Never ever say "Never ever."

94.

By the time I'd become a genuine "recording artist" in 2007, I was booking 35 to 40 musicians with my group, many at Miromar Lakes Beach Clubhouse.

The title song from my first CD, "*Where Can I Go Without You?"* was soon featured in France's *Nina Simone Fan Club Newsletter*!

Nina Simone was an American singer, songwriter, arranger, and pianist who recorded more than 40 albums between 1958 and 1974. Receiving a Grammy Hall of Fame Award in 2000, Simone was a 15-time Grammy Award nominee over the course of her career. In later years she settled in France in 1992 where her music is still popular today. To have my CD, featuring one of her favorite recorded tunes, be selected by her fan club for special mention blew me away!

I'd given the distributor permission to circulate the CD wherever they wished. I developed a website with sound clips, calendar, and photographs from my gigs. It was soon getting thousands of "visits!"

Soon, the Independent Artists Company (*IAC*) picked up two of my tunes that soon began climbing their charts.

"*The Boy from Ipanema*" and "*When October Goes*" climbed well within the magic number of 100 out of the more than 7,000 songs charted.

"*The Boy from Ipanema*," which I sang in both Portuguese and English, would eventually become one of our best sellers. Not especially one of my favorite songs, *Ipanema* was among Claude's and my most commercially successful collaborations. I had more trouble recording that song in English than Portuguese.

I was convinced that once I sang a song in its native language, it became harder to sing it in English! I re-recorded the English chorus of it too many times to recall. It just didn't "feel" right in English anymore!

I kept the promise to myself the year after Jim died in 1983. "*When October Goes*" was first on the CD.

I was floored when the CD started getting attention from some pretty big names. This kind of thing just didn't happen to 61-year-old unknowns. I kept thinking I was dreaming.

In some ways, I was.

95.

I met Jarrod shortly before leaving Connecticut. Both recently widowed, we met at a time of mutual pain and loss. We parted almost as quickly as we met.

He'd given me a dozen yellow roses. I thought it prophetic that they never bloomed.

I moved to Florida. He moved on with life in Connecticut. Years prior he'd been an amateur jazz musician, leaving music early as I did to pursue a more pragmatic career.

I was somewhat disappointed when "the roses never bloomed." But there was something about him that bothered me. I wrote it off to the fact we were both too damaged for anything serious. We were, after all, still grieving.

I suppose some part of my interest in him was that I was looking for a reason to stay in Connecticut. But in my heart, I knew it was time to go.

Jarrod and I occasionally exchanged emails since my move to Florida. He knew I'd resumed singing and asked for a copy of the CD, sending it to well-known broadcaster Dick Robinson. Robinson's *American Standards by the Sea* weekly syndicated radio/TV show was legendary for support of the "Great American Songbook."

Soon I received a phone call from Robinson's production assistant saying that the show would feature my songs on an upcoming program! It was syndicated on 40 radio stations throughout the USA and Bahamas!

Jarrod seemed eager to be a part of what was happening to me. Soon our conversations became more frequent and personal. I thought it was more than just the music. The conversations soon turned to "us."

I was often lonely. I missed my life with Albert. Jarrod was someone I thought I might care about. I suppose I was still seeking a replacement for Al and my lost life in Connecticut.

It would be a while yet before I embraced the fact that Albert would always be in a class by himself.

96.

The package with a handwritten note from Robinson's production assistant arrived in the mail.

"You're going to love this program," was all it said.

I popped the first of the two discs into my car's CD player.

My heart almost stopped when I heard Robinson's opening lines about this "new singer" he'd found.

I pulled the car into a parking lot to absorb it.

I always seemed to be in a car somewhere when I heard a song that made me pull over to the side of the road.

But in this case, the song was mine!

When Robinson's comments about my music segued into "*Where Can I Go Without You?*" I was overwhelmed.

He had devoted almost the entire program to me!

It was almost too much. At 61 years old and with a reasonably level head on my shoulders, I realized why a 19-year-old "overnight success" implodes with the shock of sudden fame.

The next few months would find me struggling to maintain a rational perspective. I wasn't always successful.

97.

The conversations between Jarrod and I grew more intense.

The memory of our brief encounter before I left Connecticut had acquired a rosier patina than reality would ultimately support. But we were living on the unexpired passion of a time when we clung to each other in hopes there really was life after bereavement.

“New love” is sometimes an intoxicating elixir of unrealistic expectations and unfulfilled dreams. It’s not really love at all.

Jarrod spent a few days in Florida, attending several gigs where I was performing.

He was the first man with whom my Florida friends had seen me.

Something still wasn’t right. Was he more interested in the heady world of my music than me? I’d seen that happen before. It was another thing about the business I didn’t like.

The feeling that something wasn’t quite right was prophetic. The fantasy of “us” wouldn’t last. We’d speak a few times after that, but it wasn’t the same.

I wasn’t ready for a serious relationship anyway. It did, however, highlight yet another thing about the music business I never liked.

Some people are more interested in what you do than who you are. The glamour of the entertainment industry draws some people like moths to flame. Music isn't the only business in which it happens, but it does seem especially vulnerable.

Almost everyone dreams of being a "star" in some way. The false hopes, failed dreams, and insincere alliances so many entertainers endure because of it are legion.

As much as I loved the music, I still didn't like the "business" at all.

98.

I was getting invitations and positive critiques from publicists and promoters as far away as Canada and France. A few were legitimate offers suggesting I was a saleable "commodity."

It was sometimes hard to distinguish between scams and legitimate offers. At least, I mused, there were strangers out there who thought my talent good enough to hustle.

Some of my tunes were "spotlighted" on various music websites. Downloads by customers were increasing.

One small record company solicited two of my songs for a promotional CD to be distributed at jazz festivals and trade shows. They got free music. I got free publicity.

I was continuing to book gigs with *AllThatJazz*, rotating musicians for variety. The individual dynamics of each group changed just enough to give regular customers a "new" group each time.

I amassed a personnel file of more than 40 local musicians whom I employed at one time or another. I paid decent wages, including a meal and beverage. I also invited talented amateurs and professionals to "sit in."

My business background helped. Displaying professional signage, flyers with photos and credentials of individual musicians, and engaging in advance promotions, I had learned that most people in the area had no idea the talent around them. No one else was promoting the musicians as I was. I felt they deserved every kudo they got.

I always believed if you take care of your people, they'll take care of you. And they did.

I could choose gigs I wanted because I was lucky enough to be able to work part-time at it. I chose only those gigs that paid well and were bound by contractual agreements. I could hire the best musicians and guarantee them payment even if that gig got cancelled, because I insisted on using contracts with clients. I rarely required musicians to sign a contract however. I trusted them to be there. They never let me down.

I gave them lots of freedom to improvise on the bandstand. I don't believe a singer should sing every song the band plays unless it's a full-blown concert instead of a dinner dance.

I also insisted that our patrons never have to compete with our music for dinner table conversation.

I invited house staff to tell me if the volume was too loud or not loud enough. I had often walked out of a place myself because too-loud music made my eardrums throb.

But the most fun of all was just being *on* the bandstand.

What was happening before and after the gigs was becoming less so.

99.

November 12, 2007

Ms. Kathryn Taubert
Miromar Lakes, Florida, 33913

Dear Kathryn,

Enclosed for your records is the signed copy of your recording contract with D and M Records.

We are so pleased to have you with us and are eagerly looking forward to the production of your first album on our label.

Please keep in touch and let us know of all the exciting things happening with your career and when you are ready to proceed with the production of your album.

Respectfully,

Dave Warren, Senior Producer
D and M Music/D and M Records

The release of "*Where Can I Go Without You?*" resulted in far more attention than I ever expected.

The day I got the letter from *D and M Records* offering me a recording contract was the onset of a whirlwind of activity that introduced me to yet another level of the music business. It was heady, exciting stuff.

Like so much else about the business, it was something of an illusion as well.

D and M Music offered what they claimed to be the best deal for a recording artist, unlike that of the "big record companies." I liked their approach.

Dave Warren was a career musician who made his name and living in Nashville. He'd seen how the artists did all of the work while everyone else got all the money. He wanted to change that. *D and M's* contract was simple, straightforward, and fair. It left a greater share of the proceeds with the artist.

I'd have complete creative control over choice of songs and arrangements. I would also locally produce and record the "master" disc of songs.

D and M would license, duplicate, package, and distribute the CD at their expense. We would share proceeds.

With the *D and M Records* recording contract, my second CD, *"Somewhere in Time,"* was born.

100.

"Can you tell me the name of that Latin rhythm you just played on air?"

I'd been stopped in my tracks yet again in the car by a song I heard on the radio.

I knew I had to sing it. I got the name of it from the station receptionist and searched online for lyrics. There weren't any!

I decided I'd write them. I downloaded a copy to my iPod, listening to it over and over again as the haunting melody "told" me what it wanted to say.

I was a writer before I was a singer, although I'd never written lyrics before. But this song begged for them. Why not, I thought? A lyric is just poetry put to music.

"*Some Other Sunset*" by five-time Grammy nominee composer/conductor/pianist David Benoit was strictly an instrumental until the day I heard it.

David Benoit later called my lyrics "just beautiful."

I wrote them for Jim Holbrook. I never saw him happier than when he was at the helm of a sailboat. We had only just begun before his sudden death at 48.

My new CD would include "*Some Other Sunset*" as well as my own lyrics to two other tunes as well.

For Harold, I wrote lyrics for "*Somewhere in Time*."

For Albert, I wrote them for "*Clair de Lune*," one of my favorite songs of all time.

I had found a way to memorialize those I had loved and lost.

I didn't realize that the writer in me was again awakening. It was only the beginning.

101.

"I want to go back to Texas, Kathryn. I'm getting better. I miss everybody. I'm so bored. I know you have a lot to do and I'm just in the way."

I had never truly convinced mother she was *never* in my way.

I loved having her live with me. Of course it was hard at times, but I enjoyed our times together. Our little drives with the top down and late afternoon dinners were as much fun for me as they were for her. But she needed her old life back. I couldn't convince her it just wouldn't be the same.

I told her she would have to go into the assisted living/nursing care wing, and that her mobility was going to be more limited than before. She said she understood, but I believe the loneliness for her old life was so acute that nothing I could say would change her mind.

I had hoped that in time, she would have realized her going back wasn't a good idea. But the more she talked with family and friends in Galveston, the more she wanted to return.

Although still in physical decline, mother was still of "sound mind." I had to honor her wishes. Her life in Florida had become a series of long and often lonely days punctuated by an hour or two out of the house with me.

I began the process of taking her back to Texas in January of 2007.

My sisters and niece beautifully decorated mother's new room in Edgewater's nursing facility. It wasn't the same as her former apartment in the independent wing, but it was cozy and comfortable. They'd even installed a small refrigerator for her midnight snacks.

Acquiring a new room at Edgewater, arranging the trip with her portable oxygen, packing and shipping her belongings, setting up her new health care arrangements, and turning her room in my home back into a guest room. It was basically the reverse of what I'd done seven months prior when bringing her to Florida. At least she was in better health this time.

I returned to Florida after seeing her settled in her new room at Edgewater. Her initial joy at being back home filled me with hope, but I was still uneasy.

The distance between her former life in Edgewater's independent living facility and her new one in skilled nursing was far greater than a mere walk across the courtyard.

I wouldn't trade anything for the seven months mother was with me in Florida. I had a chance to care for her as she had cared for me through my sometimes difficult years as a child. I helped her recover well enough to live a bit longer. I introduced her to new adventures. I had the opportunity to know her as a friend as well as parent. We had such fun together.

But she also needed to feel needed, even at 93 and in poor health. I don't think she believed I needed her as much as others in the family did.

If she could have had all her family nearby, she would have. But it wasn't possible.

I flew back and forth to Texas several times during her remaining months of life to spend time with her and take care of business.

But an awful tug-of-war over control of her care would soon render me exhausted and regretful at my decision to take her back.

102.

"Mrs. Taubert, your mother fell and broke her back," the nurse said. "We've taken her to the hospital."

It had been a difficult seven months since mother's return to Galveston. The chasm between her expectations and the reality of life back in a Galveston nursing home was just too great.

My role as her fiduciary and health care proxy was difficult to negotiate because of some difficult family dynamics. Mother was caught in the middle, as were her health care providers. Nursing home staff and administrators did their best to navigate that gauntlet, but not always successfully.

The day mother pleaded with me to take her back to Florida almost killed me.

When a nurse located me on a dive trip off the coast of Venezuela to say mother had gone into dangerously severe withdrawal after having had an important medication suddenly discontinued, I initiated serious repercussions at the highest levels of facilities involved in her care.

No one wanted to hurt mother. But misguided intentions can be deadly. It was all about control.

Through it all, mother never seemed to realize how sick she was.

The day she broke her back, she'd either forgotten or refused to call for help before getting out of bed. Her old bones snapped as she slid to the floor.

One day before her 94th birthday, my sweet little Mamma died quietly in her sleep, fulfilling the prophecy of the hospice nurse who told me, "Your mother is waiting for her 94th birthday."

All the family had all just left her room as she lay heavily sedated on morphine. I believe she didn't want us, especially her great grandson Angus, to witness her last breath. She died within minutes of our leaving.

My dear little Mamma was with her beloved husband Lee, once again.

I envied her.

103.

I believe we're here for specific reasons and keep coming back until we get it right.

Perhaps my job this time around is to recover from loss so I can help others do the same. Maybe my experiences will help others know there *is* life after loss.

I've had words roiling around inside in my head as long as I can remember. The idea of a book had been with me for some time.

I had a lot of it already written: emails, notes, and letters from the time Albert was sick and after his death.

But how could I revisit the very places I'd been trying so hard to leave behind for so many years?

It would be hard "going back" again.

I wasn't ready to write a book yet.

104.

"I'm looking for a piano player who does the old standards, jazz, and pop, who can play in any key, and works well with a singer," I said.

Claude was working nightly in Naples. I needed another piano player for my "rotating gigs." There weren't many others besides Claude and Stu with whom I was comfortable working.

"Woody Brubaker," replied the guys almost in unison at Brent's Music Store in Fort Myers.

Rick Howard and I had a gig coming up at Miromar. I wanted piano accompaniment also. I invited Brubaker to sit in with us.

Neither Rick nor I knew him. He worked mostly in and around Fort Myers while we spent most of our time in Naples or Miromar Lakes. We didn't know what to expect, but I figured the guys at Brent's would.

Brubaker was a career musician originally from Ohio. The fact that he was working steadily as a musician without requiring a day job to supplement his income said a lot. The guy must be good.

Shortly before the gig, in walked this short, compact fire-plug of a guy, dressed head-to-foot in black, beret on backwards with a gold chain around his neck. He was, unmistakably, jazz musician Forest "Woody" Brubaker.

Introducing ourselves, I asked how long he'd been a piano player.

"I'm *not* a piano player," he said somewhat abruptly. "I'm a composer, arranger, and play woodwinds. I play piano because that's where the money is."

Sitting down at the keyboard without so much as a question about song, key, tempo, or anything else, Woody segued right in tune with Rick's opening song.

The guy was great!

I'd not only found my piano player, Woody Brubaker would become one of my most reliable and faithful colleagues and friends.

For a guy whose primary instruments were woodwinds, he could do almost anything with the keyboard. He played sax, flute, and clarinet, as well as piano. He worked regularly with saxophone player-singer Skip Haynes, former backup bandleader for the old Pat Boone Show, now living and working in Fort Myers.

Soon I'd be working with both Woody and Skip as well.

Woody was a virtual one-man band with a voice as good as or better than 60's-era vocalist Bobby Darin.

Sometimes acerbic and a little too direct, Woody Brubaker was the opposite of the chronically laidback Claude Rhea.

But, like Claude, Woody had a heart of gold beneath that black outfit and terse manner.

A lot of musicians aren't what they appear to be. Brubaker was no exception. He was a teddy bear masquerading as a bulldozer.

Protecting sometimes tender hearts with *attitude*, artists often defend soft centers against the sometimes brutal world of professional music.

I couldn't believe there were so many incredible musicians in Southwest Florida!

Woody would soon regularly accompany me. We'd remain good friends long after the music stopped.

105.

"I'd like you to meet Kathryn Taubert, Miromar's resident celebrity," said a neighbor introducing me to a new resident as we gathered along the beautiful lakeside bar.

I wanted to disappear. I not only didn't think myself a celebrity, I couldn't believe anyone else did either.

I was performing regularly with my group at Miromar's new Beach Club House, a spectacular place that was winning all sorts of national awards for style and ambience. Miromar developer Margaret Antonier designed it after the beautiful resorts of her youth on the Riviera. I was proud to have a long-running contract performing there with *AllThatJazz*.

I was still swimming laps around the lake several days a week and teaching the occasional swimming and snorkeling lessons for Miromar residents and their families.

But the whole resort virtually glittered with people who'd accomplished far more than I.

"She's also the one who swims with the alligators," said another.

"I heard you carry a machete when you swim!" said one more.

I hadn't seen *that* one coming at all.

"Why don't you want to swim in the pool?" asked the new resident.

By this time I'd developed a regular spiel about my preference for open water swimming, adding to it the fact that alligators are more predictable than falling coconuts. I explained that the dive knife I wore while swimming was to remove the occasional monofilament fishing line tangled in pond weeds that could trap fish and turtles.

I quickly stole a glance at Food and Beverage Assistant Director Dean Kane, hoping somehow he could bail me out of my increasing discomfort with this conversation. He just smiled across the bar and shrugged apologetically as he juggled the 3-deep stack of customers waiting for service. I was on my own.

I was careful not to create conflict for Miromar staff because of my dual status as owner and contract employee. I'd become well-acquainted with Miromar's staff, drawn to this hard-working group of people who helped insure the residents were well attended.

Margaret Antonier had created a resort which was named number one of its kind in the nation by the National Home Builders' Association. Her strict standards were evident in every aspect of the place, extending to the employees who ran the place.

From senior management to groundskeepers, employees of Miromar Lakes Beach and Golf Club were among the best. As Miromar's part-time swimming and snorkeling instructor as well as entertainer, I identified with staff as much as property owners, of which I was also one.

Miromar's employee mantra was the "resident is always right." I didn't want to take advantage of my dual status by asking for favors when confronted by circumstances I was capable of dealing with on my own.

I struggled to make the best of this situation.

Another pause and our newest resident asked me if I had children.

"Not unless you count the four-footed ones," I joked.

People expect a woman my age to have kids and grandkids. There always seems to be the unspoken "Why not?" lurking in their eyes when they discover I don't.

After another awkward silence: "Do you like to cook?"

"I was a pretty good cook before my husband passed away. It's not as much fun cooking for one so now I eat out a lot."

I knew I'd blown it as her eyes glazed over. She had exhausted her questions. She muttered something about my probably not being interested in the Gourmet Cooking Club.

We had nothing in common. As one of the few single women at Miromar, I didn't dare start a conversation with her husband, with whom I probably had a lot more business experience in common about which to chat.

I don't know what she thought. But as a 62-year-old childless, twice-widowed, born-again jazz singer, SCUBA diver, and sometimes-swimming instructor who routinely swam miles in lakes known to have a small 'gator population, I felt even more isolated than ever.

Throw in a case of barely contained Tourette syndrome with 30,000 or so tics a day, I was becoming acutely aware of the fact that I really was a fish out of water at Miromar.

I loved the place. People were mostly friendly, and I made good friends there. But I felt more comfortable in what I'd naively believed had been the relative anonymity of a wetsuit and baseball cap as I strode around the 10,000 square foot "infinity pool" on my way to the lake.

If some thought me their "resident celebrity," with yet others assuming the knife I carried was defense against *alligators*, what *else* must they think of me?

I was starting to feel entirely too visible for comfort.

At times like that, I missed the peace and quiet of life in the woods more than ever. The lovely Connecticut summer evenings, the sounds of the owls hooting in the night, and the far off yip-yipping of coyotes coming home from the hunt in the wee hours of the dawn - how I yearned for that at times.

As much as I loved Miromar and my new life in Southwest Florida, I missed my home in Connecticut. Most of all, I missed Albert.

No matter how far I'd managed to come, some part of me was still at home on Greenleaf Farms with him. Would it always be that way?

106.

I was shocked the day I "Googled" myself.

In spite of my basic need for privacy, I'd be lying if I said I didn't derive a certain pleasure from recognition too. It's part of what propels people into the entertainment business. I just didn't seem to be able to stand it for very long.

"*Where Can I Go Without You*?" was showing up on more and more websites. Downloads by fans kept popping up from as far away as the Seychelles Islands, France, Japan, Germany, and the Netherlands, among others.

On that day I saw my name listed as a nominee in something called *The International Jazz Awards!*

The link led me to a Los Angeles-based website promoting an event to be held that summer at a premier Hollywood venue and hosted by a well-known entertainer. Associated events promised an Oscar-like glamour to the event.

I was listed as one of five nominees for *best female vocal in the Latin-Afro Cuban category*. It had to be for the tunes Claude and I recorded on "*Where Can I Go Without You*?"

I called the producers. It was legitimate, although it seemed a bit disorganized. Having planned large events myself when employed with the March of Dimes, I could tell they were a little new at producing this kind of a thing. They certainly seemed well-intentioned however.

Nominees in other categories were among the biggest names in music. The other four in my category were *real* Latinas, Cubans with fabulous songs and professionally-produced videos online.

There was no way I'd win this.

The *IJA* was scheduled a mere few months hence. Short notice might work for a relative unknown like me, but not the biggest names in music.

Just being nominated by producers in the Los Angeles entertainment industry was so heady I just went with it. They weren't asking me for money and even promised to reimburse me for my airline tickets, so I figured they weren't scammers.

Suddenly there was a buzz after I'd included the news on my website and in regular fan updates.

One day I got a call from *Naples Daily News* reporter Leslie Williams. The local newspaper wanted to do a story on me.

107.

“How come nobody ever heard of it?” he asked cynically after I’d mentioned the nomination to another local musician.

It was a fair question, but lately I’d been feeling as though some local musicians weren’t exactly enthusiastic about the attention I was getting.

I couldn’t blame them. I’d come sailing back into music after decades away, with little real experience, few credentials, and virtually no vocal training.

Suddenly my CD was getting a lot of attention, I had a growing local following, recording contract for another CD, and the “International Jazz Award” nomination.

I could understand how some musicians might resent that. They’d worked hard their entire lives without as much recognition as I was getting. I hadn’t paid the dues they had.

Suddenly I was being solicited for interviews from local news media, magazines, my college alma mater, and hometown newspaper.

Most people had no idea the reason I was doing all this. Frankly, at that time, I’m not sure I fully realized it either.

I just knew I was feeling better about life. My grief and loneliness for Albert and the life I had lost didn’t hurt quite so much anymore. Music was again helping me heal.

I was a Johnny-come-lately with a business background and some musical talent. But talent isn't always enough. Knowing how to position it can mean the difference between making it and disappearing from the scene. So many extraordinary musicians don't have the right skills to promote themselves.

I was getting attention in part because I had some of those skills due to my business experience.

But even that couldn't overcome the biggest impediment to taking my music even further.

Me.

108.

"Kathryn, are you going to sing tonight?" the patron asked as I walked past their table. "We're leaving soon to meet friends and we'd really like to hear you sing before we go."

It was spring of 2008 and I'd been sitting in regularly with this particular band from time to time when not working with *AllThatJazz*. They were terrific musicians playing in a funky little hole-in-the-wall that reminded me of a New York jazz club.

"I'll be happy to if I'm invited," I replied.

I never assumed anything, although the bandleader always invited me to sit in when I showed up. Soon, regular customers began asking for me. I'd been performing a couple of years by now. Many people remembered me from working with Claude. Others were fans of *AllThatJazz* and knew I sometimes jammed with this group.

I tried to hire this particular musician to work with me from time to time, but he didn't seem very eager to do so. I figured he was just too busy on his own.

Taking a seat near the bandstand, I watched uneasily as the woman and her companion asked the bandleader to let me sing before they left.

I thought he looked a little irritated, but after finishing his current tune, he called me up.

The woman then asked if I could sing her favorite tune as I walked past their table. Knowing it well, I told her I'd be happy to do it.

Handing me the microphone, the bandleader almost hissed: "So you're taking requests now?"

His displeasure rang loud and clear even as I hoped it was my imagination.

I was never quite sure what he thought about me. He was a wonderful, well-trained, credentialed musician.

I once asked him why he didn't hire me for one of his own gigs.

"We'll talk it about one day," he said, but we never did. He was always cordial, inviting me to the bandstand, even when he stopped inviting others.

But that night I sensed something cold and distant. I didn't feel welcome anymore.

I never went back.

109.

"So how did you become a jazz singer?" the pretty young reporter asked.

I met the *Naples Daily News* reporter, Leslie Williams, at a local diner for the interview. She was good at her job, putting me at ease immediately with her relaxed manner and open-ended questions.

We spent about an hour together, chatting as two friends might. She asked if she could take photos during my next recording session.

A few days later Leslie and a photojournalist showed up to record Stu, Rick, and I working on "*Some Other Sunset*," for my new CD.

A few days later the *Naples Daily News* published a full-page spread with photos! Leslie did a great job writing. But I learned why entertainers usually provide their own photos. I always took horrible pictures. Being photographed was almost as painful for me as hearing myself sing. I may be a little shy at times, but I'm still vain.

The *News* did print one photo I liked. It was a profile shot of my recording "*Some Other Sunset*." I was in another place at that moment. Some tunes transported me. When they did, I was lost in another world.

I was glad they'd printed my comments about the musicians with whom I was working too. Without them, I'd still be warbling alone in the shower.

I gave special mention to Claude in the article. Without his urging, none of this would have happened.

I recalled him listening one night in 2007 to our final release of my first CD. He was the one who taught me the title song, "*Where Can I Go Without You?*" after playing it one night at Truluck's.

Riveted by the lovely melody, I asked him what it was.

"The next tune you're gonna' learn, baby."

That recording would go on to become one of our best sellers.

The day "*Where Can I Go Without You?*" was released, Claude, Rick, and drummer John Lamb and I were waiting to go on stage at a local jazz concert.

Claude sat in his SUV smoking his ever-present cigarette, listening to the CD on his tape deck. I held my breath, glancing at him out of the corner of my eye, watching for the slightest expression.

"That's good, Songbird. Real good," he finally said.

That was as close to a foot-stomping cheer as Claude Rhea ever got.

It was good enough for me.

110.

I was a little uneasy about The International Jazz Awards. It was late spring of 2008 and the event was just around the corner. I still hadn't received further details from producers. That didn't bode well.

I had spoken with the producers and publicists personally. It was a legitimate attempt to produce an event that would, for the first time, be devoted exclusively to jazz artists. They didn't ask nominees to do anything but show up. In fact, the lead producer even asked me if I would be willing to perform one of my tunes on stage.

She especially liked "*The Boy From Ipanema*" with Claude on piano and me singing in Portuguese and English.

It was too good to be true. The event was postponed, then eventually put on hold indefinitely. I'd planned enough events in my fundraising career to know that getting attention in any kind of event generally requires name recognition. If the "big names" didn't appear, the event wouldn't get nearly the media buzz required.

The *IJA* producers had dreamed of producing this event for years. Like so many people in the arts, however, they were good at their craft, but not necessarily at the business end of it.

I surmised they weren't getting the sponsors they needed because they hadn't given the "big names" sufficient time or incentive to attend.

Nobody was going to pay a hefty ticket price just to see an unknown singer from Florida perform. I was one of the lesser known of the dozens of well-known headliners.

The International Jazz Awards website remains online, the hopes of its producers still apparent. I hope someday they'll realize their dream.

Just being *nominated* was enough for me. Even if it didn't come to fruition, the process of being "almost there" was rewarding.

But it was also the perfect example of the fleeting, heady, illusory nature of the entertainment business.

Some part of me was almost relieved when the event was cancelled. Along with the increasing recognition was a growing sense of unease. It was that "visibility" thing again.

111.

"Don't hire that guitar player again," he said, calling me the morning after the gig.

"Why not?" I asked.

"I don't like the chords he played last night."

Part of my job as *AllThatJazz* owner, operator, and lead singer was "personnel management." A lot of that required listening to the complaints among musicians about each other.

Artists can sometimes be edgy and easily offended. It's an ego-driven business, which is one of the reasons fans hear such incredible music. The very thing that makes musicians good at what they do is the same one that gets in the way. Sensitivity.

My business background had prepared me for it. Personnel management can be terribly frustrating.

My policy was to ask the lead instrumentalist, usually the piano player, which instruments he would like to work with on the gig.

This usually worked pretty well, although there were times I had to override their wishes due to the unavailability of a specific musician.

Without exception, all the musicians I booked were professionals. When they were on the bandstand with someone they didn't particularly like or care for, no one ever knew it but me. At times, competition between them produced even more spectacular music.

It would have been easier for me to stick with one group of musicians, but the fans loved mixing it up.

Frankly, so did I. I probably sacrificed some of the smooth, almost intuitive synergy that occurs after working together exclusively for a while. But I was customer-focused as well. No matter how good the musicians, customers always want variety.

AllThatJazz gave it to them. Clients, customers, and musicians knew our standards were high. They'd get what was promised, and more.

It took a toll on me, however. All I wanted to do was sing once in a while. Instead, I ended up running a small business.

If you want to play, you've got to pay. I guess I was paying some dues after all. But the cost to me was getting higher all the time.

112.

"Galveston, Texas, faces complete inundation from Hurricane Ike, and those who stay behind will face certain death," the National Hurricane Center said.

It was September 2008, almost exactly one year after mother passed away. I'd been glued to CNN watching the inexorable advance of what would become the third costliest hurricane to hit the United States.

Galveston was my hometown. Mother was thankfully not going to suffer what would eventually happen to it and the Edgewater Retirement Community where she had lived. However, my eldest sister Dorothy and her husband Alex would suffer terribly.

The preceding months had been increasingly difficult for them. Alex's declining health suggested rapidly advancing dementia. Having no children or other family nearby to help, Dorothy was struggling to care for him alone.

I tried to help long distance, often finding myself agonizing over the lack of adequate medical attention to the seriousness of Alex's condition.

Dorothy wasn't in the best of health either. Ten years my senior, she was struggling to handle the increasingly difficult task of caring for a husband who would suddenly end up 400 miles away from home without a clue where he was.

Alex's doctor seemed unwilling or unable to diagnose his condition and initiate treatment. One day Alex disappeared in the car. We had no idea where to look for him. Dorothy contacted the Texas "Silver Alert" program, but it would take some time to get his details into the statewide system for locating missing senior citizens with mental impairments. Although he had yet to be formally diagnosed with dementia, he was clearly confused and at risk of harm.

The day after he disappeared, I got a call from a convenience store clerk in Quemado, Texas, some 400 miles away from Galveston. He'd run the car onto a curb and not knowing where he was, wandered into the store. I was the last person to call his phone when the clerk noted my number and called me back.

"There's an Alex here with me who says he doesn't know where he is," she said.

Somehow, Alex had apparently taken a wrong turn in San Antonio on his way to California, we later believed, where his mother had lived before she passed away.

He ended up in the small Tex-Mex border town where, thanks to the kindness of the residents of Quemado and Eagle Pass, TX, we were able to finally get him home the following day. Members of the largely Hispanic community rallied behind us in ways for which Dorothy and I will be forever grateful.

Due to the relative lack of public facilities and transportation, the convenience store clerk, county sheriff, Silver Alert social worker, and owners of a small motel in Eagle Pass watched over Alex until we were able to get him by bus to San Antonio where he was met by our cousin, Melinda McDonald Lange. Melinda traveled with him the rest of the way to meet Dorothy in Houston. This event was a precursor of even worse things to come.

Increasingly concerned about Dorothy and Alex, I was just about to book a plane for Texas when the monster hurricane took direct aim at the island.

Dorothy and Alex hadn't made plans to evacuate. Two days before Hurricane Ike struck, Alex was finally diagnosed with dementia by a specialist I'd located by telephone.

Neuropsychologist Dr. Vicki Soukup agreed to see Alex on short notice. His regular physician had diagnosed Alex as "psychotic," when his rapidly declining mental status was due to Lewy body and Alzheimer's dementias.

Alex also had blood clots in his legs and bleeding in his stomach. Mere hours were all that remained before evacuation from the deadly hurricane became impossible.

Paul Fuhrhop, my first husband, remained a family friend. Marious, as we knew him, was like family. The dissolution of our marriage in 1972 had been the result of the bittersweet realization it simply wasn't going to work. But even as our divorce was being finalized, he was helping me move and we were attending movies together. We parted as friends.

He remarried, losing his wife almost 30 years later. We reconnected during mother's last days, during which time he slipped quietly back into our family as though he'd never left.

Our relationship had evolved into something more like siblings than former spouses. He was a good man. We'd just been two kids who didn't have a clue about what we really wanted. Now, however, we were adults and genuine friends with a long history.

Although we had virtually no contact for decades, Galveston's "small-town" atmosphere was such that one would hear the whereabouts of the other from time to time.

Dorothy was desperate. Alex's combative, delusional state rendered him unable as well as unwilling to evacuate. Paul was headed to Galveston to board up his sister's home. I gratefully accepted his offer to help Dorothy and Alex as well. It was quickly apparent Alex couldn't tolerate standing in line waiting for a bus with several hundred other evacuees under the hot Texas sun.

Paul loaded them into his SUV and left for Houston. I found what must have been one of the last hotel rooms available there. Evacuees had taken virtually every other room for a hundred miles.

113.

Hurricane Ike inundated Galveston, rendering 80 percent of the infrastructure damaged or destroyed. Without water, plumbing, or emergency services, the hospital would remain closed.

While Dorothy and Alex's home was spared, they couldn't return. Alex was too sick and there were no medical services available.

When the hotel ran out of food, water, and electricity, Dorothy's high school classmate, Ethel Lou Graves Macbeth, took them away to her home in East Texas. When the airports reopened, I arranged for them to fly to Fort Myers.

Dorothy and Alex would live with me at Miromar Lakes until we could decide what to do.

It was a frantic, precarious time. Alex needed immediate medical attention. They had left Galveston with little more than the clothes on their backs and a bag of medicines. Their medical and legal records were under six feet of water back on the Island.

The next months were a blizzard of doctors, laboratory tests, treatments, and worries over what was happening back on the Island to their home and friends. They had no car in Florida. Dorothy, always a nervous driver, wouldn't rent one. She was barely able to do much more than attend to Alex's rapidly declining condition.

I drove them everywhere and helped arrange appointments with doctors, lawyers, and health care facilities.

I took them out to eat, to my gigs, and Miromar special events to try to cheer them up a bit. But the strain was becoming unbearable for all of us.

Alex's dementia resulted in hallucinations and paranoid delusions as his health further declined.

Dorothy was at risk almost as much as Alex because of the strain of trying to take care of Alex during the months before Hurricane Ike. She had neglected her own health in the process. They'd been ripped away from everything they knew. I was all they had.

My doctor, Gary Pynckel, took them on as patients the day after they arrived in Florida, exhausted and confused. Dorothy still carried the box of syringes a nurse in Galveston had precipitously dropped off at their home the day they left with instructions to "give Alex one shot a day for blood clots."

A nurse also staying at their Houston hotel during the hurricane showed Dorothy how to administer the injections.

Dorothy had reverted to basic survival mode. She was afraid to dispose of what little they had in the event it might be needed. When with her friend in East Texas, she refused to throw away a paper cup thinking they might need it. She and Alex were both suffering and emotionally fragile.

The next months were difficult for all of us. Alex's rapidly deteriorating condition required his admission to an assisted living facility for "wandering" Alzheimer's patients.

Medications brought back some of what he'd lost. Before treatment, he was sometimes confused about who I was. One day he accused me of being "some lawyer," or "that realtor" trying to take their home away from them!

Another day in the doctor's office he wondered where Dorothy was even as she sat next to him.

Alex had always been kind to me. I'd known him since I was 18 years old. After Jim died, he quietly assured me he would help any way he could. I knew he meant it.

After almost 45 years, Alex and Dorothy had an unbreakable bond, even though their somewhat non-traditional marriage had at times been difficult.

Dr. Pynckel immediately issued orders for both of them.

Our sister Mary lost everything she had in the storm. Although my relationship with her had always been difficult, I admired her ability to make do with less. Minimalist by nature, the storm was just another opportunity for her to relocate, which she often did.

The 10 years in age difference between Dorothy and I complicated things. We were strangers in many ways.

While Dorothy was struggling to care for Alex, I was struggling to care for both of them. Still managing *AllThatJazz* and performing, recording songs for my new CD "*Somewhere In Time*" for its imminent release, and involved in a host of other activities, I was rapidly becoming depleted.

Living with a desperately ill family member requiring round-the-clock care is exhausting. I'd done it now three times in seven years. Dorothy's emotional state understandably often rendered her anxious and combative. I tried being patient, but found myself losing ground.

Once again facing the terminal illness of someone I loved, I was barely treading water at times.

I attributed my recent headaches to the stress. My dentist discovered seven fractured teeth from grinding them!

Something had to give.

When I read Liz Moretti's email asking me if I knew anything about Claude being in a coma in the hospital, it did.

114.

I thought it one of the most beautiful ballads ever written, and Claude played it masterfully.

The first time I performed "*How Do You Keep the Music Playing?*" was at Miromar's Blue Water Beach Grill. He'd been performing this tune for some time. I really wanted to sing it. He put a *lot* of feeling into it. I didn't want to take that away from him.

Accompanying a singer requires focusing on the singer's style and, in the process, suppressing some of the musician's own ability to improvise. I hesitated to ask him.

The gig that night was about over. As he began playing this beautiful Michel Legrand tune, I hesitantly asked if I could sing it.

"Sure, baby," he said, not hesitating at all.

It soon became one of our most requested tunes.

In late October 2008, Claude and I recorded "*How Do You Keep the Music Playing?*" for my new CD.

It would later become one of the two tunes that, figuratively speaking, took us to mainland China!

I still see him bent over the keyboard during that recording session, coaxing music out of it as only he could.

But he had seemed a little down to me then, as he had during the preceding few months. He was working pretty steadily, but not happily. We hadn't had much opportunity to work together lately. He had only recently told me about a new gig he was lining up that he hoped we'd could do together. I was all for it.

"I miss workin' with you, baby," he said. "I want to get back to our kind of music."

I missed working with Claude, too. He was always there when I needed him to lead me, and follow when it was time. He made certain tunes "ours," as no other accompaniment could. I felt safe both personally and professionally with him. It was so easy working with him.

I never felt anything from Claude Rhea but support for my efforts and pleasure at my success.

He was always proud of me. Claude didn't have a jealous, resentful bone in his body.

The man had more success with music than most would ever know. But he never boasted. The closest he ever got to that was handing me that copy of ***Sites and Sounds of Savannah Jazz***.

But the business had cost him a lot. His latest CD, "*Well-Seasoned*," with his original tunes, wasn't selling as well as hoped. Claude's "smooth jazz" scores were as good as they come. But the genre was dying, as were the old standards he and I did together.

Our audiences were dying as well, along with many of the older musicians who entertained them.

As he finished recording "*How Do You Keep the Music Playing?*" that day, he gave me a kiss on the cheek before turning to leave. I saw a tired man, saddened by recent news that a close friend was dying of cancer. But there was something else I couldn't quite define.

I didn't know what to do for him.

Neither of us realized we'd just finished the last song Claude Rhea would ever record.

A few weeks later, "*Somewhere in Time*" was completed. But before I got it to Claude, I received Liz's email.

115.

Registered under his legal name, Claude Rhea Thomas, I found him comatose in the hospital after a massive cerebral aneurysm the night before.

I knew enough about his condition to know he was already gone. His daughter Syrana had arrived to take charge of his care. A duplicate of her father, seeing her caused me to catch my breath.

I didn't have the heart to tell her the signs of recovery she thought she saw the next two weeks were reflexive responses of a dying body and a desperate need to believe her Daddy would return.

In a matter of moments after life support was removed, Claude Rhea Thomas passed away. He was 64 years old.

He died almost exactly four years to the day I first met him at Truluck's piano bar.

Claude had given me back music, encouraged and supported me as only a kindred spirit can.

He patiently taught me to sing again, urging me on with his gentle manner and good natured urging.

He never judged, criticized, demeaned, resented, or uttered an unkind word. He helped me find my way out of my grief while managing his own.

My friend, mentor, teacher, and *brother* was gone. For me, the music would never be the same.

116.

The holidays that year were a mixed bag. Although Alex's condition improved since moving to assisted living, his and Dorothy's lives were still in turmoil.

Far away from their home with only me for support, Dorothy struggled with what to do about their Galveston property, sitting unoccupied and in disrepair. Our lives were a daily struggle against the inexorable advance of Alex's dementia.

A freedom-loving man of Eastern European origins, Alex always railed at any kind of confinement.

Dorothy, accustomed to living apart from him for long periods, now spent virtually every day assisting in his care. He felt increasingly trapped in a place not of his choosing, too sick to understand why.

I was once again merely putting one foot in front of the other, doing what had to be done, losing myself temporarily in volunteer work or my remaining *AllThatJazz* contractual obligations.

I was losing interest in the latter, however, and the hassle that went with it.

It didn't help that shortly after Claude's death, we also lost two other fine musicians: former Jack Jones drummer Jim Blakemore and Tommy Dorsey alumnus Sal Sparrazza. Both succumbed to illness and old age.

Musicians of their caliber were dying like flies around me. They had become friends as well as colleagues. During the next few months there would be several memorial services. Claude's drew at least 200 people at Truluck's where we held a special "Claude Rhea Night."

The place was crowded in a way not seen since he'd left. I had Stu strip the vocals from our recordings of four of the tunes Claude and I had performed so I could sing along with him one last time at the piano bar.

The Jazz Society of Savannah held a concert in Claude's honor that was attended by hundreds of former colleagues, family, fans, and friends.

Four of us from Southwest Florida made the trip. I had a chance to get to know my friend Claude through the eyes of his former high school athletic chums, teachers, family, and his own musical mentors.

I sang two of the tunes we recorded together with the band of extraordinary jazz musicians that donated their time for his memorial. I gave copies of my CDs with our recordings to his family.

I still had Woody, Rick, Skip, Stu, and others, but Claude's death affected me more than I realized.

With everything else going on, I felt as though I was detached somehow, floating off to a place from which I might not return.

Preparing for a January concert in Miami for my *AllThatJazz* septet on top of everything else further depleted me.

"Somewhere In Time" was garnering attention, although not as much as it might have had I done more to promote it.

D and M Music was struggling to make it in the Internet world of self-publishing and voracious competition. Although their business model was an idea whose time had come, producers Dave and Mary Warren were tired of the struggle too. Soon they would close the doors of *D and M Records* to return to publishing. Within three years, they would own several Midwestern newspapers.

While they fulfilled their contractual obligations to me, neither of us had the heart to promote my new CD any further.

Dave, Mary, and I would remain friends. In some other time and place, we'd have made it work. In this one, however, it wasn't meant to be.

Few find genuine security in the music business. I'd accomplished much of what I had almost by accident. It wasn't my career as it had been for the others with whom I worked however.

For me, music had been *therapy*.

Claude's death changed the music scene for me. And when I no longer felt the need for therapy, it was time to move on.

117.

It was January 2009 when Jim Collison told me he thought it was time we finally met face-to-face. We'd been talking a lot again lately. He called to console me after Claude's death two months prior. By this time Jim was almost entirely free of the terrible vertigo he'd suffered because of the accident he had shortly before he first wrote to me.

He was planning to work again, travel the world, and volunteer his time and efforts helping others. Volunteering was one of the many things we had in common.

He sounded more positive about the future than I'd ever heard him.

Even though our communications had become sporadic the preceding few years, he was always there with supportive emails and the occasional thoughtful little gift.

He stopped calling around the time I'd been seeing Jarrod, saying later he hadn't wanted to interfere.

Now we were speaking regularly again. When I told him what I was planning to do, he was among the first to enthusiastically support it. He'd done similar things himself.

I was going to Africa to live for five weeks with the Ewe Tribe in southeastern Ghana. And I was going alone.

118.

"You're doing what?" she stammered in disbelief.

I'd just told Dorothy of my plans for Africa under the auspices of the Global Volunteer Network of New Zealand.

"I'm going to Ghana in July to help members of the Ewe Tribe in an economic development program."

"Oh my God, Kathryn. You're going to come back with worms in your eyeballs!"

And so it would be for the next six months. Most people would react either with horror or speculation about my sanity.

Soon, questions put to me evolved from the earlier "Why don't you want to swim in a pool" and "Aren't you worried about the alligators" to "Why don't you just volunteer around here somewhere?"

I felt as though I were losing myself to the demands of my life at that time. I wanted an escape, if only temporary, to something that felt more "real" to me.

Losing Albert and my life in my beloved Connecticut, relocating to Florida, performing, recording, teaching swimming lessons, organizing charity events, and taking care of mother, Dorothy, and Alex, all while trying to rebuild my life, had taken its toll. It was eight years since Albert died and although I had moved on in ways I never could have anticipated, I didn't feel "grounded."

One minute I was on cloud nine. The next I was agonizing over dying loved ones, suffering fractured teeth and losing myself in the demands of the merry-go-round of highs and lows. The years since moving to Florida had been wonderful in many ways, but I felt as though I was getting off track again. I needed to get my feet back on the ground.

Still sad over my mother's death and the increasingly deteriorating relationships with members of my family back in Texas, the loss of Claude and other musician friends, the aftermath of Hurricane Ike, and Alex's terrible decline into Alzheimer's disease was draining.

Ever since mother first took me to the Red Cross to roll bandages when I was 10 years old, volunteering had been a significant part of my life. It always helped me put my own life in perspective. I'd met some of my best friends through volunteer work. Volunteer work had done as much for me as it had those for whom I was volunteering.

The growing feeling of wanting to go to a place I'd never been on behalf of people I'd never even heard of before was as close to "bailing out" of my own life as my pragmatic nature could imagine. Somehow I knew it would help me get my own life back on track.

I started researching volunteer vacations on the Internet. Dozens of websites offered such excursions all over the world, lasting from one week to years.

I thought I might go to Brazil because I loved the music.

I'd never been to China so I thought I might go there.

I loved Hispanic culture and spoke a little of the language, so I contemplated a trip to Central or South America.

My search eventually led me to the Global Volunteer Network's (GVN) Community Service Program in Ghana.

I didn't even know where Ghana was.

But the more I learned, the more it seemed to be what I was seeking.

I wanted to stay long enough to actually accomplish something. This program lasted about a month.

The Village of Abutia-Kloe in the Ho District of southeastern Ghana needed help with their Community Based Organization's mission to make life better for themselves and their children. GVN offered more than just "vacations." They provided genuine opportunities to do serious humanitarian work. This program sought volunteers willing and able to take leadership roles, traveling alone to remote corners of this West African nation about which I knew virtually nothing.

It was 10 days from the time I first conceived the idea to the moment I booked the trip. Like so many other spontaneous decisions I'd made in the past, this one just felt *right*.

119.

I'd never been to Africa.

I had traveled, but nothing like the trip which I was about to undertake.

I had volunteered at just about everything one could. I'd even been a nonprofit executive for the March of Dimes for 10 years.

But all my volunteer and employment in the nonprofit sector had been in the USA. The closest I'd got to living with an indigenous people was the week Albert and I spent on the Blackfeet Reservation in Browning, Montana, the week after we married. I think that whet my appetite for something really different. It had been almost 20 years since that experience, but I never forgot it.

I was comfortable in my ability to take a leadership role and travel alone. But although I sang in four languages, I spoke only English fluently.

I didn't know what language Ghanaians spoke.

I didn't even know how to correctly pronounce "*Ghanaian.*"

It didn't matter. I *knew* I could do it.

But was I eligible? I was three years older than GVN's upper age limit. (The organization would eventually relax that criteria with appropriate medical releases.)

I called the Africa program coordinator to ask if GVN would waive the age limit. I was healthy, fit, and of sound mind, although some of my friends would have questioned that last one.

After completing the necessary paperwork and a few more phone and email exchanges, GVN waived the age restriction and I signed up for the trip.

It was one of those decisions that seemed right even before the idea was entirely formed. Even a few short weeks before conceiving the idea, I never anticipated I would end up doing something this bold.

Never ever say "Never ever."

120.

"I wish I could go with you," said Jim when I first told him I was going to Africa. "I'm proud of you. I think it's going to be life-changing for you. I want to hear all about it."

His faith in me was heartening. So many people were skeptical, even afraid for me. At times it made me wonder if I was out of my mind. Jim's faith and encouragement was yet another similarity between him and Albert.

Although I never had the chance to show Al all the things I could do, I had no doubt he would have encouraged me in exactly the same way. He might even have gone with me!

Jim and I were planning to meet for the first time in the spring. It was late February 2009. I was going to Ghana at the end of June. We wanted to meet before I left.

We were thinking it would be somewhere in the middle of the country, in a place neither of us had been.

I was almost afraid of it, however, so I put if off. I was still busy with what was left of my music obligations, plans for the trip to Ghana, and looking after Dorothy and Alex. Alex was declining more tragically every day. Dorothy, while stoic most of the time, had emotional meltdowns not unexpected when watching someone you love virtually "disappear" before your eyes. Alzheimer's is a horrible disease.

I'd known Jim Collison for 4 years. Although we'd never actually met, he was important to me. But I had some concerns.

How much of my interest in meeting was his resemblance to Albert? It was enough to compel me, certainly. But I had grown to accept the fact that there would never be another Al Taubert.

The traits Jim shared with Al were what I sought most in a healthy relationship. I convinced myself it was those traits I was seeking in another union, not Albert himself. Jim had more of them than any man I'd met since Al died.

He had helped me process my losses by encouraging me to talk about them. But I wanted to meet him for who he was as much as for what he'd done for me.

He wasn't particularly awed by the attention I received in music. We'd gotten to know each other before that happened. I knew he cared about me for who I was outside the spotlight. That was important to me.

This was also a man, like Albert, of whom I could be proud. His own accomplishments exceeded mine. He was not a man easily intimidated by anyone or anything, nor did I ever feel he needed to "compete" with me in any way. I never wanted to outshine anyone. I was content in the shadows of a caring partner, accomplished in his own right.

Whatever might happen between Jim Collison and I, once we met, would happen because we were both old enough to appreciate our individuality as well as whatever potential we might have for becoming true partners in a relationship.

But before I had the chance to make arrangements to meet him, I received his awful news.

"Kathryn, maybe it's a good thing we didn't meet. The cancer has returned, and it's inoperable."

121.

I hadn't been to San Francisco since a 1979 business trip not long before I'd met and married Jim Holbook. I would spend a magical weekend in the "City by the Bay," staying a few days beyond my meetings, exploring the city by trolley and Fisherman's Wharf on foot. I'd never forgotten it.

Not long out of Texas, it was the beginning of my travels, the extent to which I never imagined growing up on Galveston Island and the family farm in Texas.

If someone told me at that time about the turns my life would take over the next 30 years, I'd have thought them delusional. Then I might have crawled under the bed and stayed there.

Or, perhaps not. I've lost a lot in my life, but I've also been blessed with more than most people could ever imagine.

Losing is part of life. The more we truly live, the more we risk losing.

I've lived a lot. I've traveled widely, had wonderful careers, met many fine people and made good friends. I've done lots of interesting things, and had two good marriages with wonderful husbands. Even the marriage that didn't work out ended in a lifelong friendship. I was blessed with parents I'd have chosen for myself had I been given the opportunity before birth. I've had opportunities about which many can only dream.

These thoughts and more were going through my head as the plane landed on the tarmac in San Francisco. Jim told me not to come because he was failing fast, but I insisted. I'd made arrangements to see him just before leaving for Ghana at the end of June, 2009.

I knew our first meeting would be our last. I wanted to immerse myself in Africa not long after, distracting myself from the inevitable pain of yet another loss.

Stepping off the bus that brought me from the airport to the village at the base of the mountain upon which he lived, I found his tall, still-handsome form awaiting me with open arms.

The connection between us in person was as immediate and profound as it had been through our correspondence and phone calls.

My heart ached as he gently embraced me.

Another time, another place, another lifetime, that hug would have been merely the first of countless others.

But it was too late for us this time around.

We spent the next few days in intimate conversation. I met his lovely daughter Ursula who drove us to a party along the magnificent northern California coastline. There we mingled with their friends, as though everything were fine. I overheard someone whisper how fast he had declined. To me, however, he was the man in an earlier photo he'd sent, standing by his airplane. Tall, strong, and handsome, and ready to go on yet another adventure.

His pain was increasing. He couldn't walk without assistance. He slept a great deal. I sat by his bedside and held his hand as we talked.

I'd sit on the porch overlooking San Francisco Bay in the dawn. California had always felt slightly "alien" to me. But during those few days, it felt almost like home.

It wasn't the place. It was the *company.*

Jim would awaken and I'd fix breakfast for us both. We'd talk some more. At times, in the dark and in companionable silence, we imagined what might have been as we quietly watched the lights of that magnificent city across the bay.

There were tears.

I could have loved this man. Perhaps some part of me already did.

The day I left him in front of his home is still fixed in my memory. He wanted to accompany me to the airport. I knew it would be too hard on both of us. I wanted to remember him standing there, as he insisted on doing, with his cane instead of a walker.

It was happening, yet *again*. But I had to deal with it.

Mostly prepared after four months of planning, I still had much to do before leaving the following week for

Ghana. My trip to see Jim would be our first and last, although I told him I'd be back when I returned from Africa.

We both knew I wouldn't.

Jim Collison passed away the second week of my stay in Ghana.

The email from his daughter told me she believed he'd held on just long enough to meet me, and to see me off on my trip of a lifetime.

Jim went to Ghana with me. His encouragement from the outset helped me realize I could do it and come back better for it.

He was right. It changed my life.

AFTERWORD

It seemed as though I had barely stepped onto the plane leaving San Francisco when I stepped off a plane in Accra, the capital city of Ghana.

I spent the next five weeks immersed in a culture I never knew existed until a few short months before. The Ewe people of Abutia-Kloe welcomed me like long-lost family.

A few months before, Leslie Williams (Hale), the reporter from the *Naples Daily News,* who had written the article about me asked if I'd be willing to send the *News* a series of articles on my African experiences.

I couldn't stop writing after arriving in Ghana, even more overwhelmed with amazing sights, sounds, and experiences than I expected. The *News* would eventually publish seven of those articles.

In 2012, I would publish a book, ***Yevu (White Woman): My Five Weeks with the Ewe Tribe in Ghana, West Africa.***

I returned to the USA a more grounded woman. For the first time in a long while, I knew precisely where I was going and what I needed to do to get there.

I loved Southwest Florida, but I knew I wasn't meant to remain.

I had been living in a beautiful place with wonderful new friends, accomplishing good works as well as answering some old questions about music, and myself.

Most importantly, I had truly healed from Al's loss. When we're drowning, we become very self-centered, struggling for survival. I'm a bit embarrassed about the self-centered focus of this book. But I hope there are things in my story that might help others.

Most people had no idea the depth of my grief when Al died. But as I healed, I learned to embrace his continuing *presence* in my life. We never really lose those we love. It just takes time to realize and accept that fundamental truth of the absence of our loved ones, and our need to go on without them. That doesn't mean they aren't still with us.

I also let go of my guilt because I hadn't pursued the issue of Al's not having a CT scan soon enough to reveal the metastatic bain tumor. Even with an 80% chance of a cure had it been found before requiring invasive surgery, there was still a 20% chance of failure. Letting go of guilt is a big part of healing.

I wasn't drowning anymore. I didn't need to reaffirm my existence or search desperately for reasons to "go on." I no longer had to lose myself in anything.

Living in a remote Ghanaian village without running water, flush toilets, television, or a grocery store nearby with people who had their heads and hearts in all the right places did me more good than I had even imagined. They helped me get my feet squarely back on the ground.

I was proud of what my Ewe friends and I accomplished together. I returned from Abutia-Kloe stronger, better, and more determined than ever to live out my life in a way that would make those I had loved and lost proud.

My last contract gig with Miromar was in early June prior to the trip to Ghana. I remember my feelings that night as I sang *"I'll Be Seeing You."*

I was not only about to leave the country, I was leaving music as well.

There would be a few more performances after that, but I gradually came full circle. From the child writer struggling to get her thoughts on paper, I would evolve into a published writer for the *Naples Daily News*.

After my articles from Ghana, *News* editor Julio Ochoa asked me to write a regular blog for the *News* online edition.

I wondered if I had enough to say. As of this writing, it's been four years and counting. Julio later left the *Naples Daily News* and is now an editor with the *Tampa Bay Tribune.*

Another *Naples Daily News* editor, Jay Schlichter, has been my editor and friend since Julio's departure. Jay also edited my first book, ***Yevu***, as well as this one.

Reporter Leslie Williams Hale married and relocated to Georgia. At this writing she is executive director of *Books for Keeps*, a start-up nonprofit dedicated to putting books into the hands of children who might not otherwise have them. I always knew Leslie and I were kindred spirits, despite our age difference. Our mutual interest in nonprofit work proves it.

Writing for my blog, ***"Life in the Slow Lane,"*** helped me realize that the book I had envisioned was indeed possible. I just needed to write it one chapter at a time, much as the way I'd rewritten my life.

With the publication of ***Yevu***, most of which was written while I was in Ghana, I realized I'd also been writing ***Better To Have Loved*** for almost 12 years. Most of it was already on paper and in my head.

Rewriting it for publication was hard. Going back to things I'd been trying to leave behind often left me drained. That's why it took so long.

But I knew I had become strong enough to finish it. Like music, writing is also "therapy."

Some readers may think I progressed quickly through the grieving process after Al's death. But there are no timetables for grieving. It is what it is.

What may not be clear in this book is that Jim Holbrook's death in 1983 very nearly killed me. It took more than four years of one-on-one grief therapy and the love and support Dr. David Reed and Harold Knox. Without them, I do not believe I would have survived nearly as well, if at all.

By the time I met, married, and lost Albert, I was far stronger than I had been when Jim died. I had learned much about dealing with grief by then. I knew what I had to do to survive in spite of my wish at times *not* to go on.

I cannot urge readers strongly enough to reach out to professionals and those who love you for help when you need it. *Tell them what you need.* Those who truly care will reach back. I've included steps in the addendum that helped me through my own healing.

In December 2010, my brother-in-law Alex Karilanovic passed away. While not unexpected, the manner in which he died was horrific. The nursing home evoked a law not intended for the purpose (Florida's "Baker Act") to evict him because he was running out of insurance money and going on Medicaid. It was to the facility's advantage to expel him since his condition required a private room for which Medicaid pays only a relatively small stipend.

Alex died in fear as a result of the precipitous and frightening eviction of so-called "Medicaid dumping." It was enacted without warning or my sister's approval in a manner that evoked his most terrible fears. He died 10 days later.

I spent three months writing a grievance against the nursing home, which was eventually cited for state and federal violations by Florida's Agency for Health Care Administration (AHCA). We don't know if any substantive changes were made after those citations. We do know that three separate state agencies descended upon the facility with recommendations for change.

In the summer of 2011, Dorothy moved back to Texas, resuming her life in Galveston. She remains busy with her own music, friends and historical society activities. She is content. She recalls her three years in Florida as a nightmare. I don't blame her. Her life here consisted mostly of watching her husband die tragically with Alzheimer's disease.

I see Dorothy and my great-nephew Angus James Heartsill several times a year. Angus now has a little sister Lydia ("Sissy") and two step-brothers. I have "almost grandkids" again to share the warmth of family fun and love. I'm grateful to Angus' father, Judson Heartsill and his wife Christine, for folding me into their family as one of their own.

Al's daughter Jackie lives with her husband in Romania, where he owns a number of successful businesses. She visited me once in Florida. We keep in occasional touch through email, for which I'm grateful.

The last I heard, Adam has successfully remained in recovery since shortly before his father's death, owns his own small business and is a leader in his regional Narcotics Anonymous program.

I haven't heard from Adam, his sister Dory, or Al's grandsons since Albert's death.

Tom Holbrook (Jim's brother) and his family and I have remained close throughout the decades since Jim's death in 1983. Tom's family and Jim and Tom's parents treated me like family since the day we met. When both Dr. George E. Holbrook and his sweet wife Dorothy Krentler Holbrook passed not long after Jim's death, I lost a part of my family too.

Shortly before I moved to Florida, I was able to reconnect with Jim's youngest daughter, now a happily married woman with children of her own. It was a poignant meeting after so many years, especially considering the last time we saw each other was in a judge's chambers. She has matured into a fine young woman who recalls her father with love. I was able to give her the few remaining things of his I had retained, one of which had very special significance to her, of which I hadn't been aware at the time. It was, I think, a kind of closure for both of us. We still keep in touch now and then through social media.

Lila "Queen Mother" Astroff suffered a debilitating stroke in 2011. Ron and I helped her move from her condo into a nursing home. Unable to speak clearly and with her mobility limited, Lila passed away suddenly and shortly before the publication of this book. Lila, my most "unforgettable character," was 91 years young. Ron and his partner Bob and I remain close friends.

Claude's photo remains on the wall above the piano bar at Truluck's Steak and Seafood Restaurant in Naples, where managing partner Rick Rinella says it will stay. *Everyone* still misses him.

In October 2012, ***Yevu*** was published to good reviews. *The Global Volunteer Network* cited it as "recommended reading" for anyone interested in volunteering abroad.

Music from my two CD's continues selling well online. The "Great American Songbook" thrives overseas, especially in Europe, Japan, and many other countries around the world. Although the old standards are declining in popularity in the USA, fans who love beautiful old melodies with lyrics that tell *real* stories haven't forgotten. Gradually, however, those fans are dying off as are the musicians who made them.

However, in May 2013, I signed a contract with a major international multimedia corporation to distribute two of my tunes throughout Taiwan and mainland China!

High Note International Multi-Media Corporation promises there will be more to come after the album, "Jazz Café 4."

Judging by the response they've gotten to their first three Jazz Café albums, I anticipate mainland China is the next big market for American jazz/standards. I'm delighted to be a small part of that. While our countries may disagree on many things, perhaps the universal love of music will help us see our similarities.

I was gratified that one of the songs High Note chose was Claude's last recorded tune with me, "*How Do You Keep the Music Playing?*"

We made it all the way to China, Claude! I can almost hear him saying, "Real good, Songbird. Real good."

Without his insisting, "You gotta' do a CD, Kathy," it would never have happened.

I remain in touch with several of Claude's children, especially Syrana, Farod and Kia, as well as Mary Lee Criner and her lovely daughter, Leanne. They remain very special to me.

Rick Howard and his wife Lisa still perform regularly in the Naples area with one of his several bands. A consummate entertainer and musician, Rick plays about every kind of music there is, although jazz remains his favorite. I expect he will as long as he can hold one of his 15 or so guitars! Their sweet little dog Lallie Ann passed away in 2013. Recently they adopted little Sophie to live a life known only by pets lucky enough to find people like the Howards! The beat goes on.

Stu Shelton still performs, owns and operates Shelton Studios in Naples. This extraordinary jazz pianist is among those who continue to keep the Great American Songbook alive. Naples is fortunate to have him.

Good friend and colleague, "Maestro" Woody Brubaker keeps threatening to retire. As busy as he is playing clubs and private parties around Cape Coral and Fort Myers, Florida, I expect they'll have to carry him out on his keyboard before that happens. The maestro is busier than ever. Sadly our good friend and fellow musician Skip Haynes passed away a couple of years ago, as did Woody's partner of 20 years, Carolyn Doty. Carolyn was the perfect musician's wife and Skip the perfect musician's friend.

I correspond through email and Facebook with some of my adopted family from Abutia-Kloe, as they increasingly acquire access to the Internet and social media. I will always be grateful to them for folding me into their lives. Worlanyo Afewu, Sampson Ntifo Hayford, Queen Mother Ayipe and others remain like extended family to me.

Some of my old friends from Connecticut visit me in Florida from time to time.

Donna Esposito of Danbury Animal Welfare and I correspond regularly. She remains a dear friend, reminding me of how much DAWS meant to me. Working there helped distract me from the terrible grief of Al's illness and dying. They gave me Tony, my Belgian shepherd mix eventually adopted by Chris and Cheri Hicks Armentano, with whom I lived for four months after the sale of my Connecticut home.

Chris and Cheri now spend about five months a year not 20 minutes away from where I live in Florida! Six years after I left Tony with them, they brought him to Florida. I walked in the door, wondering if he would remember me.

From the adjacent room, Tony lifted his old head to look at me. Slowly heaving himself up off his pillow, he walked directly to me and rested his old head in my hands as he had so many years before. I still tear up recalling that moment. Tony and I had some good moments together before he passed away a few weeks later. He fell in right beside me walking through the woods as he used to so many years before. I knew he had forgiven me for leaving him. He had a wonderful life with Chris and Cheri, who were with him when he died a few weeks later.

My "adopted little sister," Anne Marie Knox, passed away in 2010 at the same age her brother Harold did. I often told her that in some future lifetime, I'd be her biggest fan, sitting in the front row of the concert hall as she, the prima ballerina, would glide gracefully across the stage, free of a wheelchair and debilitating medical conditions. I know she's counting on it. So am I.

My dear friend and attorney, Charlie Drummey, passed away peacefully at home in April 2013. Charlie was the attorney who helped me with estate matters after both Jim's and Albert's deaths. His colleagues, Irwin Hausman and Mike Ziska, helped win the lawsuit over the building lot that Al started and I finished. Charlie and I had a special relationship. He was one of those people who give lawyers a good name. He truly treated his clients like family.

Sadly, I've had less contact with a number of friends in Connecticut since moving to Florida in 2004. I don't know if they realized just how important they were to me during those dark months and years.

Denise Foster walked me through the darkest moments of Al's illness and death. She later obtained her doctorate degree in clinical psychology. Dr. Denise Foster now practices in the greater New York City area.

Sheryl Keith, who along with Denise got me out of the house for weekly lunches during the early days after Al died, now lives in Minnesota with her husband Steve.

Charlie Hupp, Pat and Rocky O'Connor, and Eddie Flynn taught me how to laugh again during those wonderful mornings at Jacqueline's Diner. Jacqueline's is gone now, but it will always remain the site of "The Breakfast Club."

Charlie DeSantis, Ron Skelton, Joe and Anne Kugielski, Dr. George Anderheggen, and others who stood by Al and I during his last days will forever remain in my heart. There are others too numerous to mention. You know who you are.

Charlie DeSantis visits me from time to time in Florida, still flying airplanes, playing golf, and recalling the good times we had with his best buddy Al, and his own beloved Josephina, who sadly passed away suddenly not long after Albert.

Peter Hearn, whose staff taught me to SCUBA dive, sold Pan Aqua and now works for the state of Connecticut. He still dives and teaches SCUBA in New Fairfield, Connecticut. I still wear my somewhat worn Pan Aqua hat on each dive excursion. It's my good luck charm.

Joanne Cohen, whom I grew to know and love through our work with the Tourette Syndrome Association, faithfully maintains contact. Rein's Deli, where we met for lunch, is gone. I haven't been back to Connecticut since I left in 2004. I never "go back" anywhere.

Never ever say "Never ever."

I may return one day to revisit places which live so clearly in memory. But now that I live in a place that reminds me of Connecticut, it's almost as though I am back!

Shortly after returning from Ghana, I began thinking about moving from Southwest Florida. I lived in or near the woods of rural Connecticut for more than half my life. I am more at home surrounded by trees and wildlife than anywhere else.

I left Connecticut in 2004 to move to a place where people were grateful for a cloudy day. I wanted to swim or dive every day. I found that and more in the magnificent resort development of Miromar Lakes Beach and Golf Club.

But gradually, I found myself missing a *community* of year-round residents, connected with each other as only full time friends and neighbors can be.

I wanted to live in a small town with easy access to basic services, with a fresh water river or lake nearby in which to swim. The older I get, the more important swimming is for health. With my genes, I'm going to live well into my 90's, if not longer. I want to leave this life still swimming.

I missed having flowers growing from the ground instead of mere pots on my lanai, complete with bugs and birds and other critters not found in the beautifully manicured lawns of Southwest Florida. I wanted to get my hands back in the dirt in as "natural" a place as I could find.

I wanted to go just far enough back to the past to find a place reminding me of rural Connecticut without the long, cold winters.

I found it in north central Florida. It was, and is precisely where I *need* to be.

In January of 2012, I left Miromar Lakes Beach and Golf Club and moved "back to the woods." Now living on a lovely acre in north central Florida, I am once again surrounded by tall trees, green fields, and thousands of blooming azaleas. I hear owls hooting in the night and coyotes yip-yipping on their way home from nightly hunts. I swim regularly in the most beautiful river in Florida. I've met many new friends and have wonderful neighbors. I volunteer for river conservation and write from my office overlooking a beautiful backyard shaded with a hundred trees.

Miromar Lakes was indeed where I wanted to be for seven and a half years, but I'm a country girl at heart.

In writing this book I realized just how many friends I do have, and how important they are to me. I was never truly alone. Drowning in grief, one often feels that way. I love you all. I always will.

In October 2011 just before I sold my home in Miromar and moved to north central Florida, I lost my old cat Biz. Albert named him "Bismarck," because he made us think of "a big gray battleship." Biz was my last link with Albert and was with me for 17 years. I will always miss him.

In July 2012, six months after relocating to north central Florida, I was adopted by two five-week-old orphaned kittens. I had only recently told friends with whom I'd started Miromar Lakes' "Trap-Neuter-Return" program, that I would never again adopt kittens. I was getting too old for infants around the house.

"Somebody," however, had other ideas. *Lewis and Clark* are now helping me explore this next stage of my life.

Never ever say "Never ever."

A year before I left Miromar Lakes, my good friends Jolene and Chris Dixon retired the Eagle Ray Dive Shop in Bonita Springs and relocated not an hour from where I now live! I had a hard time driving by the shop's former location on Bonita Beach Road after they left.

But the Eagle Ray Dive Club lives on, members gathering several times a year from all over the country for SCUBA trips to exotic places and local "eco-tourism" adventures. Chris is now a Florida state park ranger, fulfilling one of his last remaining childhood goals. Jolene is now a master gardener, also fulfilling one of hers. The best part is that they're still my neighbors!

I still see other friends from Southwest Florida, making occasional trips back to Naples and Fort Myers. My good friends at Miromar Lakes remain in my life through email and occasional visits. I'm not that far away from them and don't intend to lose touch. Sadly, Liz Davidson, my next-door neighbor who invited me to her dinner party shortly after I arrived in Florida, passed away a few years ago. Lester still lives in Fort Myers, thankfully enjoying good health.

Chuck Risch still lives in Miromar Lakes, and has progressed to occasionally driving a modified van around the "'hood." If anyone could ever overcome quadriplegia to walk again, it'll be him. I still send him the occasional article from a magazine highlighting the latest advances in rehabilitative medicine.

I now gather weekly with "The Dinner Club" of friends in my new town. These gatherings aren't as much about healing for me as they are about merely having fun.

Recently, I asked myself, if I could, would I erase the last 12 years and go back to my life with Albert in Connecticut?

The momentary hesitation I felt before answering that question spoke volumes.

I'm not the same person I was in 2001. I've been blessed to have had so much, to have loved so deeply, and to have been loved so well. I had resources allowing me to move on and rebuild my life in ways of which others might only dream. But real healing comes from within.

I was fortunate to be able to distract myself with all manner of activities, but it's what we find within ourselves that means the difference between getting stuck in the past and moving on. I've lost more than most people have ever had. But as I wrote earlier, truly living requires risk, and I've lived a lot.

I won't forget. But for those of us who have loved and lost, we eventually learn that we're the lucky ones. We at least had something or someone to lose.

I'm where I belong now, at least for the time being. I will always remember my Albert and the life we had together. He made me happy in a way I will never forget. But as I wrote in the opening pages of this book, some part of me died with him. But perhaps the best part lived on. He helped me become a better person, both during his life, and after.

Will I love again? Perhaps I already have. But if I spend the rest of my life alone, I won't truly be lonely. Not with *my* memories and so many dear and wonderful friends.

It is indeed better to have loved and been loved, than never to have loved at all.

Life is good.

I am serene.

Capt. Al Taubert, the "soccer coach who flew."
Photo Pan American World Airways
(*Below*) Albert and wolf cub Kipling, at soccer practice, 1991.
Photo by Kathryn Taubert

Mother, wearing Al's old USAF flight suit, as he demonstrates the finer points of aviation. Newtown, Connecticut, 1997
Photo by Kathryn Taubert

January 2000. Somewhere in the Atlantic on the Pan American World Airways Clipper Pioneers Reunion Cruise, five months after surgery with Dr. Olsson. The cancer was gone!
Taubert family photo

Founder of Newtown Soccer Club and Sports Hall of Fame inductee, Al Taubert.
Photo courtesy of "The Newtown Bee"

Mr. & Mrs. Albert R. Taubert, Jr. Tourette Syndrome Association Dinner Dance, Pierre Hotel, New York, New York.

Photo courtesy The Tourette Syndrome Association, Bayside, NY

The happy couch potato and her "soccer coach who flew." He once said I could stand to gain 10 or 20 pounds, so I did! *Taubert family photo*

Tenth anniversary photo as Albert gazed into the setting sun at Castle Hill Inn, Newport, Rhode Island. I felt a cold chill of prophecy as my camera flash didn't work. He would be gone in less than eight months.
Photo by Kathryn Taubert

Each week, in a dark corner of the restaurant where no one would see my tears, Denise Foster and Sheryl Keith consoled me as I grieved.

James E. (Jim) Holbrook
May 24, 1935 – Oct. 14, 1983

My lyrics to "*Some Other Sunset*" were written for Jim, who died only a few years after our marriage in 1980.

Taubert family photos

Harold "Buddy" Knox
Nov. 12, 1941 – Mar. 20, 1993.

He and Dr. David Reed probably saved my life after Jim's death. My lyrics to "*Somewhere in Time*" were written for Harold.

Photo by Kathryn Taubert

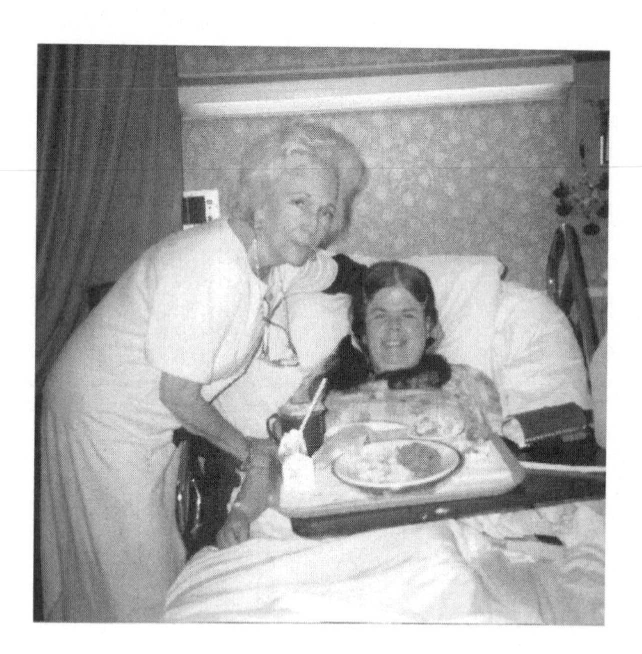

Harold's sister Annie was like my own little sister. She helped me keep my life in perspective.

Anne Marie Knox
Sept. 17, 1958-Aug. 7, 2010

Taubert family photos

The *Breakfast Club* taught me to laugh again. Charlie, Marnie, Me, Eddie, Pat and Rocky.

Shirley Smith
Feb 2, 1923-Jan 5, 2013
Rubin Smith
1920-Nov. 25, 2006
Shirley's association with TSA resulted in our enduring friendship. Rube's gourmet cooking tempted me as I'd plead with him to tell me more about his association with the "Pet Rock" craze.
Taubert family photos

Charlie DeSantis, one of Albert's oldest friends and a fellow pilot, drove us to New York City for appointments until I got the courage to drive myself. Always there to help before and after Al's death, Charlie also offered to be "on call" in the event of an emergency requiring I leave Africa on short notice. He remains a dear friend.

Photo courtesy Capt. Charlie DeSantis

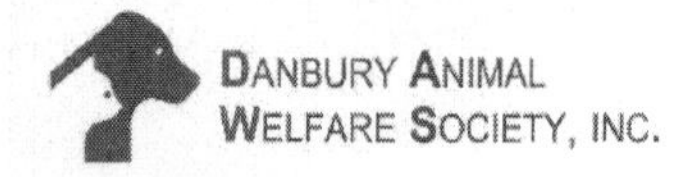

DAWS shelter dog Tony needed Kip and I as much as we needed him.

Tony
1997-2010

A new lease on life: open water swimming. "My lake" at Huntington State Park. *Photo courtesy Capt. Richard Scierka*

Swim Across America
15-mile relay for cancer research. "Rookie of the Year."

Photo courtesy "Boating World" by Janice Raber, July 2004

Kathryn Taubert, named "Rookie of the Year," poses with her prize.

Pan Aqua owner Peter Hearn and his staff taught me to SCUBA dive.
Photo by Kathryn Taubert

I'm still doing it! Chac Mool Cenotes, Mexico, July 2013

Dear friend Joanne Cohen, whom I met during our work together with TSA. Another of Albert's closest friends, Ron Skelton. Ron would eventually keep Biz for the seven months I was "homeless."
Taubert family photo

Chris and Cheri Hicks Armentano. Cheri regularly. I lived with them for 4 months after selling my Connecticut home. They now live part-time near me in Florida. *Photo courtesy of the Armentanos.*

***Left*, Donna Esposito, my good friend from DAWS.**
***Right*: Dive buddies Jolene and Chris Dixon of Eagle Ray Dive.**
Photos courtesy the Espositos and Dixons.

Thirteen-year-old Kip was alone for the first time in his life after his siblings died. Tony and Biz (below) and I were all Kip had. At times, I felt they were all I had too. Kip, 1991-2004

Biz, 1994-2011
Photos by Kathryn Taubert

Apr. 7, 2004: I left 10 years from the day Al and I moved into our lovely home on Greenleaf Farms. I would miss the beautiful woods and fields of our backyard (below).

Photos by Kathryn Taubert

Miromar Lakes Beach and Golf Club, Miromar Lakes, Florida. My new "backyard." People couldn't understand why I'd rather swim in Miromar's Lake Como than this magnificent community pool shown below. *Photos by Kathryn Taubert*

Chuck Risch, disabled due to a skiing accident, not only served on the Organizing Committee of the "GCCS," he also swam in the event, helping to raise enough money to put more than 145 disabled kids through a week of summer camp! *With the late Nancy Cleary*. *Photo courtesy Richard Cleary*

Mistress of Ceremonies, good friend Martha Gill, presenting me with a certificate as GCCS chairperson. She's much prettier than the photo, but since I looked awful too, she let me use it. It's the only one of us there together!
Photo courtesy Richard Cleary

My great nephew Angus James Heartsill helped me out of the water after my 6 mile, non-stop swim around Miromar's Lake Como in the *Gulf Coast Charity Swim.* At 60 years old, officially no longer a "couch potato." *Photo courtesy Richard Cleary*

The success of the GCCS encouraged Miromar to host the U.S.A. Swimming Open Water World Championship Trials in Oct. 2007.

U.S. Open Water Swimmers Continue Down Road to Beijing at 2008 Open Water World Championship Trials

Top Two Male and Female Finishers Advance to Olympic Selection Meet

COLORADO SPRINGS, Colo. – The nation's top open water swimmers will continue their bid for Olympic selection in the final domestic qualifying event of the quad, the USA Swimming Open Water World Championship Trials. The Trials will be held Oct. 20-21, 2007, at Miromar Lakes Beach and Golf Club in Fort Myers, Fla. There, a field of 60 swimmers will vie for four available spots in next spring's Olympic selection meet in Seville, Spain. (*USA Swimming Press Release Oct. '07*).

Claude Rhea, Naples' own *Mr. Music.*
Photo courtesy "Naples Illustrated"

Ron Yohe and Lila Astroff,
the *"Queen Mother"* of Naples.
Photo by Kathryn Taubert

Above, **Claude & I performing at Blue Water Grill.** ***Below,*** **Skip Haynes and I clowning around with *AllThatJazz* at Miromar's Beach Club Mardi Gras Dinner Dance.**

Skip Haynes
Feb 19, 1941-Jan. 8, 2012

Claude and I singing a duet at Truluck's.

Big band stint with Harris Lanzel & the MusicMakers.

Fellow vocalist seated, Gary Lavigne, passed away in 2012.

(left) **Mother in Halloween costume and (*below*) wondering what a "Geek Squad" was!**

We had *fun*!

Ron, Claude and mother on her 93rd birthday, not long after arriving to live with me in Florida.

Taubert family photos

Dorothy Catherine Cain McDonald
Sept 10, 1913-Sept 09, 2007

Claude Rhea
Apr. 13, 1941-Oct. 17.2008
Lila Astroff
July 16, 1922-July 29, 2013

My sister Dorothy cared lovingly for my brother-in-law after their evacuation to Florida from Hurricane Ike.
Aleksandar Karilanovic
May 20, 1940-Dec. 24, 2010
Photos by Kathryn Taubert

Stu Shelton, Me, George Mazzeo, below, George, Rick Howard, "Maestro" Woody Brubaker, Sir John. The *AllThatJazz* Septet, Surf Club, Miami, Fl. 1/9/09

Photos Surf Club

First CD inspired by Claude Rhea and co-produced by Rick Howard, released in 2007.

Second CD under the *D and M Music* label released in 2008.

Six months after the Miami concert, I left music, went to Africa, and wrote *Yevu*.

Shortly after returning from Africa, I moved to a lovely new home (backyard above) in a part in Florida that reminds me of my beloved Connecticut.

. . .with my new little companions, *Lewis and Clark*

. . .and a new swimming hole!
Photos by Kathryn Taubert

The man and the smile whose memory will forever light up my life.
Rest in peace, Sweetheart.

Albert R. Taubert, Jr.
September 24, 1930 - December 26, 2001
Photo by Kathryn Taubert

ADDENDUM

MANAGING A LOVED ONE'S MEDICAL CRISIS

1. **DON'T ASSUME ANYTHING**. Initial diagnoses can be wrong. Get the facts before making decisions.

2. **GET A REFERRAL** for a second and perhaps third opinion. Especially with serious disease or illness, sometimes clinicians make inaccurate assumptions about the course a disease may take. (See item 1).

3. **DO YOUR OWN RESEARCH.** If you don't know how, get a friend or family member to help. Learn everything you can about the illness and treatment options. Consider alternatives to traditional treatments, including clinical trials at major medical institutions. Don't necessarily accept the first options offered without having learned all you can about alternatives.

4. **KEEP RECORDS**. Get copies of all medical reports, lab results, X-rays, CT scans, MRIs and other films as well as the clinicians' written interpretations of them. Start a file for easy retrieval as you need them. Include insurance information and statements of expenses.

5. **TAKE COPIES WITH YOU** to all doctor appointments, especially for referrals from the original doctor's office. Reports in transit have a way of arriving late or not at all. Your copies may spare you and your loved one having to repeat tests

or appointments, losing valuable time and incurring additional stress and expense.

6. **BUILD A TEAM** of clinicians, friends, spiritual counselors, home health care aides and others who can help you interpret what's happening. You'll need help, especially if you aren't comfortable with medical jargon, procedures or alternatives under consideration. Get help from reliable, credentialed resources for help with complementary therapies to be used in conjunction with conventional treatments.

7. **INCLUDE FRIENDS AND FAMILY** in the patient's care. People want to know how they can help. Assigned tasks, no matter how small, help others feel as though they are contributing, sparing your time and energy for the most important jobs. Picking up the cleaning, grocery shopping, preparing a light meal, taking the dogs for a walk, making phone calls, driving you to appointments, taking the car in for service - the list of potentially helpful things people can do is endless. Now isn't the time to try to do it all yourself.

8. **BE PERSISTENT** but polite when dealing with clinicians' offices and medical receptionists. Don't wait longer for medical reports or phone calls than is reasonably necessary. Be polite, friendly, and persistent. Don't take your frustration out on the person with whom you are speaking. Tell them that time is critical and you need the information as quickly as possible to proceed with necessary treatment.

9. **BE SUPPORTIVE** of your loved one but not dictatorial. It is, after all, his life, and while he may actively seek your opinion, be certain that the actual decisions about the course of action remain his if at all possible.

10. **ASK BUT DON'T TELL** how your loved one is feeling. My experiences revealed that the patient will let you know how much they wish to know and when. Too much information can be discouraging, especially if it turns out to be incorrect. Too little information on the other hand doesn't give the patient full access to what's necessary to make his or her own decisions.

11. **MAINTAIN "NORMALITY"** as much as possible. To the extent the patient is able, continue as many regular activities as possible. Research shows that people do better with a certain amount of "routine" in life.

12. **SEEK DISTRACTIONS** from the trauma of serious illness. It's vitally important for the caregiver as well as the patient to get your minds on something else for a while. See a movie (or rent one). Invite friends over for a quiet evening. Go for a ride in the car, walk the dog, read, and most importantly, engage in something that makes you both laugh. Reminisce about good times and *believe* there will be more.

13. **CREATE A SCHEDULE** so that important caregiving duties are maintained while still allowing

time for visitors and other activities. Seriously ill and bedridden patients require help with daily activities.

14. **KEEP A JOURNAL** of your thoughts, feelings, and activities. Writing is cathartic, and the record may help you and others understand what was happening at the time. We don't always recall details in times of crisis. Your record of events may help in the event you wish to reprise them, either for medical or personal reasons.

15. **BE PATIENT** with your loved one, yourself and others. Dealing with serious illness puts huge burdens upon everyone involved. Expect confusion, frustration, emotional meltdowns, and sadness. These are normal and should be allowed to run their course. Holding too much in all the time isn't healthy for either caregiver or patient.

16. **TAKE CARE OF *YOU*.** There will never be enough time in the day to do everything. But nothing will get done if you aren't well enough. Eat regular, healthy meals even though you may have little appetite. Indulge yourself in a hot, soaking bath or professional massage. Get out of the house, go to a movie, or have lunch with a friend. Build some time in each day for taking care of yourself. Your patient needs you to be strong and healthy.

17. **HOPE FOR THE BEST AND PLAN FOR THE WORST**. Sadly, no matter what you do, your loved one may not survive. It's a terrible thought but one which must be addressed. If it's clear in the last

stages of his or her life that death is imminent, consult with friends, family, and spiritual advisors on final arrangements. Locate appropriate medical and legal paperwork, advance directives, powers of attorney, and the patient's original Last Will and Testament. If you cannot address these matters yourself, have a trusted friend or family member do it. Better yet, plan for these things *before* serious illness strikes so you won't have to deal with them in the middle of your grief.

WHAT TO DO WHEN SOMEONE YOU KNOW IS GRIEVING

You can help others through a loved one's life threatening illness or grief with the steps below:

1. **DON'T JUDGE** grief or the grieving person by outward appearances. Like an iceberg, two-thirds of it are out of sight. People can't and don't always reveal the depths of their pain right away.

2. **DON'T ASSUME** the loss always *registers* even though everyone knows the person is gone. The emotional impact can be so devastating that the sufferer is simply incapable of dealing with it at that moment. Accompany them as you would a sleepwalker to a place of emotional safety. Don't act surprised or stunned or shocked because they act as if nothing has happened. The tsunami will come later.

3. **BE THERE** when it does. Write, call, stop by, send cards, or whatever is appropriate for you in the relationship. Expect and even encourage tears. Like waves, they will crest and recede. Grief will subside. The bereaved will recover. All you can do is offer support in whatever way you can.

4. **SOMETIMES LESS IS MORE**. Your own experience may be helpful later, but a person in crisis may not be able to digest your stories during his

personal crisis. Simply say, "I'm here. I care. You are in my thoughts."

5. **PROVIDE HELP, NOT MORE WORK**. "I heard about someone who was cured by such-and-such" is false hope without sufficient information, creating more anxiety instead of relief. Locate the legitimate source of information and details yourself if you think it might help.

6. **KEEP YOUR VISITS SHORT**, especially if serious illness is involved. Caregivers may need time to tend the patient that your presence impedes. Ask caregivers what's the best time to come and don't overstay, unless you have been asked to do so. Be sensitive to the needs of patient and/or bereaved. Let their needs and feelings guide your actions.

7. **LISTEN TO FEELINGS, NOT JUST WORDS**. "I don't feel well myself, but I don't have time to think about it," might mean "I'm tired, feeling alone, am frustrated, angry." This is your cue to step in with an offer to run errands, grocery shop, sit with the patient while the caregiver goes for a walk, gets a haircut, or just needs to talk.

8. **JUST *DO* IT**. "Let me know if there is anything I can do to help," may be a sincere gesture of good will, but the person in crisis may not be able to know exactly what kind of help he needs. Better yet, bring a

dish of food. Call and say you'll be there to take her out for a quiet dinner together. Drive him to appointments. Even if you live afar, you might locate a local health care or grief support group and pass the information along, or send relevant literature. Better yet, get someone from that group to make personal contact.

9. **ANTICIPATE MELTDOWNS**. People under stress often react in ways you wouldn't normally expect, out of fear, guilt, frustration, or sadness. Be patient, listen carefully, and let them talk. You don't need to be a "whipping boy," but you can be a sounding board. If the tension results in hostility toward you, leave calmly with "I'll call you later." Then do it.

10. **LIVE IN THE MOMENT**. Thinking too far ahead can be overwhelming. Plans made at those times may not be the best choices. You can help by taking on some tasks for the person in crisis, and urging him to think moment to moment until he can think ahead without being overwhelmed. People grieve at their own pace.

11. **DON'T EXPECT TIMETABLES**. There are no firm guidelines for grieving. Telling someone to "let it out," or "get over it" isn't helpful. Some people grieve quietly, and alone. Others are more open about it. Sudden loss can result in a deeper, longer-lasting grief

than that after extended illness. Sometimes death after the latter brings both relief and guilt to caregivers. But be cautious about saying "He's better off now." While it may be true, the bereaved may not yet have reached the point where the loss can be rationalized.

12. **STICK TO A ROUTINE**. People in crisis may abandon routines because they are too busy, depressed, or overwhelmed. Urge the person to maintain healthy eating, sleeping habits, and to get out of the house now and then. Make a regular date to go for a drive, a walk, or have lunch.

13. **TAKE SMALL STEPS**. Remember, "denial is a developmental state." It takes time to get used to the idea that everything has changed before accepting it. After a while, urge the person in crisis to do things at times and in ways that might be less reminiscent of the past. Even little steps help. If the bereaved and her partner used to eat lunch out together regularly, encourage her to have breakfast with friends instead. If you are concerned the bereaved isn't showing some improvement after some months, gently urge him to seek medical help.

15. **GIVE IT TIME**. Don't ask a recently bereaved person what they are going to do next when they're still in the midst of dealing with the loss. Decisions such as where to live or what to do about a job are just too overwhelming at that time. Instead, say, "When the

time comes that you can think ahead, I'll be here to help. Right now, just deal with today. I'm here for you."

16. **FOLLOW UP**. The hardest time for a person in crisis is after everyone else has gone back to their own lives, and the bereaved is left to deal with hers, forever changed. Call now and then to talk. Send a card. Include her in activities you normally included her before. (Suddenly single people, especially women, often find themselves left out of couples activities in which they were once included.) Some people don't know what to say so don't say anything at all. The bereaved need to talk about their lost loved ones. Just because the deceased or terminally ill person isn't around doesn't mean they're forgotten, nor should they be. The greatest kindness you can render is helping the bereaved remember the good times too.

Whether you are friend, family, caregiver, patient or bereaved, some of these tactics will eventually apply to you. Taking a moment to think through your actions before acting might mean the difference between real help and more frustration for the person in crisis.

Being there isn't always enough. Being sensitive often is.

STARTING OVER AFTER BEREAVEMENT

1. **GIVE YOURSELF TIME**. There are no timetables. If, however, you find you cannot function very well after a few months, seek help. You may be at risk of clinical depression, which requires a doctor's help.

2. **LET YOURSELF FEEL WHAT YOU FEEL**. Emotions during bereavement are all over the map. Theories abound about the "stages" of grief, but subsequent research shows not everyone experiences all of them or in the prescribed sequence. What you feel is unique to you and should be treated that way. It's okay to vacillate between emotions. Anger, guilt, and sorrow are normal, as is relief that the terrible strain of the preceding few weeks or months is over. You will get through those feelings quicker if you allow yourself to experience them. You can't heal it unless you feel it.

3. **RECOGNIZE GUILT AS PART OF GRIEVING**. Learning to let go of guilt for something you think you should have done differently is hard, but to continue blaming yourself isn't what your loved one would want for you. Forgive yourself. There is no guarantee things would have turned out differently anyway. We are not always in total control of what happens.

4. **SURROUND YOURSELF** with people and things that ease your burden, not make it worse. Now is not the time to endure insensitive people who start off with "How are you?" and launch directly into their own tales of woe. Gently tell them you haven't the energy to attend to them right now and excuse yourself.

5. **LOVE A PET.** Research shows that people with animal companions are often healthier and live longer than those without one. If you don't want to acquire a pet of your own, ask a friend, family member, or neighbor to let you spend time with theirs now and then. Better yet, volunteer at your local animal shelter with homeless pets who need your love.

6. **LOVE FAMILY AND FRIENDS.** Even if you don't have much family, you can nurture old friendships and make new ones. Don't turn down invitations during this time. Make yourself get out of the house, and yourself for a while. Join a support group. Volunteer. Do something to get yourself "out there" with people, no matter how hard it may be at first.

7. **DEFER LIFE-CHANGING DECISIONS** until a time when you are better able to make them. There is no hard and fast rule about this one, but my experiences suggest waiting at least one, and preferably two years before deciding to sell your home, relocate, change jobs, or enter a new romantic relationship. Some decisions may need to be made sooner, depending upon your financial circumstances. Defer the ones you can.

8. **GET HELP**. Financial, legal, medical, familial, and spiritual advice are among the first things with which many bereaved require assistance. If money is an issue, ask the professional if you can arrange a payment plan. Relevant experience among friends and family may be available, sparing unnecessary fees.

9. **LIVE IN THE MOMENT**. Thinking too far ahead during the early stages of grief can be overwhelming. "How will I make it without him?" "How will I survive financially?" "What will I do for the holidays?" are among those questions that can derail your attempts to merely make it through another day. Start thinking from moment-to-moment until you are strong enough to think day-to-day and beyond.

10. **MAINTAIN YOUR HEALTH**. This isn't the time to lose weight, get a facelift, discontinue your medications, or stop exercising. While losing weight and getting a facelift might be on your list of "to do's" for the future, your focus should be on maintaining a healthy diet and lifestyle while your body is under the serious physical and mental stress caused by grief. Chances are you'll lose a little weight anyway, and you don't want to undergo any kind of major, elective surgery until your stress levels are reduced.

11. **MAKE SMALL CHANGES IN OLD ROUTINES**. Things you used to do together with your loved one may exacerbate your grief. Making small changes can help. My husband and I used to watch the evening news together before dinner. After his death I found it almost impossible to do so. Acutely aware of his absence next to me, I began listening to the news in the morning as I was getting dressed instead.

12. **THINK IN TERMS OF PROGRESS**. As days, weeks, and months pass, ask yourself how you're doing compared to before. If you're feeling even the tiniest bit better now versus several months prior, you're moving in the right direction. You may not yet

be where you want to be, but you're making progress. If not, consider seeking medical help, especially if it's been 6 months or longer.

13. **COUNT ON THE FIRST YEAR** being the hardest. That first cycle of birthdays, anniversaries, and holidays is the worst. There is almost something mystical about the end of it. The pain doesn't go away, it just seems a little easier to bear. You'll be able to think and plan a little further ahead than before. If not, see item 10.

14. **DREAM AN OLD DREAM.** Once you've gotten to the point where you can see yourself making those big changes you considered but wisely didn't implement the year before, let yourself go. If you want to relocate, change jobs, return to school, and learn a new skill or trade, now's the time to consider it. Some people will get their faster than others. Remember, there are no hard and fast rules or timetables.

15. **TAP INTO YOUR GREATEST RESOURCE: *YOU*.** Having the financial resources to make big changes in your life doesn't necessarily determine just how well you survive a loss or process your grief. It just gives you a wider range of distractions while you're doing it. What counts most is what's *within* you. Chances are if you've endured difficulty before, and while losing a spouse is among the worst things you'll ever go through, you already have what it takes to survive your loss. You can't imagine it initially. But in time, as you go forward, you'll look back and realize you are making progress.

Whatever your new life becomes is entirely up to you. You are not alone in the world, and never really were. There are many of us out here who have endured what you have. We're here. We made it. And so will you.

ON BEING WIDOWED

Originally published in "Life in the Slow Lane" by Kathryn Taubert, The Naples Daily News, September 5, 2011

"I'm sorry for your loss" is usually followed by a few moments of uneasy silence, after which the bereaved, with downcast eyes, says either, "Thank you" or "It's okay," knowing it really *isn't*.

The conversation then takes an entirely different turn, since most people have no idea what to say or do next.

Twice-widowed, I've gotten comments that, while intended to lighten the mood, ended up making it worse.

I've heard "Wow, what are you *doing* to them?" or "I'd better be careful around *you*" so often that I've become reluctant to even broach the subject.

I used to reply with something equally as "funny," until realizing there was a way to handle it that made me feel better without offending the perpetrator. People who haven't been there simply *do not know how to react*.

Now I gently say that such comments aren't funny to me, but I appreciate their attempts to lighten things up with humor.

Then I say I'm one of the luckiest people I know, because I've *lost* more than many have had; *two* good husbands.

There are things both the bereaved and others can say, or not, to help. While much of this applies to the loss of any loved one, this is primarily for widows, widowers, and those who care about them.

The widowed sometimes feel as though the others in their lives have forgotten the lost loved one, since they barely mention his or her name anymore.

People don't know what to say, and/or are afraid of hurting the bereaved, so they don't say anything at all.

If the bereaved sheds a tear at the mention of his late spouse's name, some feel guilty for having mentioned it, apologize, and move onto something else.

Sometimes they need to talk about their lost loved one. To avoid it is tantamount to pretending the person didn't exist, or wasn't important enough to discuss.

They also need to process their loss in whatever way is comfortable for them. For many, it's cathartic to talk about the loss with someone who will simply listen and understand that tears are natural, often healing.

The widowed don't need platitudes, conversational redirection, or most certainly comments such as, "Don't you think it's time to move on?" or "You'll find someone else someday."

The loss of a spouse is among the worst things one can endure. The sudden, unexpected death of a spouse results in a longer period of more intense grief.

Death after long illness is as difficult in its own way, although one has more time to prepare oneself to the extent anyone can for such a loss.

There are no guidelines to tell a person how he should or shouldn't feel at any given time.

People grieve differently. Our culture seems most often to expect the bereaved to move on in ways that aren't entirely realistic.

The person with whom one shares everything leaves an indelible imprint, whether together a few years or a lifetime. Our lost loved ones helped make us who we are, no less and perhaps even more than other people in our lives.

An acquaintance once noted both photos of both my late husbands in my home.

"That couldn't intimidate a guy, you know."

I immediately replied that such a guy wouldn't be one in whom I'd be interested anyway!

My late husband Al and I were both widowed when we met, displaying our late spouses' photos side by side after we married.

How could I resent his late wife, who during 29 years of marriage, helped shape the man with whom I fell in love? Al felt the same way about my late husband.

For the widowed, the key is knowing how much to remember while living in the present, and in time, planning for the future. For the recently bereaved, it's *minute-to-minute.* Thinking too far ahead too soon after bereavement may be overwhelming.

A friend of mine recently said of the widow he'd been dating that "her late husband seems to get more perfect all the time."

Perhaps she just needs more time, or indeed she was deifying her late husband. That's not a good thing either. Nobody is perfect!

A healthy reminiscence is, however, healthy and appropriate now and then.

I have a friend who was happily married, and widowed three times. I wouldn't dare ask her which husband she loved most, any more than I'd ask a parent which child he loves most. Yet some do.

I was 37 when my husband Jim died suddenly, sending me into a tailspin the likes of which I'd never imagined.

"This goes on every day around me and I had no idea," I recall thinking one day.

Bereavement is so common we take it for granted, until it happens to *us*.

I never thought I'd survive it, but clearly did, moving on to meet and marry Albert, with whom I had 12 wonderful years prior to his death in 2001.

I've moved on now in all the right ways, but don't intend to put away either the photos or memories of the fine men who helped make me the person I am now. While still a work in progress, I basically like the person I'm becoming.

We tell people about our friends and other family members, living and dead. Why should we be expected to avoid mentioning people to whom we were happily married?

For friends and loved ones, next time you offer "I'm sorry for your loss," follow it up with "How are you doing?" or "Tell me about him."

They'll let you know if they don't wish to talk about it.

For the widowed, *tell* people what you need and when you need it.

Take that uneasy silence in hand with "Thank you for your thoughts. It's okay to talk about her. Actually, I *need* to do that."

Don't apologize if, even years later, you still like to reminisce about the spouse who helped make you, *you*. Those who've been there will understand. The rest will learn, with your help.

For those widowed more than once (longer life-spans are increasing our numbers), gently defuse insensitive comments in ways that help people learn what's appropriate. They're not being intentionally cruel or thoughtless.

They just don't understand.

At least not *yet*.